JACKS OR BETTER

Books by T. S. Matthews

JACKS OR BETTER

A Narrative by T. S. Matthews

NEW YORK   1986   ATHENEUM

The poems on pages 32, 37, and 39 appeared in *The Book of the Tuesday Evening Club,* published by Princeton University Press. One of "Two Rhymes About Fate and Money" (page 303) by Robert Graves reprinted by permission of Curtis Brown, Ltd. Copyright © 1961 by Robert Graves. "Foreword" and poem "To Whom Else?" (page 219) appear courtesy of Estate of Robert Graves.

Library of Congress Cataloging in Publication Data
Matthews, Thomas Stanley, 1901–
  Jacks or better.
  Includes index.
  1. Matthews, Thomas Stanley, 1901– 2. Journal-
ists — United States — Biography. 3. Authors — 20th
century — Biography. I. Title.
PN4874.M4837A29   070.4′092′4 [B]   76-57874
ISBN 0-06-012842-9
Paperback:
ISBN 0-689-70705-3   LCCN 85-48120

To Pam, the happy ending

CONTENTS

Opening Remarks

We all thought we were very interesting people. We never intended.

Yes yes yes.

Well of course we didn't all think we were geniuses but we knew we were superior. We had no idea.

No no no.

You mean—*seriously?*

Mmmmmm.

That she—*really* . . . *?* And he . . . ?

Mmmmmm.

When I was young, I envied wrinkled faces.

The possiblity of sabotage should not be ruled out.

I can tell you a story.

Can you?

JACKS or BETTER

"Why don't you call him up?"

"Now? After all this time? It's been—good Lord, more than twenty years."

"But you want to see him. You do, don't you?"

I had told her pretty much the whole story, and that wise woman knew, better than I did, how much I missed him; and how persistently it gnawed at me—the non-ending, the petering-out of our story.

I unfolded the Esso map of Florida.

"Here we are—Destinn. And here he is—Wabasso. I figure it's just about 500 miles. Maybe he'd meet me halfway. Or I'd drive there and back, if he wants me to."

"Call him up."

"I will."

We were staying at a motel on the Gulf, not far from Tallahassee. Besides being on the beach, the motel had everything: swimming pool, dining room, night club, a bar. Even its own telephone operator. So she put in the call for me. Ten minutes later she reported that there was no telephone in Wabasso under his name. Of course not; he wouldn't have a telephone. I wrote out a wire and gave it to the operator to send: DO YOU WANT TO SEE ME? IF SO WIRE HOLIDAY INN, DESTINN, FLA. I signed it TOM MATTHEWS, in case he had met some other Toms during these twenty years.

That was about mid-afternoon. I went for a walk on the beach, then read for a couple of hours in my room, had an early dinner and spent the evening in the bar. I went to bed around midnight, disappointed that there had been no reply to my wire.

But there had been. While I was having breakfast next morning I got a message from the operator: he had telephoned at nine o'clock last night but for some reason they hadn't found me; he said he would call again this morning. Ten minutes later I was summoned to the telephone booth.

"Tom?"

"Schuyler!"

"I got your telegram. You didn't address it properly."

1

"Well, anyway, you got it. I figured that Wabasso—"

"You addressed me as if I were a single person."

(Well, for God's sake! As if I would have put her name on it.)

"About the question you asked. I can't give you a direct answer. In some ways, yes, I should like to see you. But I think, on the whole, the time is not yet ripe. Not until the good in you has come nearer fruition." (Then, lowering his voice—almost as if he were afraid of being overheard): "And I too."

"Well. If that's the way you want it."

"Goodbye, Tom."

"Goodbye, Schuyler."

I went back to the dining room, shaking all over, to finish my breakfast. That was Schuyler, all right. But what had happened to his voice? There was a different sort of tautness to it, a kind of niminy-piminy preciseness, like an edgy schoolmaster. And his words! "Until the good in you has come nearer fruition"—people just don't talk like that. That was the language of the manifesto. Of course! I wondered how late they had sat up, haggling away together till they got the phrase in "proper" form. I could picture him telephoning from the pay station at the corner grocery. (Consulting his notes? And was she with him? Was that why he had dropped his voice when he said, "And I too"?)

I was still shaking, fifteen minutes later. I had actually been talking to Schuyler. I remembered the last time we had met, more than twenty years ago. It was in the lobby of the Time & Life Building, in Rockefeller Center; we had walked past each other with a casual nod. An hour or so later I remembered that I had seen him and it meant nothing to me, it might have been anybody. It was as if he were dead, or I was.

But he was not dead after all; he was still alive. And so was I.

2

SCHUYLER ASCENDANT

1

The First World War is clanking to its rusty finish. A million American doughboys are in Europe; millions more are in training to be sent overseas. My classmates and I are among the last additions to this enormous (and, as it will shortly appear, unnecessary) throng. Technically we are not conscripts; but when we were accepted as Princeton freshmen we were given no choice in the matter: when the doctors have passed us we are sworn in as cadets of the Student Army Training Corps. We are bondservants to the Army and the University has no jurisdiction over us.

The only civilians on the campus are the little group of 4-Fs (physically unfit); they go to lectures and take regular courses and have to abide by all the university rules that can't be enforced on us. In order to lure us into the semblance of undergraduates, the University offers us "full credit" for any courses we can fit in and will condescend to take, no matter how miserable our performance. Thanks to this wartime rule, in my first term I get credit for two courses which I fail to pass.

Our 4-F classmates are quartered off the campus, in the student rooming houses. All the university dormitories have been turned into barracks. My company, which is made up entirely of boys under eighteen, is crammed into one building, Witherspoon, a rococo monstrosity of the 1880s. There are more than ninety of us in D Company, and the basement washroom is not nearly big enough to take us all, especially not all at once; but we have only fifteen minutes between reveille and assembly, so every morning before dawn the washroom is the scene of a frantic scrimmage. One of our number is a small, bespectacled, red-

5

haired boy named Joe Blow, who is already famous among us for his slowness of speech. One morning, for some reason, there are no lights in the washroom. From the confused and struggling darkness comes an earnest voice, unmistakably Joe Blow's: "Don't—pee—here—I'm—shit—ting—here!"

As a sergeant, I am assigned to an advance course in bayonet practice; when we have finished it we are to become instructors ourselves. This is my first sight of Schuyler. We are opposite numbers, feinting at each other with long and short jabs, at a respectful distance, and practicing a crippling swing to the crotch with the rifle butt. He is stripped to the waist. I see the intensity of his face, and admire (or envy) the muscles of his arms and shoulders and wonder whether my bayonet would go into him like butter or, more likely, hit a rib. We never exchange a word. But I know that his name is Schuyler Jackson.

All that boring military nonsense over, at the end of our first term, my friends and I take to the untasted delights of college life with a whoop and a holler. Some of us do, at least; Harry Hart, my roommate, who is determined to make Phi Beta Kappa, settles down to a four-year grind of work, which he defines in theory and in practice as "something you have to do that you hate." I discover the joys of drink and the miseries of hangovers. Whenever a visitor appears in our study, Hart retires to his bedroom, slamming the door, leaving me to deal with the time-wastrel. I am always glad to do it, being one myself.

In our first two years Schuyler is not one of our friends. We encounter him occasionally in classes, but nowhere else: he is never seen at football rallies or at the movies, or lounging along Nassau Street or shooting pool at Dad Struve's, or having a cup of coffee at Renwick's or the Balt, or in any of the places or pastimes that form the greater part of our college life. He is not completely unknown, for in Princeton no nonconformist is invisible; but he becomes, at least to some of us, a subject of speculation. What does he do with himself, and what is he up to?

The speculation about him is not confined to his classmates. There is one professor in particular who feels it his bounden duty to discover why Mr. S. B. Jackson signed up for his course on Wordsworth and Coleridge and has so far failed to appear at a single lecture or class. Professor George McLean Harper, an authority on Wordsworth and a kind of saintly Wordsworthian character himself, is an old-fashioned liberal who believes in duty. He tells the Registrar that Mr. Jackson must either appear or drop out of the course. Perhaps Professor Harper goes to see Schuyler: it would be like him. At any rate, Mr. Jackson does eventually appear, though not regularly: and whenever he comes Professor Harper, who is incapable of irony, calls attention to the fact that we have Mr. Jackson with us today and that we should all be grateful for it.

Something of the same sort, apparently, happens in other courses. There is a rumor that in one of his subjects Schuyler never shows his face at a single class—and then turns in such a brilliant examination paper that he has to be given an unquestioned First Group.

For the first two of our undergraduate years Schuyler's appearances on the campus are infrequent and brief; and it gradually becomes evident that this absentee classmate is not so much unsociable as that he has no time to waste. What he is up to is what we are all supposed to be up to: getting an education; but in his case he finds the conventional machinery of lectures and preceptorials and reading assignments an obstacle, a millstone round his neck. He has a tremendous amount of reading to do, and the University's curriculum interferes with his.

After we become friends he tells me that at Pomfret, where he went to school, he was "a red-blooded American boy," and never opened a book. He had been a successful athlete—quarterback on the football team, pitcher on the baseball nine—and had pursued excellence in this field with the headlong intensity that was characteristic of him. About the time he came to Princeton he had discovered books, a whole new world, which excited him far more than games, and he set out "to read everything." By "everything" I think he meant, in effect, poetry; at any rate, that was what he read most of. And to read the poets he wanted he had also to master Latin, Greek, Italian and French. For someone who had "never opened a book" it was a tremendous assignment. No wonder his days and nights were not long enough. His eyesight, which had been perfect, began to fail him, and soon he had to wear glasses.

The great event of our second year is the club elections. Ever since Ivy, the oldest and still considered the best of the undergraduate clubs, was founded, to be followed by twenty-odd others, the University's social life has been dominated by them. Only upperclassmen can be members, but the elections take place in one anxious week in the spring of sophomore year. Long before Bicker Week (so-called because of the bargaining and haggling it entails) its shadow lies darkly on the whole sophomore class. For weeks and months beforehand, committees from all the clubs have been calling on various sophomores. These calls, ostentatiously casual and brief, always take place in the evening. You never know when they are coming nor, sometimes, who the visitors are; for these calling committees, who are careful to introduce themselves individually, are not allowed to name the club they represent. If you don't know, you can always find out later, of course; and do. If you are called on by three or four different clubs and the interviews seem to go well, it might mean that Monday's mail in Bicker Week will bring you a couple of "original bids" (a direct invitation to become a member). But you never know. Some committees may call on you more than once. Good sign or bad sign? And is it you they come to see, or your roommate?

In a university like Harvard or Oxford or Columbia, a loose confederation of diverse kinds of men (and women), where social clubs are only a small group among many larger and more notable groups, such an overshadowing influence as Princeton's "club system" is unknown. But Princeton is not a university in the Harvard and Oxford sense; it is more like a homogeneous college, where tradition and custom apply to everyone alike, and are thwarted or neglected by any individual at his peril—the peril of being conspicuous.

For example, the few Jews who are brave enough to come to Princeton in my day are very conspicuous. The rare Jew who is elected to a good club, or in fact to any club at all, owes his good fortune to money or powerful connections or to an athletic ability that wins him popularity. In my day Princeton was quite definitely anti-Semitic: there was an unadmitted but obvious quota of Jews—a very small quota. When the gruffly jovial Dean of Admissions, Professor Magie, was interviewing me as an entering freshman, he barked, "Got an S on the end of your name?" and when I admitted it, he said, "Hmm, just saved you." No Negro, of course, ever even applied for admission to Princeton in those days.

Nowadays, they say, things have changed. Not that Princeton welcomes Jews and Negroes, but it does admit more than it used to, as "status symbols." Bicker Week itself has changed, and the club system with it (or so I am told): any sophomore can join a club who wants to and can afford it. This was far from being the case in 1920. All the clubs then were exclusive, or tried to appear so; and though there was a well-defined pecking order among them, even the lowest on the list drew the line somewhere. Every sophomore class knew that at least a quarter of its members—about 100 sophomores—would not be admitted to any club at all.

It was generally held, by those who criticized the club system, that its fundamental flaw was this exclusiveness, and that if everybody could join a club, all would be well. I think, now, that the essential trouble was the sophomoric nature of the "University" itself; and that if it had been possible to make the clubs fewer, *more* exclusive, and widely different from each other (as they would have been in a real university), they would have sunk into the background, where they belonged. But in those days "college spirit" was too fierce to allow any questioning of Princeton traditions.

Shortly before I entered college there had been a revolt against the club system: a small group of sophomores, led by Richard Cleveland (son of a former President of the United

States), publicly announced that they would not join any club, and that they were making this gesture as a protest against the "undemocratic" system. Dick Cleveland's moral courage was widely admired, since if he had kept his mouth shut he would almost certainly have "made Ivy"; some of his followers might not have made anything. Nothing came of this revolt, except that none of the rebels ever became a member of a Princeton social club—a fact that, as far as I know, did not darken any of their lives.

This was how Bicker Week worked in my day: on Monday morning the "original bids" went out, to a small minority of the class. A popular boy might get three or more; most got none. I got one, but it was from a club I didn't want to join. If you were fortunate you got the "original bid" you had hoped for and accepted it straightaway. Then, as far as you were concerned, the anxieties of Bicker Week were over. But those were a happy few. For most of us Monday was just the beginning.

Friends got together and compared bids, discussed rumors and contingencies, struck bargains, made firm alliances—sometimes with escape clauses. Groups formed. Meetings were held, sometimes with other groups, sometimes with the committee of a club that was interested enough to bargain. This went on all day and till late into the nights, for most of the week. The clubs, which were anxious to close their sections—a club that couldn't announce its new sophomore section by Thursday was obviously in trouble—kept trying to corral their little herd of sophomores before they could pick up any more mavericks, while the leader of the group was being passionately assured by L that if X weren't included, L wouldn't come along, and furthermore would take M, N and O with him.

These section leaders were not appointed by anyone, nor elected, as far as I can remember; they just emerged. I was one, and I had a stormy passage of it. The club committee that was trying to sign us up (because we were the best they could do) and my group, who were on the point of signing (because that club was the best *we* could do), came to last-minute loggerheads over

10

a school friend of mine who had been lost in the shuffle and looked like being passed over by every club on Prospect Street. The majority of my section was not too keen on him, either; but I made an issue of it, and they accepted him. Then the club committee jibbed and swore they wouldn't have him at any price. All right, I said, then you can't have me either. They gave way, and we all signed up.

On the second day of Bicker Week, when sections were still in the process of being formed, I had the happy thought of asking Schuyler Jackson to join us. I went to look for him and found him in his house on Washington Road, quietly reading away in his study. He thanked me for thinking of him, but told me that he had already joined Ivy.

2

All the men in Schuyler's family began to go bald at an early age; they were also noted for wildness in their youth, though most of them tended to settle down as they grew older. Schuyler told me that his father had a beard, perhaps to compensate for his baldness, and had been a businessman of genius. But towards the end of his life his mind gave way, and he was diddled by an Irish upstart named McCarter, who maneuvered the control of Mr. Jackson's public utility business away from him and himself became a tycoon. Schuyler and his father had shared a cabin on a liner returning from Europe, and during the journey his father went mad. He never recovered.

But Mr. Jackson had had the foresight to settle some money on his children, in trust. There were six, as I remember: three sons and three daughters. Schuyler was the youngest. Wolcott, the eldest, I saw only once. He was bald as an egg, lively and not particularly good-looking. He had become a chicken farmer in

SCHUYLER

upstate New York. The second son, Philip, was taller than Schuyler and would have been even handsomer if it had not been for his expression of settled bitterness. When Philip and Wolcott were boys one of them had dared the other to leap from the roof of their Newark house to the paved courtyard, three or four storeys below. Whichever one it was took the dare, jumped and broke both his legs. It may have been Philip, for he ended his life, years later, by jumping from the Brooklyn Bridge.

Schuyler's mother, whom I also saw only once, when she came to his graduation from Princeton (bringing him as a present an English silk umbrella), was a pretty woman, said to have been rather flighty. After her husband's death she married an Englishman named Gore, and went to live in England. Her three daughters were all good-looking; the youngest, Peggy, the closest to Schuyler's heart and the one who most resembled him, was a memorable beauty.

Peggy had many suitors, and it would hardly be an exaggeration to say that almost every man who knew her was in love with her. In her youth she had the most electrifying presence (electrifying is too prosaic but it is exact) of any woman I have ever seen; it was an exciting, vivifying, marvelous thing to be near her. When she came into a room she brought with her such a compelling light that the men all turned to moths. It was partly her eyes, and the intensity of expectation and happiness her whole face conveyed, partly her voice, which was low, thrilling, charged with an overpowering current. Not that she ever said anything in the least unusual.

"Isn't it a *lovely* day!" she would breathe.

And every man-jack there, yearning towards her, leaning towards her from the edge of his chair, would declare from his heart, *"YES!"*

From all her suitors, this nonpareil chose a man of comfortable means and assured position, and old enough to be her father; his name was Stuart Paton. When my family came to Princeton to live, I think Mr. Paton had recently died; at any rate, I never met him, although I vividly remember his young widow.

13

Though there are no Patons in Princeton now, in my day they were one of the solid families; not so rich and grand as the Moses Taylor Pynes and their in-laws, the Archibald Russells, but rich and grand enough. Another Paton family lived in a big stone house overlooking Lake Carnegie. Their son Townley was about my age, and we used to play tennis together; he was the best partner I ever had, and we won several tournaments together. He ended up as a famous eye doctor. His mother's New Year parties were an annual event which "everybody" in Princeton attended: old-fashioned formal receptions, with fiddlers in the gallery and Mrs. Paton, tall and stiff, standing underneath to receive her guests: to each she gave a slight nod as she took the proffered hand and threw it down and away with surprising force.

Peggy Paton's brother-in-law, David Paton, an Egyptologist and an old bachelor, was a sweet-faced man of gentle manners whom everyone liked. It was in his house on Washington Road that Schuyler lived during his four undergraduate years at Princeton. This was an unusual arrangement, as all students were supposed to live either in the college dormitories or in licensed rooming houses; but Schuyler was an unusual undergraduate and the Paton family had considerable influence. Old David Paton and Schuyler were devoted to one another, as they also were to Peggy.

The third member of the household was a dapper little old boy named Willie Agnew, a small, self-important bore who had never done a lick of work in his life but had "made Ivy" and was now one of the immovable pillars of the Nassau Club. A fellow member, John Cuyler, who regarded Willie with a mixture of annoyance and amusement, used to say that when he encountered him at a party, holding forth in his drawling, deadly style to a dazed knot of listeners, he simply turned him around ("Willie never notices") and he would go on talking to the new group as if nothing had happened.

Schuyler, however, found Willie Agnew not amusing but hateful, and this bad feeling was returned with interest. Though there must have been at least forty years' difference in their ages, their mutual vindictiveness brought them both down to the same schoolboy level. Things came to a head when Schuyler filled the bathtub with Willie's shoes, of which he had about thirty pairs, just at the time when Willie always took his bath. Willie demanded that Schuyler be evicted from the house. Instead David Paton read the riot act to both of them.

3

In junior year, the beginning of the last and best two years of college, my roommate and I moved to ground-floor rooms in Cuyler Hall—in those days a quiet spot near the edge of the university campus. Hart was toiling away as dourly as ever, determined to win his Phi Beta Kappa. He was also in love, which didn't make him any happier.

One evening Schuyler rapped on our door. He had come to ask Hart some question about a course they were both taking, and Hart gave him an exceptionally cordial welcome. I said hello, and went on reading my book in the corner. But I couldn't concentrate. I wished I were able to join naturally in the conversation, but I felt too shy of this admired and unknown person. I had nothing to say; besides, they were talking shop, and not my shop.

Then a silence fell. I kept on trying to read.

Schuyler said: "Why do you sit there, pretending to read, and being so tense?"

I don't remember what I stammered, or perhaps I didn't say anything. The next moment he had gone.

Hart and I looked at each other and agreed that that was an odd thing to have said. But then, as we both knew, Jackson was not an ordinary kind of person. I thought to myself: I wonder if it was me he came to see? How or when we next met I can't remember, but I think it must have been soon after that evening; and I think I took the initiative. I know I went to see him at the house on Washington Road. Was David Paton dead by then? And had Willie Agnew moved out? I don't recall seeing either of them then or on my frequent visits thereafter. But the only part of the house I remember clearly is Schuyler's ground-floor study, a small, cheerful room wainscoted with books, the walls between the bookshelves paneled, mullioned windows and a fireplace.

I had never gone out of my way to make a friend. At school, where I had been an unathletic, shy and pious misfit, few except other misfits had sought me out. At Princeton, drink to a certain extent released me from my bondage to timidity, and brought me some friends who would certainly not have come my way otherwise. Now, not for the first time but with my first determination to do something about it, I had met someone whose friendship I wanted. I decided to ask Schuyler to join the Tuesday Evening Club—so-called because our first meeting happened to be held on a Tuesday evening in my rooms. The membership was small and selected by me: Seward Collins, Louis Laflin, Henry Young, Balfour Daniels, Robert Brooke and myself. Some of us acted or wrote for the Théâtre Intime, some wrote for the *Nassau Lit.* We decided to meet once a week, at each member's rooms in turn. The purpose of the club would be to talk about writing and to read things we had written. The first meeting was not a success. Someone mentioned poetry. This was a sore subject with me, as I wrote "poems" of a kind, but not the kind that the *Nassau Lit* liked to publish. From the lame discussion that ensued it became painfully obvious that our thoughts about poetry were crass, shallow and sophomoric. I said, "What about getting Schuyler Jackson to join us?" It turned out that no one really knew him except by reputation, but that they all thought it was worth trying. I was deputed to invite him.

He accepted the invitation, and came to the next meeting. His presence made us all self-conscious and uncomfortable; various attempts were made to draw him into the limping discussion, but he kept silent, puffing furiously at his pipe and looking at the

16

floor. Even when he was directly appealed to, he took his pipe out of his mouth long enough to say that he couldn't trust himself to speak on the subject of poetry.

But at last it was too much for him, and he burst out into a tirade whose eloquence and intensity were quite beyond our powers, demolishing in a few sentences the ignorant blasphemies with which we had been baiting him, and opening our eyes to a prospect of poetry that (to me, at any rate) was like a newness of life. Poetry, it appeared, was not a mere department of writing like fiction or essays or biography; it was the essence, the distillation of writing itself, so superior to other forms in its true nature that it was of a different kind; just as the true poet was different from other men in being dedicated to the whole-souled and lifelong practice of his calling.

I was swept away by this passionate proclamation, and instantly accepted everything Schuyler said. Others raised objections or tried to pick holes in his argument: his mind was so much quicker and better armed than theirs that he scattered them like chaff. That was the real beginning of the Tuesday Evening Club, which Schuyler dominated from that time on. It was also the beginning of our friendship.

4

In those days I thought Schuyler and everything about him perfect. He seemed by so much the superior of any friend I had ever had that I could see no flaw in him, only certain peculiarities of excellence. Hart, whose eye was honester than mine, would not have agreed that Schuyler's good looks were classical and faultless. (I had told Hart that the sixteen-year-old girl I was in love with, Julie Cuyler, was "perfectly beautiful"; and after his first sight of her he solemnly corrected me: her legs were not perfect, nor her nose, and her eyes were too close together.)

Nevertheless, Schuyler in his youth was arrestingly handsome. His head was round, with a broad, high brow; cheekbones marked, mouth and jaw firm, lips thin; his eyes, like his sister Peggy's, intense—but, unlike hers, piercing. His shoulders were broad and his body well muscled. He carried himself proudly, whether standing or sitting: he had "presence." He was just my height, perhaps a shade less, which would make him about 5 feet 11. He walked with a springy gait that gave him an air of haste and at the same time had something dogged and challenging about it.

He wore his clothes well and easily, as if they had been beautifully made for him and he born to wear the best. And they *were* beautifully made, though not for him. David Paton had left him his whole wardrobe, which had come from the best tailors, bootmakers and hatters in England, and they were an exact fit for Schuyler. As long as this legacy lasted—and they were of the quality to last for years—Schuyler was without question the best-dressed undergraduate in Princeton. When he wanted to be, that is: when he made a trip to New York or went to Philadelphia to see a girl. Most of the time he didn't bother.

But he always wore a good suit when he went to Ivy, for lunch or dinner. Most club members lunched and dined at their club every day—and had breakfast there too, if they got up in time. (I usually took three meals a day at my club, Tower; although I refused to have breakfast at the same table as Hart, because he chewed with his mouth open.) Schuyler, however, rarely made an appearance at Ivy, and when he did, usually took a friend along to keep him company. I went there with him several times as his "bodyguard." I think I knew and disliked more of his Ivy classmates than he did, since I had known many of them at St. Paul's. Schuyler was barely acquainted with them; he owed his election to his friendship with upperclassmen like Freddy Lincoln—and perhaps to some graduate members who knew his family.

It was some time, however, before we were on close enough

terms for him to invite me to dinner at Ivy. After that Tuesday evening when he had exploded into eloquence about poetry we met often; we had a lot to talk about. Usually these talks went on in his study, and lasted late. We talked about everything, but mainly poetry. Or rather, he harangued me (it was almost that) and read aloud. At first I was shy of him, and fearful of disclosing the abysses of my ignorance. This was a new experience for me: hitherto I had considered myself much better read than most of my contemporaries—but Dante was only a name to me; I had the sketchiest acquaintance with French and English poetry, having read almost nothing beyond the assignments in my courses; and I had read no modern poetry at all. My taste in verse had been formed in the nursery and was based on a liking for Macaulay, Longfellow and Henry Newbolt. I regarded Butcher & Lang's translation of the Odyssey as the equivalent—no, worse: as the unmasking—of Homer.

Schuyler's familiarity with poets I had barely heard of, and the intensity of his feelings about the poems he loved dazzled and confused me. While I was being swept away by the torrent of his enthusiasm I kept struggling for a foothold. When I heard him say that poetry is written with passion, I thought I had found one.

"What about *We Are Seven?*"

His answer was to read it to me—with passion. That floored me; although later, when I first saw Beerbohm's cartoon of Yeats introducing George Moore to the Queen of the Fairies, I had to admit to myself that Moore's expression exactly echoed my own inner feeling. Schuyler could read *We Are Seven* with passion; but what about that old sheep-faced Wordsworth, tranquilly chewing his recollective cud, and sometimes embarrassing the silence by bleating like a village idiot? Such carpings, however, could not stand up against Schuyler's eager advocacy, and I found myself gladly admitting that a man who could write such sonnets and such odes was indeed one of the great ones, and must be allowed his Thursday at-homes.

Schuyler read or recited poetry like a man possessed: leaning forward in his chair, his sinewy hands rubbing his knees, shoul-

19

ders lifted and writhing, head back and eyes shut, the muscles working in his bony face, his voice a chant in monotone, sometimes mordant, sometimes yearning. His many favorites he knew by heart, and the best passages in the ones he had to follow in the book, so it was always more of a recitation than a reading.

Professor Harper, the Wordsworth scholar who had first tried to have Schuyler dropped from his course, also read aloud sometimes, to a dozen of us sitting around a classroom table. His voice, creaky and rather hoarse, and his simple, serious manner, were the antithesis of Schuyler's, but there was one occasion when I thought him no less effective. He was reading us Wordsworth's poem *Michael.* When he came to the line, *And never lifted up a single stone,* he broke off, cleared his throat gruffly, and went back a couple of lines, like the rider of a balky horse trying the fence again. No use; he couldn't do it, and after another try he gave up, and blew his nose. I never forgot that.

I kept another argument against passion in poetry up my sleeve, but of course ended by producing it: my own practice. I had been writing verses in secret for several years, not because I wanted to make something beautiful but simply as a relief from the torments of adolescence. My only qualifications were a good ear for scansion and an inexhaustible fund of self-pity. The verses were of the simplest form and as black as I could make them. Rhymes were my bane, and when in need of one I used to consult Thomas Hood's *Rhymester*—feeling as guilty about it as I afterwards felt when I went for synonyms to Roget's *Thesaurus.* Though I suspected that my verses were not very good, I hoped they were better than I thought. I hid the growing hoard in a drawer of my desk. I was torn between the desire to show them to someone who would tell me, looking at me with new eyes, "Why, these are very good! You really are a poet"; and the still, small voice that said: "If they were good, *you* would know it. Wait, and work." At last I did show some of them to my roommate, Hart; and to Julie, with whom I was then and ever after in love. And I reaped my proper reward: Hart sniffed and said they weren't much; Julie thought them "morbid."

Once bitten, twice shy. I resolved to keep my verses a secret from Schuyler. But in such a friendship there can be no secrets, and he soon got this one out of me. Before I gave them to him to read, however, I tried to hedge my bet by explaining that they couldn't be considered serious statements; after all they were only light verse, jingles; and that if they *were* to be taken seriously, they didn't fit his definition of poetry, for they certainly weren't written with passion, in his sense of the word.

He took them away and read them, and his reply was an angry lecture: by God, they certainly *were* serious—and why did I pretend they weren't? And of course they were written with passion: that was obvious in all the good lines (which he pointed out), just as the attempt to deny it was obvious in most of the bad ones (which he also pointed out). I was startled, impressed and lifted up on high. I accepted his criticism, that went without saying; I also accepted his judgment that my verses were or could be or pointed the way to a kind of poetry, in their own right. It was all and more than I could have hoped for. After that I didn't care, or didn't care so much, what other people thought.

But I never attained his certainty of taste or judgment; I could never tell, as he could, whether what I had written was good, bad or indifferent. And though it might be true (and I very much wanted to believe it was true) that I really was in some sense a poet, I knew that I was not in his class. I thought then, and still think, that the poems he wrote as an undergraduate were extraordinary, far above the undergraduate level. This opinion was corroborated by J. C. Squire, the English editor who later printed many of them in the *London Mercury*.

Schuyler's attitude towards my verse, I sometimes thought, was rather like mine towards Wordsworth's: you never knew when that mumbling old bastard's voice would ring out clear and true, in a line like minted gold—and neither, apparently, did he. Once (but this was years after we had finished college) I showed him a new version of a verse of mine in which I had changed a line—I hoped for the better, but as usual wasn't sure. Schuyler was sure: he scribbled angrily in the margin, "Throw this shit out!" And another time, when we were still undergraduates, he so admired a line of mine, *And wind high overhead,* that he asked me if he might use it in a poem he was writing. I said, of course; but I couldn't understand why he thought it was so good, or needed my permission to "borrow" it.

In our senior year I was chairman of the *Nassau Lit,* a post that in those days still brought a few hundred dollars with it, and—more important—the power to publish or reject whatever the chairman fancied. I gave Schuyler the job of picking the poetry, and naturally we published a good deal of our own. These verses, especially Schuyler's longer and more ambitious ones, and my very short ones, were not popular; but his were generally respected and mine were laughed at. At the end of the year, when the senior class traditionally chooses various egregious members ("Gloomiest," "Most respected," "Most apt to succeed"), I was overwhelmingly voted "Worst poet," and Schuyler "Most brilliant."

The high hand with which Schuyler chose the *Lit*'s verse was equally in evidence in the Tuesday Evening Club. At our meetings any member could read anything he had written, and sometimes we heard a story or a play, but poetry was the thing, and Schuyler dominated the field. It was his idea to print a small book of verse, a selection of those written by members of the club. Schuyler and I chose the ones we wanted, and gave ourselves the lion's share. Schuyler supplied the title—*The Book of the Tuesday Evening Club*—decided on the size, the typeface and the cover (as near a match as he could find to one of the Cuala Press editions of Yeats's poems) and the dedication (to Professor Harper); and wrote the brief but portentous foreword (". . . we are young, and have a long time to live. Some of us, not professing poetry, are not here represented"), which announced that we had enlisted for life in the ranks of dedicated poets. This swearing-in by proxy gave me a slight shiver; I don't think the others, even if they were meant to be included, noticed that they had been conscripted.

5

As I walked up the graveled driveway to Schuyler's house (I never thought of it as David Paton's house), I could see on my right the lighted windows of the ground-floor study. He was in, then. But when I rang the bell it was not he that opened the door but Old Mary.

"Misther Jackson? Yes, I dunno . . ."

The study door was closed. Perhaps he didn't want to be disturbed. I tapped lightly on the door, and heard him shout "Come in!" He looked up, frowning, from the desk; but when he saw it was me he jumped up, smiling, and slapped me on the shoulder. No, no; he was glad to be interrupted, it wasn't an interruption, he was very glad I'd come. Sit down, have a drink. What was it? Pure alcohol—but *pure*. A man he knew and trusted had got it for him from the Chem Lab. Not so bad, if you mixed it with grape juice.

It was pretty bad, at that; but after the first gagging swallow it went down more easily. We commented on its taste (awful), appearance (like the stuff in Mithridates' cup), immediate effect (good), long-range (non-poisonous—we hoped). In Prohibition days this kind of speculation was as unavoidable as snuffling about the weather is to the British. Being young and blessed with good constitutions, we survived this horrible Prohibition booze and even enjoyed it, at the time. Next morning was another story.

Did I know what Chesterton said about drink? No? That drink is a sacrament, to be taken only when you are happy; to drink when you're sad is a sin. No sin here! And speaking of Chesterton, remember his verses about Noah? Ah, you must hear them, then.

"What's that, Schuyler? Listen!"

In the silence there was a faint scratching sound on the closed door, and a low murmuring.

"Oh, Misther Jackson, Misther Jackson, me feet're killin' me. Oh, Misther Jackson . . ."

"Go to bed, Mary!"

The scratching and the complaining murmur died away, then threatened to begin again.

"Mary! Go to bed. "

Silence.

"It's just her way of being sociable. A kind of Irish Wailing Wall." (Or perhaps she too liked to hear him read?)

Squire's Georgian anthology once tapped, other favorite vintages poured out: Belloc's *Tarantella* and *Lines on a Dead Hostess,* Hodgson's *Eve* and *The Bull* and *A Song of Honour;* Flecker's *War Song of the Saracens,* Graves's *In the Wilderness* and *Star Talk* and *To Lucasta on Going to the Wars.* And sooner or later, Yeats: all roads led to him. The early Yeats of Cuchulain and Oisin, of Innisfree and the Phoenix and the curlew crying in the west; the aging, savage, Swift-like Yeats was still to come.

A Shropshire Lad, just published, burst on us (on me particularly) like a revelation. Housman had stolen all the thunder in my sky; yet I wasn't envious, I didn't grudge him his titanic theft. In fact, I took to him so naturally and with such admiration, his lines committed themselves to my memory so easily, that I decided he must be second-rate. My rule of thumb then was that great poetry bored me: I found it incomprehensible or dull, and in any case for me the words lay dead on the page. I thought I could recognize great poetry by the respect and the dislike, in almost equal amounts, it roused in me. Must I specify? All right: most of Shakespeare (I mean most of the sonnets and both of his long artificial poems); Milton (the epics); Spenser (everything—except for a line or two in the *Amoretti*); Shelley (except for bits and pieces). That should give an idea of my taste.

These evenings with Schuyler were usually spent in his study; when he came to our rooms Hart might break his adamantine rule and join us, or if he didn't, his silent, toiling presence beyond the closed door was like a weight on our talk. Or if someone else dropped in, Schuyler would retire into monosyllables, with puffs from his pipe like sardonic exclamation marks.

6

As a little boy, like many little boys, I had been subject to fits of hero-worship; most of my fellows shed this tendency as they began to grow up and saw the chance of becoming heroes of a sort themselves; but not I. An older boy at my first school, a master at my second, were successively adored by me. The older boy knew it; the master didn't. But the boy had been as strictly brought up as I and was nearly as innocent, so although our friendship had a homosexual tinge and might have laid us open to the charge, we never got close to being lovers, and the bonfire at which we warmed ourselves only brought a comforting flush to our faces.

Afterwards I was ashamed of both these friendships, or rather of the exaggerated emotion I felt they had roused in me. I was also thankful to have escaped, more by good luck than good management, an embarrassment that might have become a danger. As a consequence, in my undergraduate years I tried to avoid making friends with anybody; and the few who attached themselves to me did so at their own insistence, in spite of my cold-shoulder tactics, and I never allowed one of them any real intimacy.

Schuyler was an altogether different case. Our acquaintance, which began at a high pitch, intensified by alcohol, flamed almost instantly into a friendship we both acknowledged as inextinguishable. Emotionally, it was as if we were twin brothers who had somehow been separated until now, and who recognized one

another at first sight. I say "emotionally" for in every other respect we were entirely different, and in the realm of feeling too
he was my leader and elder. This difference between us was
never mentioned but we both took it for granted from the start:
that he was the major twin, superior to me in strength of character and of body, in intelligence, insight and purity of purpose. He
led and I followed. I thought him the handsomest human being,
with the most brilliant and perceptive mind, I had ever encountered. Did he share my opinion? I only know that he was as sure
of himself, as certain of his abilities and of his goal, as I was unsure
and uncertain of my own.

What was there about me, then, that he should admit me to
the position of his closest friend? I often used to ask myself that
question, and I could find no answer except that, in some way I
could never satisfactorily explain, and in spite of the obvious
discrepancy between his superior abilities and my minor ones,
we were like complementary twins. As our friendship progressed
and I got to know him better, I discovered traits in him that made
him in my eyes more human but no less lovable. For one thing,
he was anxious about losing his hair; for another, he was proud
of his legs. Since baldness was the inevitable lot, as he admitted,
of all the men in his family, anxiety on this score was a waste of
time. His legs were indeed very well shaped.

Before we were both married, I felt that his understanding
of me was deeper and more sensitive than my understanding of
him—or of myself. In affection I could hope that we were nearer
equals, though he was far warmer and more demonstrative than
I.

I was a slow developer in every way; my adolescence came
late and lasted too long, so that as a young man I still had growing
pains and suffered from black depressions for no cause that I
could fathom. When the black dog was on my back there was no
way I knew to get rid of it except wait it out; but when Schuyler
was available I sometimes visited my dismal mood on him.

I remember one evening in spring, one of those harbinger

26

days when everything seems to stir with such hope that it would hardly be surprising to see wildflowers push up through the concrete sidewalks and the asphalt streets; and by some perverse fallacy of self-pitying youth, I was in despair. I went to find Schuyler in his room. He was settled with a book, but when he saw the state I was in he dropped the book and came with me. We walked for hours through the country, at first in silence; he was amazingly patient and I was tongue-tied. There seemed to be literally nothing left to say.

"Half the time you don't need to say anything."

He knew what I meant: the other half, when you need words, you haven't got them.

That was what the agonizing problem came down to: the impossibility of putting the trouble in words, the super-impossibility of finding words that would stand up under the burden and carry them to another person. I suppose it was a foretaste of loneliness, a glimpse of "reality"—but more like a glancing, warning blow—bringing the icy news that no help or hope whatever can come to you from outside; the panic dread of discovering that you are in solitary confinement for life.

If I could have put this feeling into even such unsatisfactory words as these, it would have been some relief; but it was as if I had lost the power of speech. These half-formed thoughts went buzzing and whirring through my head like ricocheting bullets, while the observer on this mental rifle range kept coolly signaling that no shot had yet hit the target. For I was the sardonic observer as well as the inept marksman. I wondered whether I was going mad, or was there already.

With a long-suffering sympathy beyond anything I could have summoned, Schuyler bore with my lengthy, sullen silences, my occasional sighs or strangled growls of despair or rage, my preliminary clearings of the throat that were only false alarms. He said nothing, and kept tramping along beside me. When I stopped, he stopped, waiting till I went on again.

The stars that night were brilliant. We stood and looked at

them, our incredibly distant, our only neighbors.

"If you look—look at them for three minutes, you *know* there's no hope."

This was nowhere near expressing what I wanted to say, but Schuyler, I knew, would fill in the gaps.

He said nothing. And we didn't look for as long as three minutes. We walked on.

When he spoke, it was a kind of answer.

"Most things don't need to be said. And some things can't be."

"Doesn't leave much."

"Enough."

There was another silence, but this one was not uninhabitable.

Sometimes, though not often, it was the other way about. Whereas I smoldered and occasionally rumbled and grew depressingly cloudy, Schuyler erupted: when he blew his top it was rains of fire and streams of molten lava. These rare outbursts never emanated from cold blood, as mine did; they started in fury and were magnified by drink into an upheaval that was less like drunkenness than madness.

Our friendship was like an alliance between fire and ice. Schuyler was capable of Promethean rages, especially in drink: at the stage where the ordinary person would be talking thickly and making no sense Schuyler would be brilliant, eloquent, mad —and sometimes dangerous. I remember only once seeing him the worse for drink; we had ended the evening in my rooms, and perhaps the nightcap I gave him was bad stuff—at any rate, when he left I offered to see him home, but he shook me off. It was only about a quarter of a mile to his house; there had been a deep snow but the college paths were cleared. He floundered off from the path and fell in the snow. I went to help him up: I thought he had passed out. As I bent over him he said thickly but clearly: "God damn you, leave me alone!" He worked his way to his feet and faced me with a look of threatening hate. The starlight on the snow was bright enough for me to see that, and it was such a shock that I stepped back.

"Get away from me, you bastard!"

He plunged towards me; I took a step to the side, and he fell on one knee.

"Schuyler!"

"Shut up, you crummy shit!"

He got to his feet and started off again. He hadn't gone ten paces when he fell and lay still. I ran up to him, and just as I got there he pulled himself up and swung at me. I dodged and he fell again with the force of the swing. Then he hauled himself up and staggered on. I followed him; he fell several times, but I didn't try to help him. I followed him till he got to the door of his house, and I watched him go in.

When I saw him next day he was white-faced and red-eyed. He remembered nothing that had happened the evening before. When I tried to tell him, he wouldn't believe me.

The University did not encourage drunkenness among its undergraduates, especially during Prohibition, when the sale of any sort of liquor was illegal, its quality dubious and often poisonous. We were not addicts, but we would drink just about anything we could get our hands on. One of my classmates downed a bottle of lilac perfume, which impelled him to such drunken and disorderly behavior that he was expelled. Dean McClenahan was said to have told him that he had disgraced himself and the University not only by being drunk but by smelling like a cheap tart.

The university police force consisted of one proctor, Hank Bovie, and his assistant, Frank. Hank was a large, quiet-spoken, motherly man who only investigated unusually loud noises. Most of the evening he patrolled Nassau Street, occasionally dropping in to the Balt, to which drunken undergraduates were magnetically impelled to come for coffee and scrambled eggs. If they were quiet about it, Hank let them alone. I am sorry to say that I was several times admonished and at least once reported by Hank for being noticeably intoxicated (that would have been his phrase, I think). I remember Dean McClenahan, who had to deal with all such undergraduate crimes, telling me in his dry but sympathetic way that he would not send the report home, as he was bound to do, till after the approaching holiday, as he didn't want to spoil my parents' Easter.

Schuyler never once ran foul of the proctor; he seemed to be magically immune, or perhaps he was just lucky, and when I was with him his luck protected me too. One winter afternoon he and I were drinking (alcohol and plain water, this time; there was no grape juice) in his study, and had reached that stage of well-being where it seems all-important to continue feeling that way. Just in time I remembered that I was due to have dinner with Louis Laflin at his family's house, to decide on next term's plays for the Théâtre Intime. The Laflin house was on the other side of Princeton.

Schuyler insisted on escorting me there, and I needed his arm to steady me. Alcohol and plain water, I found, had a delayed but powerful effect: I was feeling drunker and drunker. Schuyler left me at the Laflins' door with an encouraging slap on the back, and I tottered carefully in. Luckily Louis's parents were out for the evening: no one else was there but Louis and the butler. I managed to get to the dining room and sit down, but I couldn't eat a mouthful of food, nor in fact open my mouth. Louis dismissed the butler and did his best to make a monologue simulate a conversation.

Halfway through dinner a strange booming sound came from the hallway, and the next moment there was Schuyler, on his hands and knees, padding through the door: I saw instantly that he was imitating a Hyrcanian tiger, and had come to rescue me. I got up and went with him without a word.

This was a disgraceful exhibition on my part; and I suppose he shouldn't have done what he did. At the time, however, I was not only tremendously grateful to him but hugely entertained.

7

We were all hopelessly in love in those days, with unattainable girls. Mine was simply unattainable. Hart's was not so much unattainable as undesirable, at least from his family's point of view. She was pretty but not an accepted Philadelphian—in fact, not a Philadelphian at all: she lived in East Orange. That was enough to rule her out, and Hart knew it. Her unacceptableness made his love a tragic affair. On spring evenings it would get him down to such an extent that he would abandon his books for half an hour and get out his fiddle. (He preferred to have the lights out, and as I wasn't studying I didn't mind.) He stood in front of the open casement window, scraping mournful sounds out into the soft night, and heaving such sighs that he had to blow his nose.

His family became alarmed, as well they might, when he wore red socks to a Philadelphia Assembly. They put their heads together and decided to give a party for the girl from East Orange. Only the flower of Philadelphia society was invited: all the girls were dowdy and all the men in white tie and tails. The girl from East Orange was dressed to the nines, and for the first hour she thought she was having the time of her life: the men queued up to cut in on her and give her a whirl. Gradually it dawned on her why all the women were whispering and watching, and she began to feel like the tart she was being made to appear. She ended the evening in tears. And that was the end of that. The party had been a great success.

Schuyler was in love with a series of girls. His first was a Philadelphian named Mary Ernestine Appleton, a beauty. She had many beaux, perhaps some more serious than Schuyler. At any rate, their affair didn't last very long. I thought at the time she was too worldly; I suppose I meant too popular. She came to

Princeton once to see him, and he gave her tea in his study. He wrote a sonnet about her which appeared first in the *Lit* and then in *The Book of the Tuesday Evening Club:*

UNREST IN LOVE

For M.E.A.

Out of the world I come to you, where strife
Is daily intercourse, and the feverous light
Of battle is the guiding-torch of life,—
Out of this world I come to you tonight.
And out of seas, ship-wrecking, salt, and gray,
Full of shrill winds, and the wild sea-bird's cry,
Where the waves cease not to rise, falling away,
My love I come to you; here let me lie.
For neither arms, nor ships tossed by the sea,
Nor age, nor winds, can reach unto your breast;
And I lie on your breast; and dream drowsily
Of love that is a sleep, and turn to my rest.
Yet love cries out, even as I kiss your lips,
To forge strange armour, and to man new ships.

Both Hart and I were in love in a painfully specific way; Schuyler seemed luckier or more sensible because his state of being in love was more general. On a maddeningly beautiful spring afternoon, when only Hart could bear to stay indoors with a book, Schuyler sometimes tucked a $5 bill in the sole of his shoe and went for a run in the country. The $5 was in case he met a pretty girl who was that easy to bribe. He didn't meet one, but if he had, I was sure she would have gone with him for nothing.

When he finally arranged something, it cost him more than $20, and might have seemed too commercial if it hadn't been for his elaborate preparations. He found out from some of his club-mates at Ivy that a youngish married woman whose husband ran a small store on Nassau Street was usually available, at that high price. I had seen her driving around town in her shiny black Model-T cabriolet, and thought her elderly (I suppose she may have been thirty); but her reputation of being a woman who sinned easily, with a husband whom I also knew by sight and wondered about—did he know? didn't he care?—gave her a wicked glamour that made up for her marceled red hair and her hard face with a nose that was too big.

Schuyler arranged a date with her to come to his house the following Saturday evening. The day before, he bought some flowers for the bedroom—they must have cost at least $5—and a small bottle of perfume; he wouldn't tell me what he'd spent on that, either. He gave Old Mary the evening off; maybe he paid for her to go to the movies.

On Saturday I went to the early movies myself, with Bill Hale. Usually we strolled up Nassau Street afterwards, smoking Bock panatelas, because they were the only cigars small enough and mild enough for us to manage—and even then we had to walk to the curb every now and then and spit in the gutter—but this time I left him, and headed down Washington Road past Schuyler's house. Sure enough, there was the shiny black Ford cabriolet standing in the drive, and no lights on upstairs. I walked back to my room, feeling very inexperienced but at the same time as if I'd escaped something.

When I saw Schuyler next day he wouldn't say anything, except that it was "all right." He looked faraway and pleased with himself, and there was a faint smell of perfume about him.

In senior year he fell in love like the rest of us; but, being Schuyler, it was worse and more of it. And in his case too the girl was unattainable, though I couldn't see why. Later I think I did see why: her mother was afraid of him, and the girl was too dutiful a daughter to break away. Perhaps she was a little afraid of him herself; though I think she could have got over that, if she'd been allowed to try.

Her name was Sarnia Marquand. Her family lived in a large, handsome-ugly stone house on the edge of Princeton; it stood in 30 acres of parkland and big trees next to the Pyne place. Her father, recently dead, was immortalized in stone in MacMonnies's monument to the Battle of Princeton: his head, under an eighteenth-century tricorn hat, was one of the most prominent

33

features of that messy masterpiece. Two buildings on the university campus, the university chapel and the art museum, bore the Marquand name, and both were stamped with the same ugly-handsome architectural hallmark as the Marquand house.

Allan Marquand was one of the small group of rich men who lived in Princeton around the turn of the century; he founded the department of Art and Archaeology, which he headed for years, and published eight books on the art of Della Robbia.

Sarnia, his youngest daughter, had goldeny-red hair, a high-arched nose, gray eyes, a profile like a Della Robbia bas-relief. She was beautiful, but she bore herself so modestly, deprecating herself and changing the subject before it even started, that it wasn't her beauty you thought of but her shyness. You wanted to say, "Oh, come on, Sarnia." No one ever did say that. If her shyness spread to you, as it always did to me, she would see it and sometimes begin to tease you gratefully, in her rather harsh, low voice that didn't go with her face or her gentleness. Her voice sounded as though she had never learned to let it go. This teasing, which was usually no more than repeating your last awkward, conversation-making remark—*quoting* it rather than repeating it, with her voice like two mocking hands holding it between them—was as much affection as she ever let herself show. But no one believed that was all of her: we knew there was much more.

Schuyler, whose poetry-name for her was "Sylvia," a name that didn't fit her, saw more in her than anybody. I don't think it was her quietness that attracted him, as much as the prospect of stirring up the quietness into something else. Anyway, it was his violence that frightened her—and her mother. I had the feeling that if Sarnia and I could bring ourselves past each other's guard, it might be a good thing if we could get married. That was out of the question, of course; not only because of Schuyler but because I was in love with Julie, although she was hardly aware of me. I felt a shy affection for Sarnia, but I wasn't a bit in love with her.

The three Marquand girls, Eleanor, Mary and Sarnia, sometimes shepherded by their formidable mother, whose smile, when she really unsheathed it, put you in fear of your life, gave tea every Sunday afternoon to a select group of undergraduates. Yes, it was select: if any weeding out had to be done, Mrs. Marquand whipped out her smile and did the job in a jiffy. Within our approved limits, this little band of regulars seldom varied. Alfred Barr (the first Director of the Museum of Modern Art in New York) was one I remember. I was often one of them, Schuyler never.

Eleanor, the oldest, was considered the best-looking; her face had a delicate dark beauty, but her faintly withering Bryn Mawr glance and manner put some people off. She reminded me of the intellectual lady in Lewis Carroll's rhyme (or the Peter Newell illustration):

> But with a tinge of bitterness
> She said, "The more exceeds the less."

Mary, the second, was the funniest and the best company. She and Julie, when they were little girls, had played a trick on Mrs. Wheaton, a mild and fluttery lady: they went to call on her while she was taking her afternoon rest, sending the maid upstairs with cards from the President and Mrs. Hibben (Mary had snitched them from her mother's collection). Mrs. Wheaton dressed herself in a hurry and wasn't much amused to find two giggling little girls in her drawing room. And years later, when Mary and I were sitting at the same table at a bridge party where the game was taken seriously, we subverted our two partners into playing, the whole evening, with the cards turned face out; and whenever I was dummy I snooped around the other tables to see what their high scores were and then raised Mary's higher, so that she won first prize. The upshot was that Mary returned the prize the next day, we both apologized to our hostess, and I was never again invited to a bridge party—which suited me.

Sarnia was much too gentle and considerate to play a practical joke on anybody. On the other hand, those same virtues of gentleness and considerateness had been so rigidly corseted by her upbringing that they often appeared as mere timidity and a conventionality that came close to becoming a bore. If I had been in love with her, I would not have put up with her conversation for a minute: this prim plodding, like a caterpillar of schoolgirls being prodded along on their afternoon promenade, would have maddened me. As it was, I just found talking to Sarnia pretty heavy going. That winter I went for several walks with her on Sunday afternoons, returning to her house for tea; but the effort of keeping up a conversation was too much for me, and after the first try I persuaded a friend of mine, Jim Brodhead, to come along with us. Jim was an irrepressible and laughing talker: words bubbled out of him continually, like a bird soliloquy. And like a bird, when the mood was on him, he sang. Sarnia took to him, as everyone did, and thereafter we were a threesome.

Schuyler would never have fitted nor allowed himself to fit into the tiresome correctness of these Marquand at-homes. Yet somehow he and Sarnia met. On her part it must have been, or felt, like a clandestine affair. Once the three of us had tea in Schuyler's study. I am sure he would have preferred to be alone with her; my being there as chaperon would have been the condition of her coming. Even so, her evident agitation made me ill at ease. Schuyler, however, was beside himself with happiness and so taken up with the delights of playing host to her that he seemed unaware of her nervousness.

Sarnia was "musical." She played the violin—I don't know how well, for I never heard her—and I used to see her at concerts in Alexander Hall. That kind of music always made me think of something else, but whenever I looked at Sarnia I could see that she was listening to it; she looked then as if she were listening with her whole heart. And she wrote a short piece for violin: she wrote it for Schuyler, and gave it to him. Or *did* she actually write it for him? It would have been an amazingly forward gesture for her to make, an almost open declaration of her interest. Whether she wrote it for him or not, I am sure she would have liked to keep the whole thing a secret from her mother, but I am equally sure she wasn't able to. Schuyler, on the other hand, was so happy that he wanted to tell the world about it. He wrote a poem which shortly afterwards appeared in the *Lit:*

To Sylvia, Who Sent Me Music of Her Own Composing

For S.M.

Sylvia, thanks in verses take,
Born in me for your sweet sake,
For music more than words can make.

You are apart from me, yet I
Wandering, a cloudy stranger, by,
Catch down a star from out of your sky.

I know not how your spirit steers
Through hopes and through wind-driven fears
Your proud, indomitable years.

I know that I can never see
That highland of serenity
From whose tall hills you came to me.

But Sylvia, my wild being take,
Broken with spiritual lust and ache
For music more than words can make.

And give it many an hour to know
How delicately proud you go,
And your good god, who made you so.

For more than music is the note—
Sung from a lyric angel's throat—
Your spirit inadvertently wrote.

Give me your peaceful hands, and then
Give me your peaceful hands again,
To be your friend. Amen! Amen!

There was another day that winter when the three of us were together, and this time too it was Schuyler who arranged it. We were to go for a walk, which was to be more than an ordinary walk: there was a sense of solemn occasion about it.

Lately Schuyler had been unusually tense; his face looked drawn and he said he had been sleeping badly. I knew him well enough by now to recognize the symptoms: there was a poem inside him struggling to be born, and by all the signs this one would cause him a supreme effort. I knew there was some connection between our walk and the gestating poem. Perhaps Sarnia did too, or perhaps she thought this expedition another step in Schuyler's odd courtship—as indeed it may have been, although I am sure his inmost concern was with the poem.

The appointed day brought a wild storm of wind and snow, a real blizzard, rare in those parts. We started off early in the afternoon, fought our way for several hours through the drifts and the stinging wind, and came back tired and tingling, with that sense of accomplishment you get from having exerted yourself, no matter how. At least, that's the way I felt; what Sarnia's feelings were I can't say, though as usual she looked cheerful and said how much she had enjoyed herself. Schuyler was in a hurry to leave us, as if he had got what he went for and now wanted to carry it home intact before it ran through his fingers. Two days later, looking ill and saying that he had not slept for two nights, he brought me the finished poem. It was dedicated to Sarnia and me.

The Walk was a set piece, a poem deliberately undertaken and consciously carried out, with the walk itself, a staged afterthought, as crudely necessary as an armature to the sort of sculpture that must have that support. But I thought it then a masterpiece (it even fulfilled my definition of first-rate poetry by going on too long, with passages in it that left me cold or bored me). I still think it an extraordinary production for a young man of twenty-one. It was derivative, though not imitative: it had echoes of Wordsworth—and (I thought) of Milton too; but in the fusion, or near-fusion, of styles I heard Schuyler's own voice beginning to emerge. The passage that moved me most, naturally, was the invocation at the poem's end:

Dear friends, who sweeten the heart that sings for you,
Whom neither age nor bitter way of the world
Can unjoin from me, let this day be one more
Bond between us, to fence off loneliness
And solitude of years. Companioned thus,
The tumultuous rigour of our lives,
After the flail of harvesting time has threshed
The vital grain from our shred, outworn husks,
Can bring us nothing sadder than gray hairs
And wrinkling masks that hide the untouched soul.
And when our malleable and ranging minds
Are steeled and rutted to the cog of things,
Until life trembles, and the sick heart fails,
Let us remember this wild day and all
The glory:—how we stood in ecstasy
On that wild summit; saw the swirl and rise
Of atoms in the womb of air; and felt
The passion of a Spirit hurtling on,
Caught in the tangles of a winter wind,
Over our heads, to plunge down blank horizons
Where old mortality is but a petulant sleep,
And birth and death are dead—forgetting not;
And, thinking and remembering, gather faith.

In spite of the solemnity of this pledge, as I took it to be, that
was the last time the three of us ever met.

8

The Théâtre Intime in our day was not one of the popular campus activities; neither was it as precious as it sounded, with all those prissy French accents. It did tend to attract aesthetes, some of whom might or might not have been queers—if such oddities had been able to exist at Princeton. The Intime's small beginnings were in a large room over the archway of Blair Hall, which could barely hold an audience of twenty or thirty, and where the stage was simply the end of the room, curtained off, with no room for any but the flattest scenery, and no wings. The Intime was too big for its diapers from the start.

Somehow or other Hart and I were roped into one of its more ambitious productions: a translation of Romain Rolland's *Lilluli*. We had no lines to speak but we were kept busy; he was supposed to represent the German Army, and I the French. We marched rapidly across the stage, crawled back at top speed under the imperfect cover of the footlights, and marched across again, to give the illusion of large bodies of troops. This must have been very funny to watch, but we took it with great seriousness, feeling that we were striking a blow for pacifism—or whatever the play was about.

When Louis Laflin took over the Intime, it began to flower. His father gave the money to convert a small auditorium in Murray-Dodge into a proper theater, with raised stage, wings, lighting, space for scenery, and even dressing rooms of a sort. Louis was passionately and permanently stage-struck, an avid Shavian who seemed fated to become himself a famous playwright. Why didn't he? I suppose that, as they say of certain overtrained boxers, "he must have left his fight in the gym." Anyhow, he made the Intime a going concern, and it was all his doing: he was impresario, director, playwright, actor-manager all in one. He wrote dozens of plays himself and encouraged others to write them. I did a few which the Intime put on: one was about Atlas (that was my favorite, and a complete flop), one about a homicidal maniac at Princeton Junction (*not* meant to be funny), and one about a man dying of DT's who at dawn, after a parson has said a prayer over him, sits up in bed and says, "I want my breakfast." That one was thought very daring and might have got me in trouble, as one professor, who had already lodged a complaint about my "socialist" activities, demanded that I be expelled from college for making a public mock of religion. That was also the first Intime play in which a real girl appeared: Sarnia took the part of the trained nurse.

The most ambitious effort the Intime ever made in our day was to stage *Samson Agonistes*. The acting version we used was cut to size by Professor Harper; Schuyler played Samson, Hyatt Mayor (who later became Curator of Prints at the Metropolitan Museum in New York) was Dalila. Hart had a minor part, and I a very small one. *Samson* ran for four nights, a long run for the Intime in those days. Schuyler was tremendous as Samson, and that was not my opinion only. He dominated the play not merely because his was the principal role but by the passionate intensity with which he spoke the great Miltonic lines. His habit of reciting poetry with his eyes shut and his head thrown back, even the writhing motion of his shoulders and his hands moving as though shackled—all this fitted the necessities of the part. Hyatt Mayor was a perfect and almost perfectly beautiful Dalila—all but his hands, which were too large; and his clear alto was pitched exactly right against Schuyler's baritone. The only time I heard the whole thing was at the dress rehearsal; during the performances I waited for my cue in the dressing room under the stage, hearing only the murmur and growl of the voices overhead, and the clanking of Samson's shuffling footsteps. (For his fetters I had borrowed the heavy iron chain looped across the andirons of the living room fireplace in my father's house: a typical Intime improvisation and a great success.)

To one of Schuyler's intense nature the strain of this nightly effort, four times repeated, added to the accumulated stresses of the weeks of rehearsal, brought him near the breaking point. Besides all this, his affair with Sarnia was not going well; in fact, it was not going at all. Mrs. Marquand's vigilant maternal eye must have seen his poem about our walk in the blizzard, which had now been published in the *Lit*, and Sarnia had been in effect forbidden to have anything more to do with him. Sarnia was a dutiful daughter, more obedient to her mother's thumb than responsive to Schuyler's rather scary spell, so for some time they hadn't met. He wrote her; her answers—that she answered at all must have frightened her and made her feel guilty—were increasingly faint. During the four nights of *Samson Agonistes* Schuyler got so little sleep that it seemed to him he hadn't slept at all. After the final performance there was a party for the cast. Schuyler was there, pale and grim, but soon disappeared. Some time after midnight the Marquand household was roused by his voice, calling under Sarnia's window. He had been drinking, but that was not evident except from the incomprehensibility of his words (he may have been reciting Dante); the sound of his voice, however, was dangerous and reckless, unpleasing to a mother's ear. Mrs. Marquand called down to him to go away.

A week or so later, as if she were posting the term's examination results, Mrs. Marquand issued invitations to various suitable young men to come for a summer visit to the Marquands' place in upper New York State, at Keene Valley. It was Bicker Week in reverse: Jim Brodhead and I were among those invited; Schuyler was not. Neither Jim nor I went.

That spring was a dry and cruel season for Schuyler, but I remember one oasis in it: an evening with him and Professor and Mrs. Harper. The Harpers, a mutually devoted, simple, old-fashioned couple, like innocent middle-aged children, were as fond and proud of Schuyler as if he had been their own talented son. That evening we sat in their small garden on Mercer Street, eating gingerbread and drinking milk, and the talk, low-toned and passionate, was of *Paradise Lost.* From the open window, where their daughter Isabel was playing the piano, the pure notes of Mozart came dropping down through our talk, like stones through water.

9

Schuyler made two lifelong friends among the Princeton faculty: George McLean Harper and Francis Charles Macdonald. Both were members of the English department; that and their affection for Schuyler were the only things they had in common. Mr. Harper was a puritan of such sweetness and simplicity that in middle age he was armored in the same bucolic innocence he must have carried as a country boy in Pennsylvania. Frank Macdonald was sophisticated, snobbish, cynical, sentimental, subversive, a gossip who was sometimes malicious, nearly always entertaining, capable of generous impulses, a self-confessed failure, increasingly prone to alcoholic melancholy. He was a bachelor, and lived in a series of large, untidy rooms cluttered by thousands of books, over a shop on Nassau Street.

In a day when the Ph.D. degree had already become the required trade-union card for every university instructor who aspired to rise in the ranks or even to keep his job, Frank Macdonald had somehow managed to become a full professor without this qualification. He was no scholar, and he played his favorites and gave mock veneration to the sacred cows of English literature, just as he singled out those whom he liked among his students and scamped those he didn't. When he was a young instructor at Princeton—or perhaps even before that, in his undergraduate days—he had been in love with one of Woodrow Wilson's daughters; Wilson was then President of the University. She had refused him, and no other woman ever again got the same chance. It may have been this comeuppance that drove him, early in his career, to the Far East, the first of several leaves of absence he spent there. He liked to tell the story of his arriving at Princeton Junction from one of these visits, which had lasted the better part of a year, and there encountering Mrs. Norris, a perpetually flustered widow who eked out a gallant living from a real-estate agency and by collecting "social items" for a local paper. Mrs. Norris had beamed at him and inquired: "Oh, Mr. Macdonald, do tell me where you're going for the summer?" Any Asian student who found his way to Princeton could be sure of Frank Macdonald's welcome and generously helping hand. For the rest, he picked his undergraduate friends with care; nearly all of them were members of Ivy.

Though he had written no scholarly works, he had published a few things: one was a romantic mystery story of which he was ashamed and which he tried to suppress by buying any copies that turned up in the University Store; the others were books of verse. The last of these appeared while Schuyler and I were at Princeton. He gave us each a copy, and alarmed me by writing in mine, after my name: "whose *doom* is to write far better books than this." I didn't see why he chose to take such a low view of himself; it seemed to me evident that he was a far more accomplished poet than I was likely to become, though his poems were not at all my style and I didn't much care for them.

I didn't think Frank Macdonald would ever have taken me up if I hadn't been Schuyler's friend, and this suspicion made me wary and critical of him. I thought him insincere and two-faced, which to a certain extent he was, at least with me; but Schuyler saw more deeply into him and forgave him his deviousness as I did not. I know he loved Schuyler with an affection that held also a completely unenvious admiration: he counted on Schuyler to become the kind of writer he knew himself incapable of being. Then why did he write that inscription in the book of verse he gave me? I suppose it may have been one of his characteristic bursts of generosity, the sort of thing that always surprises me and shames my too-hasty judgment—or it might have been a form of insurance!

If it had not been for Schuyler, who was in his confidence to an extent that I never was, I would not have known about the two central secrets of Frank Macdonald's life. The first was his unhappy love affair with Wilson's daughter; the second—which interested me far more, because it was alive and continuing—was his diary. Schuyler told me that ever since the Wilson days Frank Macdonald had kept a regular journal, copious, scandalous, indiscreet gossip of the goings-on in the University and the town. Nobody, not even Schuyler, had seen this secret history, nor would while its author was alive; but it was to be published after his death. This, I thought, was a real *magnum opus,* and would more than make up for all Frank Macdonald's shortcomings and self-pitying failures. And I still think so, though now it can never be proved; for during his last, increasingly unhappy, sentimental and alcoholic years, in a fit of despair or revulsion he put the whole record in the fire.

On the ship that brought him back from one of his trips to Asia (this one must have been in 1919 or thereabouts) Frank Macdonald made the acquaintance of a fellow passenger, a young Cossack officer named Vladimir Perfilieff. This young White Russian had been carrying a message to General Denikin, had been cut off by the Reds, and to make his escape had boarded the ship to San Francisco. He spoke no English, so he and the American professor conversed in halting French. Vovo (that was the nickname he liked his friends to use) had no money and no plans. Frank Macdonald himself had very little money to spare, but before the voyage was over he invited Vovo to come to Princeton and be his guest there until he could find his feet. Vovo had a keen intelligence, some education, and an enormous talent, like an insatiable appetite, for getting on with people. If he felt like it, and he usually did, he could make himself popular in no time at all, in any sort of company. This talent, which brought him fame though not fortune and was eventually to spell his ruin, was often exercised at the expense of someone else. But this fact was not immediately apparent in his early days, when he was still feeling his way in a foreign tongue.

When Frank Macdonald first brought him to Princeton, Vovo was in his late twenties—a square, powerfully built Russian of medium height, with full face, imperturbable gray eyes, black

45

hair and a small, closely clipped mustache. Except for his schooling as a cadet, his only training was his brief career as a Cossack officer. The first job he got was mowing Dr. Spaeth's lawn. Vovo went at it as if he were leading a Cossack charge. The lawn itself presented few difficulties, but there was also a grassy bank between the sidewalk and Edgehill Street, under the trees, which had unsightly bald patches. Vovo was determined to do this job to rights. And so he did. Dr. Spaeth was delighted; the greens committee of the Springdale Golf Club, when they saw that some vandal had scalped their 18th green, were furious.

Schuyler, in whose life Vovo played a brief but indelible part, must have met him through Mr. Mac in these early days at Princeton. By the time I first saw Vovo he had moved to Philadelphia and was definitely going up in the world. He was then established as a fashionable painter in a large, dark and ornate studio on Sansom Street, and had become the center of the local Russian colony. It was Julie who took me there and introduced me; she had met Vovo at several Philadelphia parties and was proud to be able to show him off to me. Vovo traveled a good deal, often by milk train, at hours that suited his convenience. He once told me that he had made a card catalogue of his friends, and that there were 4,000 cards in the file.

He may indeed have had 4,000 friends—and I don't doubt the existence of that card catalogue—but was Schuyler ever really one of them? In those days, when I thought of friendship as a lifelong affair, I might have doubted it. For a while they were companions and fellow travelers, and it was through Vovo that Schuyler met the girl he married. But all that comes later.

10

In June of 1922 we graduated. We were a famous class: in our four years we had beaten Yale two or three times in football—or something like that. Hart won his Phi Beta Kappa key, with gloomy satisfaction but no evident joy. Schuyler was awarded one too; although technically he had not qualified, the University felt obliged to confer this mark of distinction on the most brilliant member of our class. Neither he nor I was chosen to write the Class Ode: that honor went to a more prominent and popular classmate, whose verses we had always scorned to publish in the *Lit.*

And now what? Of all the professed poets of the Tuesday Evening Club, Schuyler was the only real one. There was no question of what he was going to do, only of where he would do it. For myself, all I was sure of was what I would *not* do: I would not work in an office. So I headed for Oxford, for two more years of being an undergraduate, thus postponing the necessity of making up my mind. Hart was going on to three more years of his accustomed drudgery, this time at the Harvard Law School—not, of course, because he wanted to but because it was expected of him.

Two years before, my father had taken me to call on Canon Spooner, the Warden of New College, Oxford, and then and there the old man had promised to admit me in Michaelmas Term (the autumn term) of 1922. That was the way it was done in those days. I took no entrance examination and had no further interview with anybody. When I arrived in Oxford in October my name was on the college books as a Senior Foreign Student. This meant that I was excused from all examinations until "Schools" (the finals) but had to pay £50 "caution money"—an insurance the college required from all foreign barbarians, in case they turned out to be vandals, window-smashers or worse. If you didn't turn out that way, the money was refunded before you "went down" (left Oxford for good).

I arrived, by ignorance or miscalculation, a day or two early: term had not yet officially begun, and a "gaudy" (the stately Oxford version of a graduates' reunion) was in progress. The college porter, Churchill, emerged from his lodge to set me straight on these matters. He could not have been said to welcome me, but he accepted me. With an archi-episcopal wave of the hand he indicated the general direction of my rooms, and turned away to more pressing duties. Half an hour later, after burrowing through a rabbit warren of medieval passages, entryways and blind alleys, I discovered a doorway in which a list of names, including mine, was neatly painted in white letters on a japanned tin plate. My rooms were at the top of a tower overlooking Holywell Street.

That evening I dined with Dudley Hughes, a Princeton friend and an Oxford veteran of three years' standing, who spent some time admonishing and informing me about correct behavior. One piece of advice he gave me I still remember: if we passed one another on the street I could expect him to nod or even say "hello"—but only the first time; if we met again that day he would simply ignore me.

When I got back to college there was a note at the porter's lodge from Schuyler, to say that he was coming to Oxford next day and would meet me for tea. He had arrived in England a couple of months ahead of me, to visit his mother and favorite sister Peggy, who had also married an Englishman and had settled over here; and had then found himself rooms in a cottage on Boar's Hill, a few miles outside Oxford. We had so much to talk about that he stayed on for dinner; afterwards we went back to my rooms and talked some more. Before we knew it, it was midnight, and he had missed his last bus. So he spent the night on the couch in my study.

This was apparently a grave breach of regulations on my

part, though nothing came of it. When, a few days later, I casually mentioned this small misadventure to Dudley Hughes (he knew Schuyler and disapproved of him), he was appalled: I could thank my stars, he said, that term had not yet officially begun, or I should infallibly have been "sent down" (expelled). To have another man spend the night in your rooms was regarded as tantamount to being caught in the homosexual act. This shocked me even more than Dudley's warning that he would not speak to me if he saw me a second time on the street.

Schuyler had come to England to start his literary career. Squire, the editor of the *London Mercury,* had put it into his head when they had met in Princeton the year before: I don't know whether Squire had suggested it himself or merely agreed that it would be a good idea. He and Schuyler had taken to each other. The *Mercury* was then in its heyday, and a young writer could hardly ask for anything better than to appear in its pages. T. S. Eliot's *Criterion* in London and the *Dial* in New York were more respected by the intelligentsia, but the *Mercury* combined a high standard with a much larger circulation than either of those highbrow magazines. Besides reprinting many of Schuyler's undergraduate poems and several new ones, Squire commissioned him to write some articles. The first was on Yeats.

Schuyler went to Ireland to meet his admired poet, and there was such attunement between them that they found themselves getting up and sitting down in unison and beginning to talk at the same instant. He also made occasional trips to London, where Squire introduced him to Chesterton and Belloc and other panjandrums of the literary world. I think he also went to see Mrs. C. M. Doughty, the widow of the author of *Arabia Deserta,* whose epic poems, never recognized and now forgotten, were one of Schuyler's great admirations; he intended to bring out a new edition of these epics, with notes and a glossary.

Doughty, who is now remembered mainly for his massive *Arabia Deserta,* himself regarded that masterpiece as only a trial heat for the supreme race to which he had dedicated his life and in which he hoped to win an immortal garland; the course he had set himself was the rescue of his beloved mother tongue. The English language, he believed, had begun to be blighted in the sixteenth century, and since then the rot had spread to its very roots. Latinity was the corrupting worm and Anglo-Saxonry was to be the vermifuge. His multi-volume and unread epic poems —*The Dawn in Britain, The Clouds, The Cliffs, The Titans, Adam Cast Forth*—for the writing of which he had trained himself by that arduous pilgrimage through the deserts of Arabia and the dry nobilities of his antique prose, were intended not only as patriotic acts in themselves but as examples of the English tongue as it should be written. Having set his face against the course the language had taken, Doughty would have nothing to do with any word he considered un-English, and this stubborn puritanism drove him into some narrow paths. When he could not lay his hand on a word of Anglo-Saxon lineage to say what he meant, rather than fall back on the corrupt expedient of using a non-English word he would invent what he needed, roots and all. This made his poems difficult, if not impossible, to read without a glossary, which he had been too unbending to supply. With Mrs. Doughty's permission and even blessing, both of which he obtained, Schuyler was to fill this need.

Boar's Hill was itself a nest of poets. The Laureate, Robert Bridges, lived there; so did John Masefield, who was to succeed him. Gilbert Murray, a kind of scholar-poet, had his house halfway up the hill. Robert Graves, whose disastrous meeting with Schuyler was still sixteen years in the future, had just left Boar's Hill for the village of Islip, on the other side of Oxford. Another American and fellow Princetonian, Henry Chapin, who was writing a long poem on Leif Ericsson based on the Norse sagas, was already there with his wife and baby, in a cottage near Schuyler's. I planned to move out there myself for the six-week Christmas vacation; Schuyler got me a room in a cottage not far from his, and I was to have my meals with him.

It was my first taste of the English countryside in winter: long nights, black as pitch; misty, rainy, frosty days; a ghostly sun (when it was visible) sliding in a low arc above a short horizon;

roads and paths slippery with mucous mud; rooms so chilly you could see your breath 10 feet from the fire. It was a long six weeks.

Mornings and afternoons I read Spenser, and it was like chopping knotty firewood (not for me the poet's poet). Unless it was raining hard I went for a walk, a form of exercise I find very boring, usually with Schuyler and sometimes with Henry Chapin. Meals were a bright spot in the day, for Mrs. Trinder, Schuyler's landlady, was a good cook, though she gave us more than we could comfortably eat. One night at supper, faced with an enormous dish of spaghetti, we wrapped up half of it in an old newspaper and hid it behind a book on Schuyler's shelves. It was still there when he went off to spend Christmas with his married sister at Cambridge; his last words to me were to get rid of it, for God's sake. And his first words when he got back were to ask me if I had. I had forgotten it—and when we went to look for it, it was gone.

On Christmas Day the Chapins and I were invited to tea at the Gilbert Murrays'. We hadn't been to church that day, and decided to go in to Evensong at the Cathedral, stopping for half an hour at the Murrays on the way. We got a chilly reception. It appeared that we were three-quarters of an hour late for a sit-down tea, with place cards. At my table there was a very pretty girl, to whom I was not introduced, and who sat in shy silence, with downcast eyes. I kept passing her bread-and-butter and cake, but couldn't get a word out of her. At last it dawned on me that she must be the scullery maid; looking around the room I could see that the rest of the staff were also having tea with us, and not enjoying it much either. It must have been a dreadful annual occasion. Though we were in disgrace for being so late we also had to leave early if we were to get to Oxford for Evensong. We edged out of the room, stammering our apologies. Just behind us a small Murray child repeated as if to himself but quite audibly: "Don't make excuses, don't make excuses."

Schuyler's friend among the poets on Boar's Hill was Robert Bridges, the Poet Laureate. His poetry-writing days were over,

51

but Schuyler much admired some of his past performance, especially the poem on nightingales,

Beautiful must be the mountains whence ye come . . .

and the one beginning

Whither, O splendid ship, thy white sails crowding . . .

Bridges's theory of prosody, which attempted to apply the same sort of quantitative values to the syllables of English verse as in Latin, and which most people thought overcomplicated or nonsensical, interested Schuyler, and he tried to explain it to me, but I couldn't understand it. His opinion of this theory, if I remember it right, was that in practice it was too idiosyncratic to be made a general rule, but that it fitted Bridges's own poems beautifully.

Schuyler had no high opinion of John Masefield as a poet, though he liked some of his things, particularly the early dramatic poems; and I remember his reading *The Everlasting Mercy* aloud with gusto. We both thought Squire's dual parody of Masefield and Wordsworth ("as if Wordsworth had written *The Everlasting Mercy*") very funny:

> . . . and I turned homeward, meditating much
> Upon the single transferable tax.

We also thought there was something endearingly funny about Masefield himself. He and Lillah McCarthy had organized a company of amateur players who gave performances of Shakespeare and sometimes of Masefield's plays in the villages near Oxford and in Oxford itself. I remember seeing *A Midsummer Night's Dream* in the village hall in Wootton, in which the yokel parts were played to perfection by yokels themselves. Occasionally Masefield took one of the minor roles: we saw him as the ghost in his play about Ahasuerus. In his stage directions he has the ghost haunting the bedside of the sleeping king and "hinnying like a snipe." We saw and heard him do that. This performance was in the hall at Keble College, and went on so long that we missed the last bus to Boar's Hill and had to walk back.

It was a still winter night, with no stars. As we plodded up the hill we both saw it at the same moment: something luminous in the sky, like an enormous triplane from another planet, rushing towards us silently and at incredible speed. We were both about to take to the fields and run for our lives when simultaneously we saw—and heard—what this ghost-plane was: a telephone pole whose three crossbeams had caught the light of a car climbing the hill behind us, too far away for us to hear the sound of its motor.

11

Schuyler's stay in England was to be for an indefinite time, but we both thought (and I hoped) that it would last at least a year. When I had said goodbye to Julie it was with the understanding that I would be away for two years, and I hoped I had nerved myself to that long an absence. The prospect of Schuyler's presence in England for at least half that time helped to harden my resolve. But in the early spring of 1923 two things happened to him that conspired to send him unexpectedly home. One was a book and the other was a girl. Which came first?

The book was *The Rediscovery of America,* by Waldo Frank. In general its theme was the challenge and opportunity of America, and it lit in Schuyler's mind a sudden flare of specific purpose. The girl was Jo James. Jo had entered Oxford at the same time I had and was reading English, as I was. I knew her by sight—as who didn't? she was the Zuleika Dobson of our day—but had avoided meeting her. She was already famously popular, which was reason enough for me, whose shyness was grounded in conceit, to give her a wide berth. Schuyler too, up to this point and for reasons of his own—he might have been thought conceited but he was certainly not shy—had steered clear of her. Then (I have an idea that Jo engineered it) they met, and it was like an explosion.

Although Schuyler talked to me about her, and told me more details of the affair than I either desired or deserved to know, I never altogether understood what happened nor why it ended so abruptly. The whole thing was as violent and as brief as a thunderclap. At their first meeting, he told me, nothing particular was said by either of them, in words: they looked at each other, he took her in his arms, and she fainted. If this sounds like a scene from a Gothic romance, I can't help it; that's what he told me. If she *hadn't* fainted, he said, they would have—as he put it —"come together" there and then, on the spot. As the spot was a semi-private living room or a completely public street (I was not clear on this point either, but I think it was one of these two places) it was just as well Jo fainted. Schuyler was certain that this swoon was perfectly genuine. Anyhow, they met again in a somewhat calmer frame of mind and arranged a meeting which was to consummate their love: this time there was to be no fainting.

At the appointed evening hour he went to Jo's lodgings. The sitting room was in semi-darkness but the flickering light showed her to him: she was lying naked in front of the fire on a sheepskin rug, waiting for him. What more could any man want? It should have been wonderful; but it wasn't: something went wrong. Jo ended in tears, and Schuyler's frame of mind, when I next saw him, was bitter and despairing. "She loves me but it's no good." That was as much as he told me.

Why this one disappointment should have been accepted by both of them as disastrous and final I couldn't make out, either then or later; that was the way they did accept it, though. They met once again before Schuyler left for America, but only to say their sad farewells. Shaken as they both were, it was Jo who was apparently resigned to their parting; Schuyler's grief seemed to me to verge on the suicidal. In our last talk before he left, I said what I could to revive his enthusiasm for the mission that was taking him back to America, the purpose that had been lit in his mind by Waldo Frank's book. This mission was the discovery of young, unknown American writers, especially poets, who were there, waiting to be found (Schuyler was convinced of it), in every state of the Union. Their discovery and publication would bring American writing, at one tremendous forward step, into the forefront of the world's literature.

But, although he still clung grimly to his purpose and his sense of mission and the patriotic rightness of his idea, the mood in which he set off was less quixotic than Luciferian:

> And courage never to submit or yield
> And what is else, not to be overcome.

When I saw him off on the train to Southampton I was terribly anxious about him. I really feared that he might not reach the other side.

His final word to me was to "look after" Jo. Though as yet I had not even met her, I promised him solemnly that I would.

I didn't much like the prospect. In my mixed feelings about Jo, jealousy was predominant. I hated her for making Schuyler miserable, but I hated her more for being able to. And yet the idea of being on terms of intimate friendship with this popular beauty tickled my vanity—and in the event very nearly turned my head.

Our first meeting was at a tea party in Tui Kinsolving's rooms. Tui was a Rhodes Scholar from Virginia; all his family were good-looking, social parsons, and so many of them were called "Tui" (pronounced *Too*-ee, the Brazilian diminutive of Arthur, first bestowed on one who had been a missionary bishop in Brazil) that they were differentiated as "Big Tui," "Little Tui," and so on. This Tui was in his last year at Christ Church and was headed for a typical Kinsolving career—Trinity Church, Boston, where he would be one of the most sought-after bachelors in town, then Trinity Church, Princeton, and finally St. James', the second most fashionable church in New York. Everyone in Oxford liked Tui, in a not very serious way, and he gave the impression of liking all of them in the same light manner.

When I got there, Tui's rooms were crowded, but Jo had not

yet arrived. I knew some of the Americans, and Tui greeted me
jovially as an old friend; I think we had met once before. Soon
after, Jo came in, escorted by several men. Tui introduced her to
me, with an air of amazement that we didn't know each other.
Jo gave me a small conspiratorial smile and raised her hand to
show me the backs of three books she was carrying: the middle
one was *The Book of the Tuesday Evening Club.* I felt myself
flushing with pleasure. She was immediately hailed and swept
away by a clamant posse of social vigilantes.

The following week I had tea alone with her in her rooms,
and soon we were meeting often—coffee at the Cadena, lunch at
the George, a cigarette in my rooms between lectures. Our conversation was always on the same subject, Schuyler. She wanted
me to tell her everything I knew about him. I did my halting best,
and gradually, as I got to know her better—or became more used
to her—my jealousy of her evaporated. She spoke of Schuyler
with sadness and love, as if he were dead. Imperceptibly other
people crept into our talk—Johnny Martin, Erd Harris: all of
them seemed to be beaux of Jo's, or ex-beaux. They were scattered all over the world but most of them were Americans, and
all of them wrote her long and intimate letters. The more earnest
passages often made her laugh, and she would read them out
loud to me so that I could share her amusement. This shocked me
at first—how would I like it if Julie did the same with *my* letters,
holding me up to a stranger's—or worse, a rival's—ridicule? Jo
brushed my scruples aside and went on reading the best bits
aloud, with giggles and snorts of laughter. I succumbed: it was
flattering to be made a party to such secrets.

Jo seemed to have such a maddening effect on her English
beaux that they would give her or lend her anything they had,
and apparently for no return whatever. One such acquisition
(this one, luckily, was temporary) was a motorbike with a sidecar.
She came to fetch me in it one day. She had never driven one
before, she cried happily, so get in quickly. I scrambled into the
sidecar, and off we went. We drove up Boar's Hill to Mrs.

56

Trinder's cottage, which Jo had heard of and wanted to see. We got there all right, with a few narrow escapes. Mrs. Trinder came out of her kitchen, wiping her hands on her apron, and showed us a postcard she had had from Schuyler.

On the way back, just before the road turned and dipped down the long hill to Oxford, we were chugging along beside a high fence made of solid board uprights when Jo lost control of the motorbike. The front wheel swerved off the road, and the next moment the sidecar, with me in it, was being swept along the board fence the way a boy rattles a stick along palings. Jo was shouting with laughter but managed to wrestle the motorbike back on the road: no harm done except a few scrapes and dents in the sidecar.

We made other excursions. We took a picnic lunch to Bagley Wood, famous as the haunt of nightingales, although I never heard one there. Jo brought some books of poetry along, including the *Tuesday Evening Club,* and we took turns reading them aloud. She lay on the ground with her head on my lap, and more than once I became troublingly aware of her warm weight. This shameful sensation seemed to me literally incestuous, and I fought against it with horror, hoping—and believing—that Jo remained unaware of it. Later, coming out of the wood to the Oxford road, we met Henry Chapin walking up the hill, and he greeted us with such a knowing smirk that I felt guilty all over again. Jo gave him her blandest smile and said to me, when he was barely out of earshot: "Henry has a dirty mind, hasn't he?"

New College
June 10, 1923

Dear Schuyler

I have been trying to answer your letter for several days. I haven't mentioned Jo before, but I am going to now. Please forgive me if it hurts you, I don't mean to. We met finally, though so many accidents postponed it that I began to have a queer feeling. She came to the Holywell Gate one morning, and we went into the garden, and sat under that big copper beech in the far end. She was carrying the Spectator with *Wild*

*Birds** in it, and gave it to me. It was rather desperate, that first meeting. All I can ever do for her is to make my profession of faith, which I cannot always do simply and with love, and which chimes such a wild discord with what I am. I cannot understand a woman's heart, and her emotions seem agonizingly subtle. But my faith is that you love each other, which means that you are alive in one another, and my hope is that you will some day marry altogether. I love her, and it has not been hard to do that, first for your sake and then for herself. I didn't think I could bear to love anyone more after you and Julie, and my heart is pretty crowded, but I think perhaps they are growing pains. Though we have not talked much about Julie, I somehow love Julie better because of her.

Your letter heartened me unspeakably. I knew, Schuyler, but I was afraid, because I am a coward, and my bravery is mostly in you. But I am not afraid now. Thank you for telling me of my mother. I believe what you saw, though I cannot see it, because I am a great part of the suffering that her life is measured by.

I am sure that life, though living may be, is not a desperate complication. I don't know what I would say to you exactly, except to echo what your love and others' have taught me—that nothing true is ever finished, and that love is alive. God does lean out of heaven, and sometimes we see him, though I suppose he is always leaning out. Oh Schuyler, forgive me for talking at all; I cannot write poetry.

Love brings peace at the last; I am sure of it, though I never find it.

The other day at Cambridge I had lunch with Forbes, a don there. He gave me the name of Bruce Rogers (c/o Harvard University Press) who I understand is one of the leading authorities on printing. According to Forbes, he is discontented with America and with everything, but would be sympathetic with a scheme like yours, and might come in on it. I should think he's worth looking up. I called on your sister, but she was not very well, so I couldn't see her. I'm glad the speech went off so well; wish to God I could have been there. Can't you possibly stay in the East, if not Princeton, till early in July? I shall be back by then,

*The last poem, I think, Schuyler ever published. It first appeared in the *New Republic*.

58

with luck, and I can't afford the carfare to Arizona. Write me your schedule, if any.

Give my love to the Harpers, and my best to Frank MacDonald. Write me when you can. I will do it oftener after this.

Tom

My assignment to "look after Jo" might have been considered at an abrupt end when, one April morning, I got a cable from Schuyler saying that he was engaged to a girl I had never heard of named Katharine Townsend, and please to tell Jo. I didn't know how I could go through with this cruel task. I thought the news would break her heart. How could I bring myself to do it? But it had to be done. I telephoned to Jo, and arranged to meet her at noon in New College Gardens. Then I went back to my room and walked up and down for a long time. I hadn't said my prayers for years, but now I felt the need for some wiser help than I could find in myself. I decided to go into some church and try to pray. The college chapel was too familiar: I needed some shrine where, as an anonymous stranger, I might forget myself and think only of Jo. I went into St. Mary's on the High, a church I had never entered before, and for half an hour I prayed, or tried to pray. It wasn't a success. By the time I was to meet Jo I was so wrought up that I knew I would make a mess of it.

I needn't have worried, however. How I blurted out my news I can't remember, but I'll never forget how she took it. We were sitting on the grass under the big copper beech. Jo said nothing, but she wept. I had seen other girls weep—my sisters and Julie—and it was an unpleasant sight; their faces crumpled, their eyes crinkled almost shut, the corners of their mouths drew down, then their mouths opened wide and they bawled like calves. That was not Jo's way. Her great wide eyes filled and brimmed with tears, and her perfect little mouth trembled and gasped like a goldfish, with no sound. It wasn't a pleasure to see —though it is, to remember—but she wept beautifully.

And Katharine Townsend, the unknown girl in the cable?

My only feeling about her was of freezing resentment and dislike. That was my cold introduction to Kit.

12

Schuyler had had a rough voyage home, although the sea was calm. As I had feared, he thought of suicide. But with every sea-mile that took him away from Jo and brought him nearer America his despair dwindled and his resolution grew. By the time his ship docked in New York he had thought of a name for his project (The Open Road Press), had drafted a one-page Manifesto to announce it, and had begun a list of writers who might lend him their names or their services (Robert Frost, Hervey Allen, DuBose Heyward, Vachel Lindsay, Edgar Lee Masters . . .). As soon as he had his board of editors set up, he would start on his transcontinental journey of discovery.

There was no trouble about enlisting the board. All the writers he talked or wrote to were sympathetic with his scheme, and some were enthusiastic. He got his Manifesto printed (a beautiful job). He bought a Model-T Ford and converted it into a truck, so that he not only had room for supplies and piles of the Manifesto but a place to sleep. In Princeton he ran into Vovo, who was bored with Philadelphia, tired of painting portraits (which in any case were pretty poor), and volunteered to come along on the expedition. He could do the navigating while Schuyler drove; he could also cook. Schuyler agreed to take him.

It was a tremendous journey for those days. They covered tens of thousands of miles and went through nearly every state in the Union. By the time they reached the Southwest they were sometimes mistaken for Mormon missionaries, partly because they had both grown beards and partly because of the biblical-looking book on Vovo's lap—the automobile guide called a Blue

Book which was almost a necessity then, before the days of road maps, interstate roads and national highways.

In the earlier stages of their journey they fetched a circuit through New England, then headed west through upper New York State. In Cooperstown, as in many other haunts of the rich and social, Vovo had friends to whom he was pleased to present a still-presentable Schuyler. They had drinks at the Ryersons and dinner at the Townsends, who lived in a big, pillared house called "Brookwood" on the shores of Lake Otsego. There were three handsome and lively girls in the Townsend family, and they had a jolly evening. Vovo's keen social eye noticed that Schuyler seemed to be much taken by the next-to-youngest daughter, Kit.

Two mornings later Vovo woke to find a note pinned to his sleeping bag: Schuyler had gone back to Cooperstown and would return shortly. When he did, he told Vovo that he was engaged to Katharine Townsend. Vovo gravely congratulated him, and they continued their journey.

Why do I remember, or think I remember, an encounter in a railway station—and, of all railway stations, Princeton Junction —between Vovo and Jo, Julie and me? That was the first time Vovo and Jo had met, and mostly for her benefit he was describing Kit, whom the rest of us had never seen. He said she was a tall girl, an outdoors girl; then with a man-of-the-world stare at Jo he added that she had rather full lips—"and ve all know vot zat means." I wasn't at all sure that I did know but didn't like to show my ignorance. I supposed he meant that she had a passionate nature; but why did he say it in that superior tone, as if having a passionate nature was like a physical handicap?

I think Vovo had ideas about Jo, if not designs on her. I remember clearly a chance meeting with him on a later occasion —and this time I am sure it was at Princeton Junction. He was in such a bitterly didactic mood and lectured me so roundly on the subject of women that I could only suppose he had recently suffered a stinging rebuff. Why do I think it was Jo, and not some other girl, who had repulsed him? Anyway, I remember thinking so at the time. Vovo was well aware, like everyone else who knew

me, that I was in love with Julie and had been courting her for
years. Nevertheless, he talked to me as if I were on the verge of
making a disastrous match with a foreigner. I should always remember, said Vovo, in his most earnest and deepest growl, that
it would be an act of folly and an almost certain disaster for a man
to marry a woman who was not of his own nation. He went on
and on about it. This scolding admonition made no sense at all,
I thought—unless he was really talking to himself. And why
should he be talking to himself like that unless he had just tried,
and failed, to make the same mistake he was lecturing me about?

Jo and Julie met only twice: neither time was a success. Julie
had been at the dock when Jo and I came back from England on
the same ship. Julie's first remark to me was: where had I got that
hat, and why? The hat was a bowler, recently bought in London
at Jo's suggestion and with her help. She was pleased with the
result; she thought it suited me. Julie didn't. Even I, who had
been looking forward for some time to the meeting of these two
beloved creatures, could feel a certain chill in the air; and I saw
uneasily that neither of them was putting her best foot forward.
Julie was edgy and untalkative; Jo, in a self-conscious drawl,
talked too much.

Back in Oxford again, a month later, Jo was full of praise for
"little Julie." I knew she meant it affectionately, but all the same
I wished she wouldn't call Julie "little." And I soon knew that
something was wrong, for Julie stopped answering my letters.
For five months I didn't hear a word from her. I did, however,
get a number of veiled warnings from well-meaning friends,
which were no help at all, as I hadn't the slightest idea of what
they were warning me about. I began to have inklings of what
it might be like to be insane. I suppose I was morally insane, for
everyone but me knew what the trouble was. Did Jo? I don't
know. The worse things got, the more I saw of her, and she must
have figured frequently in my letters to Julie. Towards the end
of this interminable time I took to calling on Jo nearly every
evening just to kiss her good night, which I found comforting.

13

In midwinter of 1924, shortly after Christmas, Schuyler and Kit were married in Cooperstown. Kit's mother was a generous and impulsive woman, and the cost of the celebrations, which went on for several days, must have eaten into her dwindling capital —although as long as she had money (originally some $7 million) she never gave it a thought. Julie and I arrived by train with the vanguard of guests a couple of days before the wedding. Kit was at the station to meet us, and that was our first sight of her. She was wearing a fur hat, which looked natural on her, a fur coat and galoshes. She had a big nose and fine eyes, and her face was alight with friendly happiness. She strode through the creaking snow on the platform, a welcoming grin on her face, shouting to friends getting off the train. She gave us a hearty handshake, then an impulsive kiss on the cheek.

As Schuyler's best man I was quartered with the out-of-town ushers in a hunting lodge in the woods about a mile outside Cooperstown; Julie was staying at Brookwood. The Townsends were a worldly and social family, and the wedding party was a typical cross section of their world. Most of the Princeton ushers were members of Ivy, and the Yale men Skull & Bones. The bridesmaids, except for her sister, were all schoolmates of Kit's —Izzy Rockefeller, Lila Talbot, Janie Hickok. Kit's father and mother had been divorced years ago and had both married again. Mr. Townsend, a tall, raw-boned, rough-hewn man with a sleepily angry expression, had come with his wife from Mystic for the occasion. Kit's stepfather, whose name was Edgar Chapman but whom they all called "Steppy," was a small, neat, precise Albany lawyer who looked completely out of place among these worldlings; in fact, they and their doings delighted and endlessly

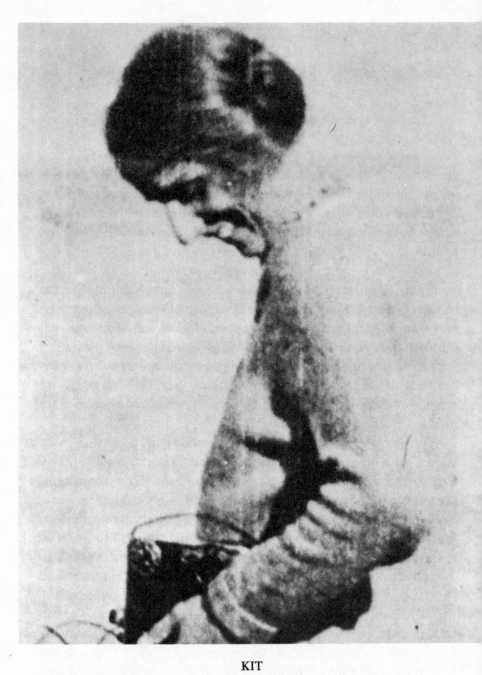

KIT

amused him. He never said much, and in any case could hardly hope to make himself heard above the bawling ribaldries and roars of laughter with which the big rooms and spacious hallways of his wife's house hummed and vibrated. He sat or moved quietly through the din, smiling, short and upright, like a renegade deacon who genuinely welcomes the invasion of a riot of demons in his meetinghouse, or like a banker who has finally abandoned his lifelong program of thrift and prudence for the saturnalian disorder he has always secretly desired, which he cannot quite bring himself to join but can only look on and applaud as a sympathetic observer.

Schuyler's family was not so well represented as the Townsend side; his father was dead and his mother and his favorite sister lived too far away to make the journey. Neither of his brothers showed up. But I seem to remember that his other two sisters came on the day itself; and his Uncle Freddy Jackson was there, very much in evidence, throughout the three-day celebration. To look at, Uncle Freddy and Schuyler were uncannily alike; this facial resemblance was misleading. Uncle Freddy was a Presbyterian parson, earnest, simple, humorless, stubborn. He liked young people and made the mistake of supposing that this feeling must be mutual. They might have liked him more if he had been less demanding of their attention; but he couldn't leave them alone.

Except for the wedding ceremony itself and our agonizing wait beforehand, I hardly remember Schuyler being there at all. He must have taken part in the rehearsal of the wedding service, and if there was a bachelor dinner—but was there?—he would have been the host.

On the morning of the wedding, an hour and a half before we were due at the church, I went to Schuyler's room to help him get ready. He was pale and tense, and was having trouble with his Ascot tie. The wedding party were wearing full dress: cutaway, spats, stiff collars and gloves, but Schuyler and I had decided to dispense with top hats. Just before we left for the church, Schuyler poured himself three-quarters of a tumbler of neat

Scotch, and downed it. He offered me some, but I couldn't face a drink that morning. The only effect it seemed to have on him was to bring out red blotches all over his face. I hoped they would fade before he appeared in church.

Thanks to my nervousness, we got to the church nearly half an hour early, and went to the vestry to wait. I was glad to sit down, but Schuyler paced back and forth, silent and frowning. I put the ring, which I hadn't trusted him with till then, in his left-hand waistcoat pocket, and called his attention to the fact. He said nothing but nodded absently. Then he said he wanted a smoke. I said no, not in the vestry. He said he would just step outside.

"You'll ruin your shoes." There was deep snow everywhere.

He took off his shoes, which meant removing his spats as well. He put a cigarette in his mouth and disappeared through the vestry door. I watched him go with great misgivings.

He hadn't been gone two minutes, it seemed to me, when I heard the organ blare the first notes of "Here Comes the Bride." I dashed to the vestry door and stuck my head out. No sign of him anywhere. I called "Schuyler! Schuyler!"

My God, I thought, he's made a run for it. What the hell am I supposed to do now?

To my unspeakable relief, he materialized. His feet were soaking and there was snow on the bottom of his trousers. I brushed the snow off with my hands and somehow we got his shoes and spats on. All this time the organ was growling threateningly, now and then repeating "Here Comes the Bride." When we stepped to our position at the chancel rail the bride's party was still at the bottom of the nave; they were waiting for us.

The bride and groom had made their escape; the wedding, properly speaking, was over, but most of the guests lingered on for one more night. That evening there was a party in a big house at the other end of the lake, and we were taken there in horse-drawn sledges. We sat or lay, packed as close together on the straw-covered floor as our bundled clothes would permit, covered to the chins by rough horse-blankets. It was a still, moonlit night; the sledges slid along quickly and silently except for the occasional creak of a runner, the muffled clopping of hooves and the jingling of harness. We had had just enough to drink and some of us were in love. Julie and I said nothing but our hands had found each other's bodies. I wished this drive would go on all night.

Haven Page, a schoolmate of Schuyler's and one of his ushers, had fallen head over heels in love with Kit's sister Mary Anne. Both of them had lovely voices—Haven sang in the Yale quartet and Mary Anne had the makings of an opera singer—and now the two of them tried a duet. It broke off in a laugh and a murmur, and our sledge fell silent.

A good-looking light-haired boy, whose name I can't remember, suddenly stood up, poised one foot on the sideboard of the sledge, and made a neat swan-dive into a passing snowbank. Someone cheered, and there was a brief murmuration that sounded like applause. The driver didn't turn his head nor slow the horses. This boy, it appeared, was a disappointed suitor of Kit's, and had chosen this tragicomic gesture (he came to no harm but had to walk home) as his farewell to the girl who had broken his heart. This was my final memory of Kit and Schuyler's wedding.

"YOU'RE ALIVE, MY DARLING!"

1

I never knew Julie as a little girl. By all accounts she must have been delicious. She was small, dark, pretty and completely feminine. She had four brothers, two older and two younger than herself, and no sisters. After her two older brothers had outgrown the barbarous period in which they looked upon her as only a nuisance who cried and told her mother when they hit her, and had to be shut up with the pet goat to keep her from tagging along and getting in their way, they became immensely proud and protective of her. Even in her tagging-along days there was nothing of the tomboy about her. From the crown of her dark head to the soles of her pretty little feet she was all female, and was never for a moment tempted to be anything else.

At three she was a chatterbox, and when she had no better audience would talk a blue streak to her dolls, all of whom she had named herself: Jack Wigglelolly, Jane Buffle, Feather-huncas (that one was an Indian squaw), Vazinir Brinsby, and Ragdraggle (a rag doll). When she was asked at the age of eight what she wanted to be when she grew up, she said, "A long green feather that tickles." Her father and mother both adored her, but she was not a spoiled child; she aroused affection as naturally as a kitten, and the love that surrounded her enhanced her inherent sweetness and minimized her kitten-like cruelties. She had a quick hot temper like her father and a mischievous streak like his.

Though she inherited her mother's coloring and, in her very different way, something of her mother's looks, Mrs. Cuyler's dark charm of face trembled on the very brink of beauty; behind her high cheekbones and her full mild eyes one was often aware of an almost-presence, something deep, serene and far away.

71

People used to say of Mrs. Cuyler that she wasn't beautiful, exactly, but there was something about her . . .

Her daughter Julie, pretty as she was, never came quite so close to beauty. As she grew older her likenesses to her father were more apparent. Her eyes, like his, were a little too close together; and she sometimes told herself despairingly, as she gazed into her mirror, that she even had his *nose!* That was not true; Mr. Cuyler's nose was large and rather bulbous, whereas Julie's was small and neat and, though not perfectly shaped, fitted innocuously into her charming face. She and her father were more alike within themselves. Their flashes of temper dissolved easily into a cloud of laughter, and their fiercest outbursts always ended in a clearing of the air; neither of them could hold a grudge or willingly protract a quarrel.

There was an extraordinary sympathy between father and daughter: they shared an instant perception of why certain people made them laugh and why certain happenings made them angry or sad. They could always put themselves into the other's shoes, and were constantly doing it. Occasionally their hot tempers flared up at each other, but these failures of understanding were temporary and rare. It would not have been fair to call either Julie or her father an irritable person, but both of them were subject to irritable spells. Though Julie loved her mother deeply, their differing temperaments sometimes grated, and in spite of the fact that Mrs. Cuyler was never known to lose her temper, every now and then Julie found her mother extremely irritating.

There were times when Mrs. Cuyler's serenity looked to Julie like a sleazy cloak for mere absence of mind or shiftless woolgathering. Her mother's hopeless and helpless attempts to keep house, the rickety makeshifts she employed just to keep the household going, baffled and offended Julie's yearning for order and roused in her a passionate determination to be *different* (which she was already) and some day to have a house of her own which she would run *properly*. This deep disapproval of her mother's domestic ways troubled Julie, for Mrs. Cuyler's obvious goodness and kindness to every person and animal that came near her made Julie warm with approving pride, though as often as not her mother's quixotic acts reduced her to demoralized laughter or tears of vexation.

As soon as she was old enough to notice and compare, Julie became aware that her family didn't live the way other people lived—and she wanted, or thought she did, to live "like everybody else." The main trouble was, she decided, that her family was poor. And so they were, in comparison with most of their social peers in Princeton. They lived on a broken-down farm whose few weedy acres had lain fallow ever since Julie could remember. The house was in bad repair, and they had only one car, a second-hand Dodge. Mr. Cuyler came from a good Savannah family who had Northern connections; he and Mrs. Cuyler were both related to the Potters, and shared a Conover great-grandmother. John Cuyler had been at school at St. Paul's, where he was a bad boy, always in hot water; my father, who was a good boy and applied himself to his books, was there at the same time, but they had no recollection of each other. Further attempts had been made to educate Mr. Cuyler at a school in Germany, which he hated, and at the University of the South, at Sewanee, where he had a good time. His happiest days had been spent as an art student in Paris in the nineties. He had a small talent for painting, and enough money to indulge it, until he found himself burdened with the cares of a family.

Now and again, though at rarer and rarer intervals, the spirit moved Mr. Cuyler to a burst of painting. On one such occasion he tacked a notice on his studio door:

> I will not go to Mrs. Jones' tea.
> Please do not tell me it's lunchtime.
>   "   "   " disturb.
>   "   "   " otherwise annoy.

Once when he was hard at it there was such a racket outside his studio and even on the roof that he finally flung the door open and stuck out his head, his mustache bristling with anger. There was a small crowd in his little courtyard: his wife, his daughter, and several small boys, one of whom was trying to swarm up the drainpipe to the studio roof.

His daughter said apologetically: "The fish has fallen in the gutter."

"*What fish?*"

Eventually they were able to explain to him that a half-grown cat had climbed the tree at the corner of the studio and couldn't get down; Mrs. Cuyler, seeing its predicament, had sent a small boy to the fishmonger's to get a fish head, which she then stuck on a fishing pole and with which she hoped to lure the cat; unfortunately the fish head had fallen off the pole and landed in the gutter. That was the situation at the moment.

Incredible as it may seem, this same thing happened several times, with different cats. Mrs. Cuyler's first move was always the fish head—although it never worked. After that she would find a small boy who was willing (and light enough) to climb the tree. As the cat usually kept retreating to a higher branch, this required an exceptionally light and courageous small boy. If the boy failed, the last resort was the fire department, who brought a ladder. On each of these occasions, as luck would have it, Mr. Cuyler was painting. He got it firmly into his head that it was always the same cat, driven by some sort of crazy cat death-wish. The last time it happened he charged out of his studio with a despairing cry: "How can I paint when this damn cat keeps going up the tree?"

A man of volatile temper, subject to occasional moods of gloom but more often wafted into high spirits on updrafts of unreasonable but infectious hope, Mr. Cuyler would perhaps have been a failure in any calling. When he was not weighed down by one of his infrequent depressions he was a good companion, an affectionate if inefficient husband and father; in his odd, disengaged way, a wise man. His wife loved and forgave him as if he were her favorite child; his sons were defensive and protective of him; his daughter, who understood him best, laughed and cried with him, was fiercely proud of him and fiercely ashamed for him. The thing he dreamed about was making a pile by inventing something. One of his forebears had been a successful inventor (the family legend was that he had been the first to build a steamboat, though Robert Fulton somehow got the credit) and Mr. Cuyler felt that the knack was in his blood.

Julie could always tell when the inventive spell was on him by the faraway look in his eye: he admitted to her that in those moments he was figuring out how to spend the first million dollars his royalties would bring him. He was, on the whole, a happy man.

And Mrs. Cuyler? In her way, she was a better companion than her husband; not that she was entertaining or witty or a teller of stories, as he was. But it was such a delight to be with her that it took her most of the morning to get her marketing done, for everyone she met wanted to talk to her and delay her, just for the pleasure of her company. She loved people and gave them not merely the small change of courtesy but all she had in her pocket. She was devout, not pious, a woman of the world, conventional and tolerant. In repose her lovely face was sad. It was generally assumed that she must be happy, because she gave so much happiness to others.

When Mrs. Cuyler at last acquired a refrigerator (which ran by gas instead of electricity, and none of the family understood how it worked), she was always trying to make it do more than it could. She got the notion that the ice trays could make ice cream and frozen puddings. Though none of the experiments ever turned out successfully, she kept on trying, and her defensive explanations of their failure became famous in her family.

An outsider would not have thought any of the Cuyler possessions very valuable. But at the Farm there were four chairs and a sofa with upholstered seats in *petit point* known as "the tapestry furniture": they were supposed to have come from the Palace of the Tuileries and no one was ever allowed to sit on them. Mrs. Cuyler considered them priceless and said that some day they would be sold and save the family fortunes.

Though she was not a worrier, she was burglar-conscious,

and every night before going to bed used to hide all the silver. She tried to hide it in a different place each night, until once she forgot where she had put it and jumped to the conclusion that the burglars had taken it. After that she always put it under the soiled clothes in the laundry hamper.

Shortly after Daylight Saving Time was introduced, Mrs. Cuyler wrote to her daughter, who was away at school, to say that she was coming to see her. Most of the letter was an argument with herself about Daylight Saving Time: what time her train would leave Princeton (the railways stuck to Standard Time, which was an hour earlier or an hour later than Daylight Saving Time—Mrs. Cuyler was never quite sure which); what time it would be *on the street* in New York, and then what time it would be at Grand Central Station, where she would take the train to Peekskill; what time it would be in Peekskill when the train got there. On the flap of the envelope she had written not to expect her after all, as she wouldn't be able to come that day.

Even more famous in the family was her telegram to her eldest son, Dick, who was then teaching at a school in Connecticut. He kept the telegram and Julie copied it:

I WOULD HAVE A SHORT STAY WHETHER I CAME WEDNESDAY AND RETURNED FRIDAY OR WENT BACK WITH YOU SUNDAY AND RETURNED TUESDAY WHICH I WOULD HAVE TO DO. JULIE'S NURSE LEAVES WEDNESDAY AND RETURNS FRIDAY OR GOES BACK WITH YOU SUNDAY AND RETURNS TUESDAY WHICH I WOULD HAVE TO DO. JULIE'S NURSE LEAVES WEDNESDAY THE 15TH AND RETURNS FRIDAY. I MUST BE HERE THURSDAY, SO EXPECT ME WEDNESDAY AFTERNOON AND WE WILL COME DOWN FRIDAY.

Dick answered this telegram with a briefer one, saying WHAT? This came close to annoying Mrs. Cuyler, who said it was really too bad of Dick; she had told him *exactly* what she was going to do.

Her domestic life was one long rescue operation, and she was always having to devise impromptu defenses against hopeless odds. She would tackle anything, although she wasn't very good with her hands and never achieved more than a partial and temporary success. Though she knew I was quite unable to fix or repair anything whatever, no matter how simple, she sometimes appealed to me to help her, just because I was there.

I remember particularly one repair job on a piano leg. The leg had lost a good deal of the veneer that originally covered it. Mrs. Cuyler had collected some of the pieces that had been knocked off or fallen off: they should have been flat, but many of them were warped into a shallow curve. She proposed to glue these pieces to the bare parts of the piano leg, holding them in place with rubber bands till the glue hardened. I did what she told me, as far as I could, but I could see it wasn't going to work and it didn't.

Mrs. Cuyler had a special feeling about pianos. She played them, a little, herself; but it wasn't so much their musical aspect that appealed to her: she liked them as pieces of furniture. At one point she had four pianos in her house. Only one of them would play, and that one needed tuning. One had had its insides taken out, and its keyboard leveled down to a mere black-and-white pattern: it was a *trompe l'oeil* piano that had been made into a desk. A third, that Mrs. Cuyler had picked up for a few dollars at a country sale, had proved too big to go through the door or the window and so was left on the side porch. When Mr. Cuyler came home and found it there he voiced the general opinion by saying: "What this family needs is another piano."

Mrs. Cuyler may not have been very good with her hands but she did manage to get through a mass of darning socks and mending shirts and underclothes. And she somehow found the time to work away at a stool cover in *petit point*, a job that seemed as endless as Penelope's web. When it was finished at last, everyone felt relieved—and correspondingly depressed when Mrs. Cuyler lost it, before it was attached to its footstool. She thought she must have dropped it on Nassau Street, on her way to Bamman's, the grocery store at which all the Princeton ladies forgathered every morning.

It was winter when the stool cover disappeared, and it

turned into one of the snowiest winters on record. When the spring thaws melted the snow, someone spotted the missing stool cover, lying on the street where Mrs. Cuyler had dropped it months before, and returned it to her: everyone in town knew about it by that time. It was none the worse for wear, with a bit of cleaning, and ended up in triumph on its stool.

With all her makeshift ways, it was Mrs. Cuyler who kept the family going. Prices went up, but not her husband's income, and it was she who had to beg or borrow the difference. She preferred begging to borrowing. Her husband, who didn't mind asking a friend for a loan to pay a poker debt, simply could not bring himself to do the same thing when it was a question of groceries or a school bill, so this necessary fund-raising became one of Mrs. Cuyler's domestic chores. It was never spoken of nor even hinted at, least of all by herself.

Partly, perhaps, because he was ashamed of not providing enough money for his family's wants and even more ashamed of shifting this burden to his wife's shoulders, Mr. Cuyler found a good deal to laugh at in the way Mrs. Cuyler managed or failed to manage their household. The children followed his lead; and their mother, after a few increasingly feeble attempts to defend herself, usually gave up and joined her laughter to theirs.

Though Julie was too much her father's daughter not to laugh too, she "hated the whole thing," and although she felt herself the fierce opponent of her mother's feeble governance of the family life, she was also, and more deeply, her mother's devoted ally. She knew, in a more personal way than her brothers, that her mother's absurd shifts and ingenious devices were the desperate rearguard action of a harried army in constant retreat. She also knew, although this fact was too painful for her to face squarely, that her mother had been forced into this impossible situation only because her father had given up the struggle.

As her mother's supporter and helper she threw herself into the family battle—the archaic stove, the well which did duty for an icebox (except that when you put things in an icebox you didn't have to suspend them by pieces of string, which sometimes broke), the sleazy, slapdash colored cooks who came when they felt like it and left the same way, the kerosene lamps, the rickety furniture, the cheap screens (a bargain) that didn't fit the windows and failed to keep the flies out; the piano, yellow-keyed and hopelessly out of tune, with some of the felt hammers eaten away by mice. The list was too long, the obstacles listed kept growing in size and number. Every time she thought of it, which was at least once every day, Julie swore to herself that some day she would have a house where everything *worked*, a house with *good* furniture, a house that could be kept clean. When her mother found her in tears, she would take Julie in her arms and tell her, with a little shake in her voice, not to take things so hard.

As a girl in Philadelphia, Mrs. Cuyler had been something of a belle. She would have been more of one if her parson father had had fewer children and more money. As it was, she attracted a small crowd of beaux but almost no serious suitors until Mr. Cuyler came along. He fell so head over heels in love that he never noticed until it was too late the fact that neither of them had enough money to live on. And in those days he still had "prospects." All in all, it was a happy marriage. Mr. Cuyler, who didn't mind repeating himself when he had a good thing to say, as he often did, liked to tell his children that if he had to do it over again he would marry someone as much like their mother as possible, but with a lot more money.

Remembering her own triumphant days as a girl much sought after, Mrs. Cuyler wanted Julie to have the same opportunities. They wouldn't be able to afford a conventional coming-out party, but Julie would certainly go to the Thursday Evenings and the Assembly, and perhaps, when the time came, they might after all manage something . . . Meantime Julie must go to a proper school. Here she was, almost fourteen, getting prettier all the time and already beginning to attract boys to the house. Too many boys, Mrs. Cuyler said to herself; and one or two of them (how surprised they would have been if they knew what she thought of them) not exactly the kind of boy she wanted Julie to see too much of. It was time she went off to boarding school. Mrs.

Cuyler knew of one she thought would be suitable: a convent school run by an order of Episcopalian nuns, at Peekskill, on the banks of the Hudson.

Mr. Cuyler concurred, as he always did with his wife's serious decisions. But where was the money to come from? They looked at one another for a brief instant; Mr. Cuyler silently concurred again. His wife took even longer than usual at her marketing the following morning, and when she got home she broke the news to Julie that she would be going away to school in September. Julie's immediate response was rebellious tears.

After she had grown up, Julie would have said that she enjoyed her schooldays, and if she had had a daughter herself she would no doubt have sent her to St. Mary's. But at first she was so homesick and wept so much that she earned the nickname of "the Weeping Willow." In her second term she began to settle down, make eternal friendships with other girls and decide which of the nuns were old dears and which were horrors. School spirit was cultivated at St. Mary's as a kind of secondary religion, and Julie became a thoroughgoing convert to it. She was too feminine to excel in the girlish rough-and-tumble of basketball or field hockey—playing Lady Teazle in *The School for Scandal* was the high point in her career at St. Mary's—but from the sidelines she screamed her class cheer with the best of them:

> Con-*found* those girls, why can't they see
> That they can't play as well as we?
> With a *vee*-vo
> And a *vi*-vo
> And a *vee*-vo *vi*-vo *vum*
> Rit-tail, rat-tail, hangin' on a cat-tail,
> Vum, vum, vum!

Mrs. Cuyler's ideas about education, as far as she had any, were conventional; she thought it better, for the good of both sexes, that boys and girls should be kept apart a good deal of the time while they were growing up. Otherwise girls sometimes tended to become "boy-crazy"; and everyone knew what boys tended to become. Mrs. Cuyler did not consider her Julie boy-crazy, but she was certainly interested in boys, and since the interest was so obviously mutual, it was just as well to have her out of circulation for most of the next few years. Julie more than made up for lost time in the holidays; the telephone never stopped ringing when she was home, and on the evenings when she was not off to the movies or out for a spin in a Stutz Bearcat (her mother had to be reasonably sure about *that* boy), she would hold court on the front porch of the Farm, surrounded by four or five guffawing swains.

It was a hard-and-fast rule at St. Mary's that none of the girls was allowed to get letters from any boys but their brothers. In Julie's case, two of her brothers wrote to her with amazing frequency and regularity, and the envelopes were usually so fat they had to have extra postage. More than one of Julie's beaux had discovered this way around the rule and had persuaded her brothers to act as go-betweens.

By the time she was sixteen, in her last year at school, Julie had acquired half a dozen "steadies," several of whom considered themselves serious suitors. Julie thought of them as her property, which was not quite the same thing. She knew that one day she would have to make up her mind, just as they said they had; but when she did it would end the delightful, exciting, fascinating game, and she was in no hurry to do that. Besides, how could she possibly make up her mind? The ones she liked best were all as different as they could be, and she liked each one so much, when she was with him, that she almost thought she was in love with him. And you can't love three different boys at the same time, can you? Her mother smilingly agreed, and encouraged her, in her roundabout, apparently easygoing way, to take her time.

Bill, the handsomest of the three—and very handsome he was—was president of his class at Princeton, president of one of the best undergraduate clubs, captain of the track team, intercollegiate champion in the quarter-mile. He was also very funny, and the things he said kept Julie in stitches. She had a sort of

81

feeling that she would probably end up by marrying him, and she was pretty sure her mother saw this more clearly than she did and would be glad to have it happen—when it happened. Bill was going to be a lawyer, and she knew he would be a great success and probably make a lot of money.

Murray was not nearly so good-looking as Bill, but he was sweet. He was in his first year at medical school in Baltimore, and worked very hard. He would be a wonderful doctor. He was tall and rather gangly, and shy—he even stammered sometimes—with rather a plain face, but sweet. She really thought she loved Murray. Sometimes she wanted to put her arms around him, he looked so sort of touching.

Then there was Francis. He was almost as good-looking as Bill, and terribly attractive, but there was something kind of bitter about him. He was the son of a famous man: his father had been President of the United States. Francis was still at Harvard and his father wanted him to go to law school, but he said he was going to be an actor. He could be very funny sometimes too. Julie liked him a lot. She even thought he was kind of fascinating, but he also made her uneasy. He was pretty definitely No. 3.

There were others who wanted to marry her, or said they were in love with her, but those three were the serious contenders. Some of the others were fun to be with occasionally, and she felt good friends with them; but some were *pathetic*. Bob was so shy he grinned all the time, and could hardly open his mouth without turning red. And that *pill* Tom! He had been after her for years, or it seemed like years. He was just a nuisance. Such a gloom. He wrote poems, and showed them to her—some of them, he said, were *about* her—but Julie didn't like them; they were morbid.

I was Tom; and it was me, after all, that Julie married.

Mrs. Cuyler's vagueness grew on her with age. She became more and more absent-minded with the years, and even gentler. It began to worry her that she couldn't always remember the names of all the people who spoke to her in the street. After Mr.

Cuyler died, she went to live with a married son—whose house was well within the sound of Trinity Church bells, and very convenient to the Parish House. Mr. Cuyler was buried in the little walled graveyard at the east end of the church. It was almost a family graveyard, as no one could be buried there who was not a Potter or had been married to a Potter. It was known as "Potter's Field."

Some time after the headstone had been set up at Mr. Cuyler's grave, someone discovered that a mistake of ten years had been made in his birth date. This tickled everybody, and didn't overly distress Mrs. Cuyler, who simply told her son that he must have the date corrected. But changing a date on a tombstone is not as simple a matter as correcting a typographical error. After the change was made it was quite noticeable that in the line "Born March 29, 1867," 1867 stood in a sunken square by itself.

Mrs. Cuyler's death seemed as gentle and serene as her life had been, though it was cancer that took her off, as it had taken her husband. She was buried by his side in "Potter's Field." Later her children wanted to put up a memorial to her in Trinity Church, and decided on a stained-glass window. After looking around the church for an appropriate place they finally hit on the vestibule. That was where people coming out of church began to chat with each other; as one of her sons said, it combined the best features of Trinity Church and Bamman's.

The quality we call, in our crude modern shorthand, "a social sense" was strongly developed in Julie, as in her father. Her brother Lewis, always known as "Buzz," was famous—after a rickety start as a miserable small boy—for his good company and for the way he could always put life, if not soul, into a party. He had the same gift his sister had of warming the atmosphere; I owe him many happy hours and I am grateful for them, but where he set the whole table on a roar she would bring a smile of affection to a single face. Buzz, like his father, was noted for his stories, but his taste in them was more catholic than discriminating. Julie's stories, like her mother's letters, were Chekhov, not O. Henry—

a warm and salty commentary on everyday life.

One of my earliest mental pictures of her shows her sitting on the front steps at the Farm, surrounded by three or four swains (she would be then about fourteen and they a year or so older); some unsympathetic observer—not I—had dubbed them "titty-birds." Julie is in the midst of telling a story, the titty-birds all wear expectant grins, but I—yes, I too am there, on the outskirts—know what is going to happen, I can see it coming: she is going to forget the point of the story! And sure enough, she does —to the whooping hilarity of all titty-birds, in which she heartily joins. *I* am the only one who is embarrassed.

She really liked to give other people pleasure, and she did not feel, as I did, surrounded by a world of probably hostile strangers ("Who are all those others?"). I don't think she thought of them as strangers, but as people like herself whom she had not yet met. And she was always ready and willing to meet them, and prepared to like them too. Although I gradually got more or less accustomed to meeting new people—I had to, on account of my job—I was never prepared, and never expected, to like them.

2

I fell in love with Julie when I was sixteen; she was three years younger. My courtship of her went doggedly on for nine years. Or that's the way it stuck in my memory. In fact it didn't last quite that long, and I was not continually faithful. Half that time we were apart, and in her absence I carried on other adolescent affairs.

Alice (pronounced A-*leece*) was the most sophisticated girl in town, snub-nosed but rather pretty, with a mocking manner. We exchanged stilted letters during my last year at St. Paul's, which consisted mostly of compliments on the other's handwriting. I was impressed by her letter paper, which had a distinct smell to it: it reminded me of her breath, which was bad. Not that I had ever kissed her (in later years, at our rare meetings, she used to present an old friend's cheek), but I often danced with her at Princeton parties.

She was an accomplished dancer. The only daughter of a rich and worldly widower, she was so precocious and so spoiled that she was allowed to go to her first Princeton Prom when she was only thirteen—to the huge disgust of all the local mothers and the envy of their daughters. At the small dances we all went to at the Peacock Inn Alice was as conspicuous and as glamorous as a wicked fairy princess. During a Paul Jones, when Harry Fine had the whistle, I would persuade him to blow it as I came opposite Alice.

She married young, an Englishman, an old Etonian, in the Foreign Office. Julie and I spent a very social weekend with them at their first post, in Washington. But long before that she took to traveling, and was seldom in Princeton. We met once on the *Aquitania,* I think it was: she was in first class and I in third; in those days of many transatlantic crossings I had learned the art of trespassing. She had one son and was never divorced, but I don't think her marriage was happy. She seemed increasingly blasé and mocking, and she drank a lot. The last time I saw her, in the bar at the River Club in New York, she asked me how Julie was, and I had to tell her that Julie was dead (which she knew and would have remembered if she had been sober). She died herself a few years later, from a fatal combination of barbiturates and cocktails. The coroner's verdict was death from accidental causes.

Neither Julie nor Alice was the first girl I kissed. I can't remember that girl's name, or anything much about her except that she was lively and dark and attractive. We were sitting together on the steps of a tennis club in Staten Island, where I had just played well in an exhausting and successful team match. I was tired, happy, and bemused with victory and drink. And all of a sudden this girl kissed me. I wish I could remember that it was I who kissed her. That was all there was to it, and I never saw her again. But I never forgot it, or her, altogether; and I did make some shy inquiries about her, in the vague hope that we might meet. The last I heard of her, she was married and had several children. I don't like to think that, if she's still alive, she's a grandmother and probably has rheumatism and perhaps a mustache.

I kissed two other girls while I was waiting for Julie. One was a strapping blonde, bigger and older than I was. She came from St. Louis and had the reputation of being "fast." When we met at a party in Princeton I somehow knew she would let me kiss her if the circumstances were right. She asked me to come and see her. She was staying at the house of Gerry Lambert, whom I regarded as one of Princeton's *parvenus:* he had made his name and increased his fortune by inventing the "halitosis" campaign to sell his family mouthwash, Listerine. He had moved to Princeton and built a neocolonial mansion outside the town.

I nerved myself for this encounter by buying a half-pint of fiery brown sherry, and choked down several mouthfuls before boarding the Johnson Line trolley, which in those days ran between Princeton and Trenton and would take me to the Province Line Road, the nearest stop to the Lambert house. On the long plod up the driveway my Dutch courage faded nearly away, and I had another couple of swigs. But the girl (was her name Connie?) met me at the door, thus saving me the unspeakable embarrassment of inquiring for her, face to face with a butler or perhaps Gerry Lambert himself, and took me off to an isolated sitting room.

Must I remember what happened next? I must. Instead of throwing a carelessly masterful arm around her and pressing a firm kiss on her yielding lips, I was seized by this powerful girl and gently seated on her lap, where for the next half hour she dandled me like a rag doll or a baby. She mothered me. She must have thought I was "cute." She kissed me occasionally and coolly, with some amusement but certainly no passion; and I got away as soon as I could break her maternal grip. Waiting at the trolley stop, I felt a confused sense of relief at having escaped her and shame for my inability to dominate her.

One other idyll from these days of innocence: a perfect example (for it came to nothing but was everything for the few weeks it lasted) of what we crassly smudge by calling it "puppy love"—the shy and wordless longing of a boy and a girl for what they dare not and cannot express. Romeo and Juliet in bud: comical to their elders but pure, incoherent tragedy to themselves. (When I was taken to see Booth Tarkington's play *Seventeen*, being seventeen myself at the time, I was enraged nearly to tears by the audience's roars of laughter; and later, when I read William Saroyan's story about sitting sadly through a farcical movie, asking himself, Why are they laughing?, I well understood him. Apparently we learn to develop a "sense of humor" as a defense against our deeper feelings; and towards the end of our lives we find the defense getting flimsier.)

Lieschen Gray was her name. I remember the freckles on her pretty nose, and her eyes (were they gray, like her name?) and her gentle voice—which I wouldn't find gentle now, for she came from Detroit, and my years in England have made the Midwestern accent seem harsh and uncouth. We met at Harwich Port, on the Cape, where that summer I was visiting my married sister for a fortnight, and where the Grays too had a cottage. We sailed and swam and went on picnics and clambakes on Monomoy; Lieschen and I did everything together. When the time came for me to go, Lieschen came with us to the train at Hyannis, and when we said goodbye there were tears in her eyes. We were too shy to kiss. We promised to write to each other but I don't think we did; and I never saw her again.

3

In the jawbreaking lingo of dentistry, I am a case of "malocclusion"; meaning that my jaws don't fit together like the two parts of a steel trap. Though there must be millions of people who have gone through life happily enough with jaws more ill-fitting than mine (the Crooked-Mouth Family was one of my mother's favorite stories), I was not allowed to. As the only son of wealthy and anxious parents, I was put through five years of torture in order that my crooked teeth should be made straight.

Years later, when I was middle-aged, an ear doctor at Johns Hopkins was discussing the possibility of an operation on my deaf ear. "If you were a beautiful deb," he said, "I'd recommend it. But you're not." I wish my parents had had the sense to take a similar view about my teeth. But they didn't, so from the time I was eleven until I was sixteen I endured the miseries of "teeth-straightening"; and I must say that at the end of the process my teeth were apparently no crookeder than they had been.

"Orthodontistry," as the dentists who specialized in this racket called it, was then in its infancy, and its various practitioners were trying out various methods. As my family moved three times in these five years, my jaws became the experimental battleground for three (no, four) different tacticians: first in Cincinnati, then in Faribault, Minnesota; then Trenton, then Philadelphia. Though each of these experts favored his own pet treatment—one preferring the thumbscrew, as it were, to the rack—they all based their practice on the same assumption: that if enough pressure is applied to a tooth it will eventually move.

It wasn't till years later that I realized the fallacy in this assumption. Every week I sat myself cringing in the dentist's chair while he tightened the two parabolas of heavy wire that were bent around my teeth and cemented solidly to a contraption anchored to my molars. The result of this weekly tightening was that every tooth in my head ached for four or five days afterwards and I couldn't chew properly until the day before I went back for the next tightening. The fallacy of the orthodontists' theory—that the wires pulled the teeth into shape—was borne out by the final result: after five years of this excruciating, weekly renewed pressure, my teeth were just as crooked as they had been. It hurt them to bend the wires to *their* shape, but they'd done it!

A child whose mouth is harnessed with this apparatus may learn to forget his own grotesque appearance, but not so an adolescent. During the last years of my "tooth-straightening" I was an acutely self-conscious adolescent; and to make things worse, I was in love.

Julie, the unconscious object of my love (but was she unconscious of it, even at that age? Little girls are very precocious), was being prepared for confirmation, and my older sister Charlotte was coaching her. I think the first time I saw Julie was on one of her visits to our house, for a lesson with Charlotte. But the occasion that is burnt into my memory is the day she first came to lunch. I sat opposite her, my eyes on my plate, trying to eat without exposing my cluttered teeth. They were more cluttered than usual, for besides the accustomed armature of gold wires I now had heavy rubber bands stretched between my upper and lower jaws, held in place by hooks cemented to my teeth.

My father was in great form, telling his favorite stories. Most unfairly, he told one I had never heard that was so funny I couldn't help opening my mouth in a shout of laughter. This dislocated one of my rubber bands, which shot across the table and landed on Julie's butter plate. Everyone except me thought this was even funnier than my father's story. Merciful memory refuses to tell me what my feelings were; all I can remember is the dreadful fact.

4

I had baited a trap for Julie two years in advance; and she walked into it and out again uncaught. In 1920 I invited her to the Senior Prom that wouldn't take place till 1922, and she accepted; what else could she do? By June of my senior year we were not on very good terms. In fact, I was close to the bottom of the totem pole. And there were several other boys she would much rather have gone to the Prom with. But I held her to her promise, and against all the probabilities stuck to my resolve to ask her, at some appropriate point in the evening, to marry me.

Nothing worked out the way I had planned. No sooner were we launched on the dance floor than someone cut in, and it seemed to me I hardly saw her again. For one dreadful period, more than an hour, I searched for her, walking round and round the great hall against the stream of dancers; she was nowhere to be seen. When at last I found her she swore she had been on the dance floor the whole time. I insisted on my rights as her partner to take her to supper, but she haled two other couples along with us. She danced the rest of the night, but almost never with me, and when at last dawn brought an end to this interminable ordeal, I drove her home in a silent, sullen rage. She thanked me for a *heavenly* party but didn't even kiss me. So much for my hopeful schemes: I could see now, in the dull light of early morning, how unrealistic and ridiculous they had been.

But what happened then? I can't remember or explain it: all I know is that somehow during that summer, like the mysterious changing of the tide, my affair with Julie began to go better. Was it because we both stayed in Princeton, while my glamorous rivals took themselves off to their glamorous summer resorts?

Did her mother favor me and help my suit along? Or was it because Julie herself had a change of heart, or began to tell herself that she would, after all, miss me when I went away to Oxford? Whatever the cause, the new dispensation was so much more favorable—favorable? so intoxicatingly heady!—that I hardly cared or dared to hope whether it would last out the summer. In short, I kissed her. And not only that: I woke each morning to the great expectation or at least the heart-lifting possibility that today, or this evening, or some time soon, I would kiss her again.

This was the more marvelous to me because my first attempt had been a disaster. I had taken the advice of an expert, and it had turned out all wrong. Her brother Buzz was my confidant and well-wisher. Although he was a year younger than I, he had already won a firm reputation as a great hand at kissing girls, and when in my despair I had turned to him for help he had told me: "Why, just take hold of her and kiss her." I must have left out some essential factor in this solid formula, for when I tried it with Julie she slapped my face.

Then how had it ever come about that I did kiss her, after all? It was a mystery I couldn't fathom; but I remembered when it happened, if not why. That afternoon about a dozen of us had been swimming at the Pardees' pool, a favorite meeting place for those of us who were lucky enough to have a standing invitation. I was never much of a swimmer, but I could do a feeble imitation of a swan-dive and a passable jackknife. My best dive, when I could nerve myself to try it, was the back jackknife, in which you stand on the end of the springboard with your back to the pool, and jump backwards as well as up, doubling over and just missing the springboard as you go straight down. When I tried this dive I always had to stand and wait for several seconds, to get my balance and my nerve.

While I was standing there, Julie called out to me; being intent on my dive, I didn't actually take in what she said, though I heard her mocking tone of voice. But the dive went all right, and I didn't mind; as long as she noticed me, I thought, let her say what she likes. Besides, she had already promised to go for a drive with me that evening.

As a reward for having graduated from the University, though not with honors, and in recognition of my new status as a legally if not actually mature man, that summer my parents allowed me the use of the Chandler, the lesser of their two cars. This gave me a position, a standing, or rather a place to sit that was more advantageous than being merely one of the chattering group on the front steps of the Cuyler Farm that might move on, always as a body, to the movies or a bowling alley or a piled-together, aimless ride-to-nowhere in someone's car.

My constant purpose, to get Julie to myself, was sometimes thwarted by the chance that mine was the only car available and that I had not succeeded in pinning her down to the pledge of an evening by ourselves. She preferred—I cannot blame her now, though I did then—the boisterous, giggling, puppy-and-kitten romping of a crowd of boys and girls to the gloomy silences and bitter sighs of a hapless, hopeless adorer. Nevertheless I did occasionally have the luck during that all-too-short summer to take her for a drive, "just for an hour," alone. Getting her to come with me was only the first step. The second, which then became my entire purpose, was to find an appropriate place where she would agree to stop. She almost always wanted to keep going; so at least half the time these expeditions ended in blank failure. We must have driven hundreds of miles on these summer evenings, often over roads I never saw before or since. Once, on a country lane that meandered through a wood, we both instantly concurred in stopping: in the dazzle of the headlights we saw a skunk and her four little ones pacing deliberately across the road, manifesting their right of way.

One alarming incident nearly put an end to these rides. In Lovers' Lane, which in those days was on the bosky outskirts of Princeton, I persuaded Julie to let me stop the car "just for a minute," and then I had my arms around her. At that moment a man stepped out of the bushes and put his foot on the running board. Somehow I started the engine and wrenched the car ahead, shaking him off. As we made our getaway we heard him shouting something: we couldn't make out the words. Though the shock of this ugly surprise left us both breathless, it was also a secret we shared and puzzled over. Who could it have been? A policeman? A robber? A voyeur?

The events of that summer have left no clear sequence in my mind, so I cannot be sure when the greatest of them all took place: the night I first kissed Julie. I think it was the evening of the same day she had called out her mocking remark to me at the Pardees' pool. When I came for her at the Farm she was ready and waiting. This punctuality, a characteristic of my family but not of hers, surprised and encouraged me. And she seemed to be in a subdued frame of mind: I put this down to her natural disappointment in having to sacrifice a whole evening to me. But I was mistaken. As we were passing the Canoe House on Carnegie Lake—I remember the exact spot—she said she had written me "a letter," and handed me an envelope.

I stopped the car. In the dim light from the dashboard I could see my name on the envelope but I couldn't read the message inside, so I got out and held the letter under the headlights. It was an apology! That afternoon, when I was standing on the springboard, she had apparently called out a taunting reference to my bandy legs, about which she knew I was sensitive. In her note she confessed that this had been inexcusable behavior and that she was very sorry.

I could have laughed with relief and delight. I assured her that I had taken no offense whatever, that I hadn't even heard what she said but that it would have made absolutely no difference if I had; that it was terribly nice of her to apologize but that really it was nothing, etc., etc. The upshot was that she cried a little, I put a comforting arm around her, and we kissed. Yes, she did more than merely let me kiss her; she did her part and kissed me as well.

That was why the whole future, or at least the nearer view of it, suddenly took a different direction and a rosier hue.

5

On one of the last days of September, a sparkling, blue-and-gold morning with a faint frosty nip in the clear fall air, I left my father's house and Princeton and Julie for a new and unknown life in England. I was to be at Oxford for two years, and I didn't intend to come back until that time was up. It seemed then that I was saying a long farewell.

My ship sailed from New York at noon, and I took a train from Princeton that morning so early that most people were still in bed. I had said goodbye to my parents the night before, but my mother and sisters were up to see me off. Walter, my father's chauffeur, who was to drive me to Princeton Junction, grumbled that I was starting too early and would have a long wait at the station.

"I want to stop at the Cuyler Farm for a minute," I said.

Walter said nothing but the back of his neck was eloquent. He knew all about it.

I had Mrs. Cuyler's permission, and of course Julie's, to come and say goodbye that morning. This meant that I would see her in bed; the prospect was bitter-sweet.

The front door of the Farm was locked. I rang the bell, which was probably out of order, and pounded the knocker. Presently the door jerked open and there was Mr. Cuyler, in nightshirt and slippers, his hair on end, glaring at me with sleepy eyes. Obviously neither his wife nor his daughter had warned him that I was coming. But as soon as he saw who it was the glare turned into an expression of puzzled benevolence. My emotions were so near the surface that I couldn't trust myself to speak. I gave him a wave of the hand that was intended to be explanatory and dived past him into the hall and up the stairs.

Julie was lying in a big four-poster. She held up her arms to me as I sat on the creaking edge. She was rosy from sleep, her nightgown was pink; I had never seen anything so heartbreakingly beautiful. Her father used to say, "All women are prettier in bed." He was right, but what an understatement!

What did we say? I think I said, "I can only stay a minute." I *must* have said, "I love you." I don't remember that Julie said anything; but she kissed me, and smiled, with her eyes brimming.

I tore myself away and clattered downstairs, the tears streaming down my face.

We drove off. After a while Walter said, "Well, you got a nice morning."

6

As it turned out, it was only a long six months, not an eternity of two years, before I saw Julie again. I simply couldn't stay away. The six weeks Christmas vacation on Boar's Hill, in spite of Schuyler's company, had been a lonely vigil; and the prospect of another such time at Easter, especially since Schuyler had now left for America, was too grim to face. I half-knew that I was missing the chance of a lifetime, the coincidence of my youth and Europe; but I told myself that every decision is a spermatozoon that can come to life only at the cost of the millions of other spermatozoa that come to nothing.

Julie was glad to see me, but not glad enough to suit me. She wouldn't say Yes and she wouldn't say No; she wanted to keep me dangling and she didn't want to choose. Again I can't blame her; but I did then. I left her a second time, but this time in anger, telling her that if she ever changed her mind she would have to let me know it. And the extraordinary thing is that she did.

Even then, however, although it was understood between us

that we were engaged and one of these days would be married, she didn't want it made public, and our engagement wasn't announced till more than a year later. A few members of our families were informed: Julie took me to call formally on her most important cousin, a grand and dowdy lady named Mrs. Moses Taylor Pyne ("Cousin Etta"—or "Yawnetta" as she was called behind her back, from her habit of punctuating her small conversation with enormous yawns); I remember that she didn't seem much impressed. And Mr. Cuyler, whom by rights I should have waited on to ask for the hand of his daughter—except that it never occurred to either of us that I should. I knew that he was on my side, although he took the somewhat perverse view that it was my reluctance rather than Julie's that was holding up our affair; and he took to leaving a Sears, Roebuck catalogue on the hall table at the Farm, opened at the page that showed engagement rings.

Our aged ex-governess, Miss Miller, now a family retainer in my father's house, had nutcracker jaws that gave her a strong resemblance to Mr. Punch. When Mr. Cuyler was told that Julie and I were at last engaged, though unofficially, he heaved a sigh and said, "Will I have to kiss Miss Miller?"

When I went back to Oxford for the summer term of 1923, I had already decided that I would return to America that summer (another rendezvous with Europe missed) to be with Julie. But I reckoned without my anxious elders. I am sure they never discussed the situation in so many words; I am equally sure they understood each other clearly, and thoroughly agreed on the strategy that was called for, though they may have differed about tactics. Since Tom and Julie obviously couldn't be married for some time (he had to finish at Oxford and get a job, though the poor fellow didn't seem to realize that yet) and were therefore in for a long engagement, it would be best if they didn't see *too much* of one another. An engagement should be a testing time, in more ways than one: they were very young—too young, really, to know their own minds. And perhaps, after all . . . Time will tell, etc.

All very sensible. It might have been more sensible, and less cruel, to keep us entirely apart until we could come entirely together, as the practice is in wiser societies. The frustrations of a long engagement—ours lasted two whole years—were not a good preparation for a happy marriage. We emerged from this "testing time" as sexual opponents: Julie having stubbornly defended her virginity, and kept it unbroken if not intact, against all my assaults; and both of us feeling guilty and inadequate for the wrong reason—for what we had done, not for what we had failed to do.

During those two years I tried many times to seduce her, and never quite succeeded; I still regret it. If we had loved each other more—if I had loved *her* more—would I have been successful? Yes! I believe that; but then it would not have been a seduction, it would have been mutual consent. I was unable to persuade her, so the failure was mainly mine.

We were both brought up under the same sexual taboos, which in our Christian society were supposed to supplement and parallel love but which usually cut across and negated love's true morality. Is it any wonder that we felt ourselves wrapped and scored by the barbed wire of this moral tangle? Well, wonder or not, we did feel it. In those days I often thought that, like Mrs. Gummidge, I felt it more; but I may well have been mistaken. Julie had a warm heart, warmer than mine, and our endless kissing, our furtive, groping caresses, roused her passions no less than mine.

It was hateful to be apart; it was sometimes a torture to be together. If our families had been wiser, or if we had all been more outspoken, they would have been more aware of our inflammable situation. Perhaps they were more aware than we thought. At any rate, Julie was sent off on visits; my parents took me on a Western trip, which did not improve my temper and seemed to slow down the passage of time to an almost agonizing degree. But at last the long summer was over, and I went back to Oxford for my second and last year.

By this time it had been decided by the parental authorities, or with their approval, that the fact of our engagement was incorrigible and might as well be publicly admitted. An announcement was to appear in *The New York Times* on the day after I sailed. I found four or five other Princetonians aboard, also heading for Oxford. The second day out we were sitting together in the tourist smoking room. The talk was mainly of Oxford and its peculiarities. I could think of nothing but Julie and the stupendous fact of our engagement. At a pause in the conversation, I plucked up my courage and said in a small voice, "I'm engaged." Nobody heard me. It took me several days to nerve myself to repeat this remark; but that time it hit the target and I was overwhelmed with congratulations.

Julie's schooling had ended at St. Mary's; she was never even tempted to go on to college. She was far too concerned with being alive to be a bluestocking. She could never get through *War and Peace* (and she very much wanted to) although she made several attempts, because she always bogged down in that long explanation of the Masonic Order. In vain I told her to skip it, that it was quite irrelevant and unnecessary. She was determined to plow through it, but she never did. She wrote and spoke the rather sprawling and exaggerated hand and dialect of her generation and class. Her spelling was a delight to me. One of her favorite words, *huge,* she invariably spelt *hugh,* giving this giant word a personality of its own.

After she left school and was supposed to be "settling down," her mother arranged a job for her (with little or no pay) as secretary to the Rector. Robert Williams, the Rector, had come late to the Church, as he came late to everything. He was a slow man, famous for his tactless sermons ("Some of you who were here last Easter are no longer with us, and some of you here today will not be here next Easter") and his booming laugh, which went off half-cock most of the time because he was afraid he would miss the point, and usually did. He really had no need of a secretary, or rather, was unable to employ one to good effect; and Julie could neither type nor write shorthand, so they were a pretty pair. There was a monthly parish paper, the *Trinity Bulletin*, of which Mr. Williams was in charge and for which he wrote a Rector's letter. For a time he tried to dictate this letter to Julie.

Instead of the desired speeding-up of the work, this dictation seemed to slow it down. For instance, Mr. Williams would roll out the word *imminent*.

"How do you spell that, Mr. Williams?"

Mr. Williams, after some casting about, would confess that he didn't know.

"Look it up, Julie!"

"Well, what letter does it begin with?"

It would then turn out that neither of them knew that either.

7

On the way back from our honeymoon, Julie and I were not speaking to each other. It never occurred to me that this might be a normal state of affairs or even that it might ever have happened before in the whole history of marriage. This quarrel appeared to me monstrous and tragic—in the sense that it was the inevitable result (I thought) of a fatal, irreconcilable difference in our natures. I had made the enormous and despairing discovery that we were an incompatible couple.

I didn't know that this is the necessary first hurdle, which is not necessarily the finish, of married life. And at that point I wouldn't for a moment have believed it. Even so, at this early and passionately committed stage of our marriage I didn't and couldn't feel that the chasm between us, a chasm that seemed to yawn wider every minute, was unbridgeable. In fact, I thought it was nonsense.

What was the quarrel about? I couldn't remember, and I was sure that even if Julie could, she wouldn't be able to state the case articulately. Anyhow, the cause of it didn't matter: the real issue now was how to end the war. Julie might have said, if she had thought in those terms, that the only settlement she would accept was my unconditional surrender, with punitive reparations for the outrageous suffering that had been inflicted on her. Though perhaps she would have been more deeply satisfied with exactly the opposite: a peace enforced by her own unconditional surrender.

But I was even less aware than she of these conflicting desires in her. Even if I had suspected the existence of a peace party in the enemy camp, I wouldn't have known how to get into contact with it. Besides, I was in the position of a general who knows that his own disaffected troops are on the point of mutiny, and whose one hope is to end the war quickly—by a negotiated peace if possible, but at all costs. Had I only known it, my best and only chance was an immediate and all-out attack. Instead of that, I sent out a flag of truce and made feeble and defeatist overtures.

Julie was sitting beside me in the car but as far away as possible. I put a cautious hand along the top of the seat; timidly I touched her shoulder. With a violent shrug she flung off my hand. We were just coming into the unlovely outskirts of Bridgeport. Nothing further was attempted by me, and nothing was said between us, for the rest of the way into New York.

Two weeks before, almost to the day, we had been married. In spite of the miseries and disappointments of the honeymoon we were emerging from, I remembered our wedding day with gratitude and awe. I had lived for it, prayed for it, waited for it, it seemed to me, forever. Even though, when it finally, unbelievably came, I didn't *enjoy* it, that seemed to me beside the point; perhaps it was too much to hope that a bridegroom should enjoy his bride's wedding. It certainly hadn't been my day. That was all hers, and the fullness thereof; I didn't grudge her a moment of it. But it hadn't seemed to me so much full as exhaustingly empty.

It wasn't that I had a hangover either. I had foregone the traditional bachelor dinner the night before, partly on the grounds of expense but largely on account of my unpredictable best man, Schuyler. I knew it would be hard enough looking after Schuyler (whose job as best man was supposed to be looking after *me*) even if he stayed sober. If he got drunk, as he most certainly would have done at a bachelor dinner, there was no telling what he might not do. Schuyler presented certain other difficulties. When I had asked him to be my best man, he had been reluctant. In the first place, he wasn't sure he believed in marriage, and, having been through them himself, he was dead set against the flummeries of a formal wedding. Was I sure I was marrying the right girl, or that I should marry at all? Furthermore, he didn't have the proper clothes for such an affair and he wouldn't lift a finger to get any. I borrowed a cutaway that was a reasonably good fit, and we dispensed with top hats. I don't remember how I answered his questions about marriage, or whether I attempted to.

When Schuyler arrived in Princeton, the day before the wedding, I almost wished I hadn't asked him. He had shaved the top of his head and had grown a straggly beard. He explained to me that his family baldness was threatening to overtake him and that these drastic measures were intended to halt or at least delay the loss of his hair. There was nothing to be done about his shaved head, and the most he would do about his beard was to let a barber trim it. He had arrived too late for the wedding rehearsal, but I went over it with him in the room we shared. We were both staying at my family's house, and I had asked to have Schuyler in my room, so that I could keep an eye on him. (Why didn't Kit come too? It was only a few months after her own wedding, so she can't have been prevented by one of the series of miscarriages that haunted her early married life and that Schuyler

101

turned into a kind of awful joke. She was very much under Schuyler's thumb, and I suppose he simply didn't want to bring her.)

Next day, the great day, dawned cool but sunny. I hardly dared let Schuyler out of my sight, but I desperately wanted to see Julie for a moment. When I got to the Rectory she was being photographed in her wedding dress, so I was not allowed to see her (it was considered bad luck) until she had changed. She was nervous, distraught, I thought she was almost at the end of her tether. For weeks she had been working night and day on all the details of the wedding, determined that it should be perfect in every smallest particular, and now she was in a state where the slightest mischance irritated her. She had weighed herself that morning, and seemed more pleased than not that she was down to 98 pounds; but it worried me. She scolded me for nearly interrupting her wedding picture.

I gave her a hasty and apologetic kiss and took myself off. Mr. Cuyler walked to the gate with me, put his arm around my shoulders and told me not to worry, everything would sort itself out. It wasn't till afterwards that I realized that he was not only trying to cheer me up but might have been warning me that Julie probably had the curse.

I got Schuyler and myself properly dressed, far ahead of time. He wanted a drink. So did I, but I had decided to be absolutely sober for this great event in my life, so I refrained. I watched anxiously while Schuyler put down nearly a tumbler of neat whiskey, in a few gulps. In the sacristy, while we were waiting for the organist's signal, Schuyler began to show symptoms of alarming euphoria: a far-off happy look came over his face, his eyes seemed to turn glassy, and he began to hum "The Volga Boat Song"—always a bad sign with him.

I hissed at him to shut up, and asked him if he had the ring. He poked a relaxed finger into his waistcoat pocket, and gently said "No." I could have killed him. I swung him around and searched him. I found the ring in another pocket to which he had absent-mindedly transferred it. At that moment the organ burst into "Here Comes the Bride."

JULIE

The wedding went off all right; I suppose weddings always do. Julie rose to the occasion, as she had intended, and looked meltingly pretty. I amazed myself and others by speaking up in resonant tones; my responses, I was told, were clearly audible all through the church. In the exhausting hours that followed I thought I understood the *realpolitik* of a formal wedding: a day of triumph for the bride, and equally important, an experience for the bridegroom so punishing and painful that he will never again willingly submit himself to the ordeal. A public wedding, I saw now, was the community's way of warning all hands that a marriage had better be for keeps.

The reception at the Cuyler Farm was unbelievably crowded. The receiving line, which was meant to take its stand in the drawing room, never got there; the first wave of heavy dowagers knocked it apart while it was still forming, and the small pockets of resistance that were left were cut off from one another and overwhelmed piecemeal. Julie and I were pushed into a narrow corner of the front hall, between the stairs and a side wall. The din was deafening, and the pressure of screaming middle-aged women, terrible in broad-brimmed hats, incredible, not to be borne.

I tried to shield Julie but I was helpless against that weight of pushing bodies, elbowing, clawing to get at her, screaming "Where's the little bride? Let me at the little bride!" Whenever I saw a familiar or even friendly-seeming face I shouted hoarsely for help. Nobody heard me.

By some miracle Julie survived this hour-long assault, not merely unscathed but apparently unruffled. She even seemed to enjoy it. As for me, I was in an almost fainting condition. As the assault lightened, drew off and at length died away, one of my hoarse cries of distress attracted a friend, who brought me my first drink of the day, a half-spilled glass of warm champagne. Someone steered me to the bridal table. There were roars of embarrassed laughter when Schuyler proposed a toast to "Miss Julie Cuyler!" He couldn't even get *that* right. Julie hissed in my ear, and I rose and mumbled a toast to the bride's mother.

Finally it was over. Julie and I made our getaway amidst showers of rice and a chorus of vinous yells—they sounded to me like derisive cheers from the victorious enemy. Our car was borrowed from my father. Julie, still riding the crest of her great day, still keyed up, chattered on and on, reliving every moment of those past hours whose memory made me wince. Getting no support from me, her enthusiasm faltered, exhaustion overtook her, and she too fell silent.

Perhaps this was the point at which our quarrel began. How dreadful silence can be; into what cavernous deeps it descends. When nothing is being said, at last there is nothing to say. All you can do is listen for the small, subterranean, inhuman echoes and drippings, the faint scurrying of bats or rats, the muffled sliding of no longer steadfast rock.

We spent our wedding night in Newark, at the Robert Treat Hotel. We were heading for Cape Cod, where my married sister had lent us her summer cottage. I wanted to make the trip in easy stages. Except for this first night I had made no hotel reservations, and that small chore I had entrusted not to Schuyler but to one of Julie's brothers—who had forgotten all about it. No, said the room clerk, we have no double room reserved in the name of Matthews. Cuyler? No, not that either. And the hotel is full up. At last he took pity on our desperation and told us we could have a maid's room on the top floor.

The room was small and dreary, and not very clean. And it turned out that Julie did have the curse. But the actuality of being in bed with that beloved small bony body (though she wouldn't take off her nightgown), and lying with my arms around her, was the most acute pleasure I had ever known. I had waited years for her, I could wait a little longer. Both of us were exhausted and soon fell asleep. I was roused—it seemed to me only a few minutes later—by a disagreeable but not unfamiliar sensation: something was biting me.

I had always attracted insects, especially those that bite, and whatever it was that had bitten me this time had settled on me and spared Julie. But the sudden start with which I woke and my

105

frantic efforts to find the insect woke her as well. Together we searched the bed. It was Julie's keen eye that spotted the bedbug, my slipper that squashed it flat. I carefully put the corpse into an envelope, to show the clerk in the morning.

But in the morning I lost my nerve. Anyhow, as I pointed out to Julie, the man to whom I paid the bill would not be the same one who had given us the room—and what could he have done about it anyhow, except say he was sorry, or laugh? By the time we had got to our second hotel, at New Milford, I felt that I had almost lived down this humiliating incident. It took us three days to get to Cape Cod. Julie still had the curse but gradually grew less edgy. I wondered whether other honeymooners ever got on each other's nerves.

The Cape Cod cottage, which my sister had built the year before and which I had never seen, was like a little fairy tale house; cheerful, pretty, and stocked with everything we could want. A local woman named Ella came in and cooked our lunch and dinner for us. She was large and loquacious, and we were shy in her presence. She was a continual reminder that we were a raw newly married pair who couldn't look after ourselves and who probably needed instructions on how to behave when we were alone together. At least that's how she made me feel.

Julie and I were well brought up: that is, neither of us knew, except in the sketchiest and most theoretical manner, how to perform the act of love. Julie was a virgin and thought there must be something wrong with her. I was in no better case: I had had one brutal experience with a professional tart which had only weakened my self-confidence. I knew I should be Julie's guide and teacher, but I didn't know how to guide or teach anybody.

So Julie was frustrated and bitterly disappointed, but feared that she was somehow to blame; and I, who was passionately in love with her, felt guiltily that my frustration was nothing to hers, and that the responsibility for our failure was entirely mine. It was not a matter we could *discuss*, brought up as we had been, but in moments of stress it was mentioned between us in muttered exclamations or in broken phrases.

Our problems were physical and ludicrous but seemed to us tragic; not only to fit our ignorant and unaccustomed bodies together in love but also how to sleep with some degree of comfort in the same bed. On our first night in the cottage, when we were in bed together, Julie disappeared under the covers with a flashlight, and sat there, humped under the blanket tent, for long and motionless minutes. I lay perfectly still, enduring this shy and lubricious inspection with shame and delight, wondering what would happen now. Nothing happened. When Julie emerged from under the covers she said not a word, but lay beside me, rigid and shivering. I took her in my arms, caressed her, and made another clumsy attempt.

I wanted to make love so often in those first days that I sometimes wondered whether I was abnormal. It didn't seem to make any difference where we were or what time of day it was: I always wanted her. I would lure her down to the deserted beach, pretending that we were only going for a walk, and then try to get her into a sheltered spot in the dunes. That was never successful; she was always afraid somebody might see us. Or I would pull her down with me on the couch in the living room. That was not much better.

Julie resisted all these advances with quiet fury: she would hiss at me that we could be *seen,* or to wait for the night. It was only in bed that she felt even relatively secure from prying eyes. The only time she did give in, one rainy afternoon after Ella had washed the lunch dishes and gone home, we were interrupted by a rapping on the door knocker. We leaped from the couch, frenziedly buttoning and rearranging our disordered clothes, and I, with flushed face and rumpled hair, went to the door to admit a friendly and unwelcome neighbor, come to call.

I had imagined our honeymoon very differently: we were to be alone together, completely alone, with nothing to do but make love, by day and by night. But we never seemed to be alone; there was Ella, and our few neighbors, frequently visible, and the peeping Toms conjured up by Julie. Our only privacy was at night, in our bedroom—and even then Julie "heard things."

Once I heard something too. I had been asleep or dozing; the sound scared me into instant and frozen wakefulness. Someone had just flushed the can in the bathroom across the tiny hall. There was—or should be—no one else in the house but Julie and me, and Julie was asleep beside me. Some marauder had got in, and to show his contempt for me had flushed the can. What other explanation could there be?

I told myself to be a man and get up and investigate. I didn't want to do either. Julie slept peacefully on. I lay stiff with fright, trying to nerve myself to get out of bed. The can flushed again! This was too much. Galvanized by despair, I leapt out of bed, wrenched open the bedroom door, switched on the lights—and confronted an empty bathroom, the water still gurgling in the pan. I whirled to look behind me. No one there. A consoling explanation began to dawn on me. I stood in the bathroom door and waited, watching the can. Sure enough, as soon as its tank was full it flushed again. I took off the lid and poked around among the rods and plungers, but I was hopeless at anything mechanical. I soon gave up and went back to bed. All night long, at intervals of a few minutes, the can flushed itself.

For most of every day, it seemed to me, Julie wrote letters. She had brought a list of everyone who had sent a wedding present, about 250 all together, and she was determined to write a thank-you note to each one. This Herculean chore did not improve her temper, nor mine. In her view it was a hardship but her duty, and duty must always come first. My feeling was that she had brought it on herself—she and her mother between them—by insisting on "that kind of wedding"; and that on the precious two weeks of our honeymoon it was us (I meant me) who should come first. She would never get all those notes written in two weeks, anyway, so why not put off writing them until we were home?

Was *that* how the quarrel began? Hadn't I gone on from there to condemn "big weddings," whose real purpose was to get a lot of wedding presents—like a mail-order campaign? Yes, I remembered saying something like that, and that we had had a row about it. But that must have been only the start of it. We surely couldn't have reached this silent and hostile impasse just because I had criticized her family's taste in weddings. The thing that ruins marriage, I thought gloomily, is sex. Or is it the other way about?

As we neared New York the weather grew hotter and hotter. It was a Sunday in early June, and should have been lovely, but we were coming into the first heat-wave of the summer. I had rented a small furnished flat on East 49th Street. It was on the fourth floor, over a bookshop, and there was no elevator. We would have to share the bathroom with two trained nurses.

We had made an early start that day, and hadn't yet had any breakfast. We drove through nearly empty streets to the bookshop and parked the car. I suggested that we have breakfast first and carry up our bags later. Julie silently agreed. We set off through the shimmering heat to find a restaurant that was open. The first two Julie didn't like. After walking another half-mile without finding anything, I said savagely that we might as well go back to the Childs we had considered first.

We did, but Julie said she felt sick; she ate hardly anything. By the time we had clambered wearily up the four flights of stairs to our baking hot apartment and sketchily unpacked, Julie had to lie down. Then she went to the bathroom and was sick. I pounded on the door of the trained nurses' bedroom and got one of them to come and take a look at Julie.

The nurse reported to me that she thought Julie had colitis and had better see a doctor. It took me quite a while to get one. The doctor confirmed the trained nurse's report. The honeymoon was over.

8

When I was first in love with Julie, in my undergraduate days, I was once shocked and offended by a friend of mine who said that if you were in love with a girl you wanted to go to bed with her. I indignantly denied that I wanted to go to bed with Julie—and at that point the idea did seem so shameful to me that I suppose I couldn't face it. Or wouldn't, rather.

And in spite of the fact that later we did go to bed together, and in spite of the fact that by then I knew she shared an animal nature no less hungry than mine, I never altogether succeeded in marrying lust and love. No, that is not quite true: in her case I did, but it was a clandestine affair and she would not be an open partner to it. I could seduce her into what she regarded (and I too) as animal behavior, but afterwards she felt betrayed—by herself as much as by me. So I too felt shame, and sometimes even the kind of *horror feminae* that haunted Swift, and which he expressed with such brutal disgust.

Like most of the "well-brought-up" boys of my generation and background, I was taught to believe that God himself had made sexual knowledge shameful and furtive (that was the gist of the story of Adam and Eve as it was expounded to us). In consequence, when we ourselves grew old enough for fig leaves, we too became shameful and furtive. In my case, I was so alarmed by adolescence that when its first signs appeared I took them as proof that something was wrong with me, and when other signs were slow in appearing, I took them as further proof.

Would I have agonized less over the mystery of sex if I had grown up in a franker and more open-minded generation, as the present one is said to be? Perhaps; although both frankness and furtiveness seem to have proved an equally luckless way into the heart of the sexual labyrinth. Like Adam naming the animals, our words run ahead of our knowledge.

Take the unlovely modern phrase, "penis-envy"—a solemnly ludicrous concept characteristic of our day. And, may I add, a libel against the female sex, on whom the notion has been foisted. This sort of envy exists much more among men than among women. We cannot resist comparing ourselves with our fellows, secretly fearing (although we should know better) that the size of our member is the infallible indication of our virility. The sight of a stallion's extended prong should be enough to throw all of us into despair. If we are slow developers we regard with dismay our more precocious rivals, whose voices have deepened and whose private parts are huge and hairy; we wonder how that little tassel of ours, sparsely topped by a few silken threads, will ever be able to play a man's part.

This misapprehensive envy is ages old: remember the story in *The Arabian Nights* (Burton's translation, of course) about the fat young man whom the jealous husband foolishly left alone with his lovely wife, because the husband had seen the young man naked and had written him off as a harmless eunuch, since his member was no bigger than a filbert? And it still goes on.

The secret all men know, however, is that dress rehearsals don't count. The only thing that counts is to be all right on the night. And no matter how triumphant the performance is then (the press agent always exaggerates the number of curtain calls), we can never be sufficiently reassured—we are not only gluttons for the act but greedily anxious for applause. And for the kind of long run that will satisfy us (temporarily) and allay our fears that our powers are failing, we know what is needed: the outward and visible sign of our manhood will droop and fail without inward and invisible support. The Spaniards, who have thought long and felt deeply on the subject, have a word for it: *cojones.* What makes a man virile is his balls.

9

I had loved her terribly, painfully, for years and years, and at last she had said Yes, and now it was all legal, open and aboveboard. Those endless years of courtship, which had been like waiting forever in a queue, the purgatory of our too-long engagement, the miseries and disappointments of our over-anticipated honeymoon—all were ended now. Now at last we were actually married, and we were going to live happily ever after.

It was a hot Sunday afternoon in July, and we were alone in our two-room apartment (no private bath) in New York. She was pretending to be asleep; I was almost sure she was pretending. And I was sitting beside the bed, looking at her. I remember that as if it were yesterday. And I can remember, being by then accustomed to suffering on account of her, though never used to it, feeling that now the pain was finished and the happiness was at last about to begin. Looking at her was like being the eyewitness to my own joy; I didn't know then what an eyewitness is worth or what it was that I was looking at.

What did I see? For I certainly saw something extraordinary and not to be denied, either then or later. I saw a girl's naked body, the first I had ever beheld and the one I had always longed to see. Those facts I can be sure of. She was lying face down on the bed, her head turned away from me and pillowed in her arms. The sunlight, broken into horizontal bars by the slatted shutters, laid two stripes of gold across her back.

Her arms were touchingly thin, a child's arms. She was too thin altogether; her ribs and the sharp triangle of a shoulder-blade, the knobbly curve of her spine, the blunt protuberance of a hipbone, stood out under the taut skin. The curves of her back, of croup and thigh and shoulder, were like a preliminary and faltering sketch for the bold lines of maturity; the bony armature showed through.

And yet I had never seen nor imagined anything so heart-breakingly beautiful. This thin, unfinished body was to me the most beloved and most desirable of all bodies, and in my eyes it was perfect. This was the final revelation of the girl I had worshipped under her various protective disguises, for the past nine years. I had become agonizingly accustomed to holding her light scantiness in my arms at dances, although never for long enough. During the stormy two years of our precarious engagement, with its strained and anxious embraces, impeded by our clothes and by the heavier trappings of convention, to all of which she fiercely clung in spite of my urgent pleas, I had won piecemeal more torturing bits of knowledge of that adored body. But only in the last few weeks, to my insatiable ecstasy, had I been permitted a tenant's rights, to view, to entry, to full possession, and I was still abashed by my incredible good fortune.

And she? I knew she didn't adore me, or my body either; how could she? But she had married me. When I had pressed her for the reasons she had said she didn't really know; she supposed she hadn't liked the idea of somebody else getting me. I might have preferred a fancier reason, or a less grudging statement of it, but she *had* married me; that was the all-important fact.

Now she was pretending to be asleep, I thought, because she didn't worship my body as I worshipped hers. She was still afraid there was something wrong, perhaps blasphemously wrong, in the ravening constancy of my desire for her, which she certainly didn't reciprocate. She was shy of her own body, she was even shyer of mine. I had been brought up to feel the same sort of shame, but now all that training was being undermined and swept away by a force I was glad to acknowledge as more powerful than my well-tutored self.

I could no longer keep up the pretense that the mere sight of her was enough. Though I knew she might rebuff me—we were still on those terms, and furthermore we had not yet made up our latest quarrel—I couldn't help risking it. Besides, if I hesitated she might really fall asleep. I laid a gentle hand, which I prayed might seem more persuasive than pleading, on the cool skin of her dearly beloved girlish rump.

She shook herself and I heard a muffled, "Don't!" At least she was awake.

I withdrew my hand, but only to put it on her shoulder, and the next moment I lay beside her on the bed, my mouth at her ear . . .

And what happened then? Ah, if only I could remember; but it was all too long ago. I would give anything to recall those golden hours out of the past, but I haven't enough to give.

I know that what happened was a marvel and a wonder, and that it is still one of the buried treasures of my life. I remember where it was buried, and when; though I've forgotten all the rest.

MUSE IN MALLORCA

1

I remember my first sight of Robert Graves as vividly as my first sight of Schuyler. It was some time during the winter of 1923 or early in the following spring, at a meeting of a literary club in Hertford College, at Oxford. My friend Dudley Hughes, an eccentric member of that undistinguished college, took me as his guest.

Graves was already a name to me: I had read a good many of his poems and liked most of them. I liked their tone of voice, which fitted the face I now saw for the first time—masculine, gnarled and quick with intelligence. He was the speaker of the evening, which was an informal, crowded affair. He talked about his theory of poetry (later I learned that his theories were subject to change without notice, though his practice developed in a steady progression). His current theory was that a poem is the resultant of a conflict in the poet's mind. The text he chose to talk from seemed about as difficult and unlikely an example as could be found: the Mother Goose rhyme

> How many miles to Babylon?
> Three score miles and ten.
> Will I get there by candle-light?
> Yes, and back again.

To defend this text he had, of course, to invent the unknown author and the circumstances of his life that might have led to the poetic result of these lines; and this he did with such smiling ingenuity that I felt myself on his side and wanted him to win. Even so I was divided between admiration of his cleverness and disbelief in his evidence, which was of necessity wholly circumstantial. The stirring and muttering in the room showed that

117

others were moved by a like skepticism. There were several attempts to interrupt him but he insisted on his right to finish what he had to say.

The moment he stopped, they were on him. His first attacker was an older man, evidently one of a strong scatteration of dons among us. This academic, in a voice of mingled scorn and fury, wished Mr. Graves to enlighten us, if he would be so kind, on the conflict in Tennyson's mind which produced *The Charge of the Light Brigade*. Mr. Graves did so—to general applause, if not to the satisfaction of his questioner. *The Sinking of the Royal George? Tyger! Tyger! Burning Bright?* Kipling? Eyes rolling with mischief, smiling almost apologetically, Graves fielded these hard-hit questions with deft ease, and no runs were scored by the other side. This was a game at which he excelled any of his present competitors, and it was a pleasure to watch him play.

I came away from that evening bemused, impressed, mentally stirred—and vaguely irritated: whether by Graves's too easy victory, the ineptness of his opponents, or the nature of the game itself, I didn't know. It never occurred to me to speak to Graves or to introduce myself. Perhaps if I had known then that he had been a recent inhabitant of Boar's Hill, I would have.

It was through Maisie Somerville that I met him. Maisie was a large, blond, slow-spoken, catlike creature, with a cat's equivocal smile, who was a slightly older contemporary of mine at Oxford. She was an undergraduate (we called them "undergraduettes") at Somerville, a college founded, I think she said, by her grandmother. She had been charged by a mutual friend to keep a guardianly eye on me. And when she remembered to, she did.

Some time during my second term at Oxford I received a note from Somerville College inviting me to tea; the note was signed "Mary Somerville." I went. It was a large party, more girls than men, and most of us had to sit on the floor in Maisie's crowded sitting room. Maisie did almost all the talking, and it was almost all about Edmund Gosse, who was not even a name to me. I didn't enjoy the party and added nothing to it. Nevertheless, when Maisie invited me again, I went. Same sort of thing, so the next time she asked me I made my excuses.

It must have been mainly from a sense of duty that she tried me once more, this time inviting me to go with her to have tea with Robert Graves. I accepted with alacrity. Robert was living in a cottage called World's End, in Islip, a village near Oxford, with his wife Nancy and three children. When she heard we were coming, Nancy went to bed with a headache. The children were sent out to play; I helped them on with their galoshes. There was plenty of margarine for tea but not much butter, and Robert called this to our attention. While we were having tea (and listening to Robert talk about a book he was writing on dreams) there was a commotion outside: a crowd of children all shouting and accusing each other. Someone had hit someone else with a stick. Robert commandeered the stick, broke it in two and tossed the pieces over the hedge.

That memorable afternoon—memorable to me, at least— was the only occasion when Robert and I met during my time at Oxford. It was eight years until our next meeting. Meanwhile he had left his wife Nancy and their four children and had gone off with a woman named Laura Riding. Rumors of this, but vague and uncertain, reached me; it was years before I got the whole story straight. By then he had naturally forgotten me, and I had almost forgotten him.

Laura Riding was born in New York City on January 16, 1901 (the same day I was born in Cincinnati). Her father was an Austrian Jew named Reichenthal: she later changed her name by deed poll to Riding. Except for these bare facts her early life is still unknown to me. She went to college at Cornell, where she met and married Louis Gottschalk, two years older than she, an instructor in modern history.* (Although Professor Gottschalk's biography in *Who's Who* named his present wife as "second," he made no mention of Laura.) Laura's first published book, a long

*He died, after years of teaching at the University of Chicago, in June 1975.

119

ROBERT

poem entitled *Voltaire: A Biographical Fantasy,* brought out by Leonard and Virginia Woolf's Hogarth Press in 1927, was signed Laura Riding Gottschalk—with the Gottschalk overprinted but still legible.

That pamphlet was published the year after she had joined Robert Graves's household. It was an earlier and much shorter bit of verse that brought about their meeting. In Nashville, Tennessee, a group of poets led by John Crowe Ransom and including Allen Tate and Robert Penn Warren, who called themselves The Fugitives, were publishing a literary magazine. Some time in 1925 or 1926 they offered a prize, $100, I think, for the best unpublished poem. Laura won the prize with *The Quids,* a few lines of which ran:

> The quids, that had never done anything before
> But be, be, be, be, be—
> The quids resolved to predicate,
> To dissipate themselves in grammar . . .

Years later, John Crowe Ransom told me in his urbane and circumspect way what happened then. To the astonishment of the Nashville poets, Laura appeared in person to claim her prize. Furthermore she proposed herself for a job: secretary to the board of editors. I gathered from Mr. Ransom that they didn't need and couldn't afford a secretary, and moreover that their wives did not take kindly to the idea. Had Laura burnt her bridges and left her professor husband? At any rate, she seems to have stayed in Nashville long enough to become estranged from him.

Robert Graves and his wife Nancy, 3,000 miles away in their Oxfordshire village, saw a copy of the magazine and were much taken by Laura's "teasing" poem. Robert wrote to her, asking her to come and visit them. At this point the facts grow misty again, but according to the version of the story I have heard, Laura didn't answer the letter and in time Robert and Nancy almost forgot about her.

As they were preparing to pack up and go to Egypt, where

Robert was to teach English literature for a year at the Egyptian University in Cairo, a cable arrived from Laura, saying that she was on her way. Robert went up to London to meet her boat train, and (according to this version), his father-in-law, Sir William Nicholson the painter, went with him. As they waited behind the barrier on the platform at Waterloo, they spotted her at once: a small, bedizened woman in gaudy make-up.

"O my God," said Robert. "What am I going to do?"

"I know what *I'm* going to do," said Sir William. He turned on his heel and left.

Robert and Laura returned together to Nancy and the four children in the cottage at Islip, and when, shortly after, the Graves family set out for Egypt, Laura went with them. They stayed in Egypt until the end of the academic year, when Robert resigned from his job and they all returned to England. This time they settled in London: Nancy and the children on a barge in the Thames at Hammersmith; Laura and Robert in a flat in St. Peter's Square, not far away.

What happened next? Laura's own Authorized Version* shows a kind of shadow dance of what happened, but the action is only hinted at and the actors themselves unnamed. They are, in a way, described: "myself" (Laura), "the Virgin Mary who was also Medea and so on" (Nancy), "the Devil who was also Judas and so on" (the nameless villain), and "a third who was about to finish with that kind of thing" (Robert). There was, apparently, an altercation which whirled up to a deadly quarrel between truth (Laura) and "underhandedness" (the Devil and so on). The quarrel was victoriously ended by Laura's leaving the room—"by the window, of course."

There is also a Talmudic commentary on this Authorized Version written by Robert: it appears—or rather, did appear†— at the end of *Goodbye to All That,* in a "Dedicatory Epilogue":

---

*In the Preface to *Poems A Joking Word,* by Laura Riding (Jonathan Cape, 1930).
†It was expunged, with all other references to Laura, from the revised edition of 1957.

After which.

After which, anecdotes of yours, travesties of the parable and so precious to me as vulgar glosses on it. How on April 27th, 1929 it was a fourth-storey window and a stone area and you were dying. And how it was a joke between Harold the stretcher-bearer and myself that you did not die, but survived your dying, lucid interval.

After which.

After which, may I recall, since you would not care to do so yourself, with what professional appreciation (on May 16th) Mr. Lake is reported to have observed to those that stood by him in the operating theatre: "It is rarely that one sees the spinal-cord exposed to view—especially at right-angles to itself."

Now what would an investigating police sergeant make of this evidence? Not much, perhaps; but something:

That on April 27, 1929, in a fourth-floor (U.S.: fifth-floor) flat in St. Peter's Square, London, four people were having some sort of discussion—two women, a man and a shadowy fourth figure. The discussion became acrimonious; various accusations were made and denied; finally Laura Riding, the woman who made the statement, brought the discussion to an end by leaping from the window, suffering a nearly fatal compound fracture of the spine on the stone courtyard below. By the evidence of Graves's Epilogue he was the fourth person present. But who were the other two? And why did Laura Riding throw herself from the window?

In another version, which has never been made public but which has at least the virtues of clarity and coherence, the story goes like this:

The four people in the room were Laura, Robert, Nancy Nicholson and a young Irish poet named Geoffrey Phibbs. Whether Laura was in love with this young Irishman or regarded him as her property or merely demanded a statement of allegiance from him is not clear; she certainly wanted something from him that he was unwilling or unable to give, and his obvious unwillingness finally put her in such a passion of fury that she leaped from the window, landing on her coccyx and fracturing

123

her spine. Robert, beside himself, ran down one storey and then jumped himself; he broke no bones and was able to help carry Laura to the ambulance.

During the three months that Laura was in hospital, Robert wrote all or most of *Goodbye to All That,* besides spending as much time as he could at Laura's bedside and making frequent visits to Nancy and the four children, who were living on the barge at Hammersmith. Many of his old friends dropped him and he quarreled with those who didn't. When Laura was well enough, she and Robert left England and went to Mallorca, where they took a small stone cottage in the mountains near the village of Deya.

Nancy and the four children (the oldest, Jenny, was about ten) remained on the barge. They were very hard up: according to Jenny, who told me this version of the story, at one point they had almost nothing left to eat. They were sitting in the cabin of the barge, and Nancy was weeping. A shadow fell on the companionway, and there was the Irish poet Geoffrey Taylor, with an armful of food. Out of gratitude or loneliness or propinquity, Nancy soon took him as her lover—a fact that, in those days before the English divorce law was liberalized, effectively prevented her from divorcing Robert, even if she had wanted to: a punitive feature of the law being that no divorce could be granted to a guilty party, and now both she and Robert were legally guilty.

By 1931 I had endured only the first two years of my twenty-four-year servitude on *Time,* but already it seemed an eternity, and my job, while not as utterly hateful as it had been at first, was still only a poor imitation of what I wanted to do. Writing acceptable copy, learning to be a competent journalist of sorts, gave me a certain satisfaction, but the more of this kind of journalism I wrote, the more I wanted to write something that would be acceptable to myself. The writer I most admired at that point was Katherine Mansfield, partly I suppose because of the poignancy of her early death, only a few years before, with the promise of her best work to come. Poring over the few published photographs I had seen of her, and reading her stories and *Journals,* I came to the sentimental conclusion that I knew her well and was more than half in love with her. I decided to write a novel in which she would be the principal figure. So I got a six-month leave of absence from *Time* and in January 1932 went off with my wife and two small sons to Mallorca.

The only way we could get there was by ship; we booked passage on the *Resolute* of the Hamburg-Amerika Line. The *Resolute* sailed from New York in January on a cruise around the world; the third port of call, where we would get off, was Palma. For the first three days after we sailed we were left in peace in our deck chairs; then the cruise staff moved in, to bully and dragoon us into entertaining ourselves. Julie, who knew how I hated such forced-draft fun and games, bought me immunity by explaining to the "cruise director" that I was recovering from a nervous breakdown and should be left alone, by doctor's orders; she offered herself as sacrificial substitute, and duly appeared in an evening show, dressed as a female bootlegger, as New Jersey. The theme of that evening was "Come and Boost Your State!"

The road from Palma to Valldemosa runs for 10 miles or so through flat farmland, the fields studded with almond and olive trees and *algarrobas;* then it begins to climb through craggy gorges into the mountains. After Valldemosa the road comes out 1,000 feet above the coast, noble with rocky headlands, and from here to Deya curves high along the Mediterranean.

We were looking for a house—something small, cheap, and away from people. As the road began to twist towards Deya, whose houses we could see a mile away, clustered on a hill in a cup-shaped valley, we noticed a small stone cottage, half-hidden in trees, above the road. I stopped the car, got out and climbed the steps to the cottage.

A Mallorquin girl answered my knock. I asked her if she

knew where Señor Robert Graves lived. (He was the only person in the island whose name I knew; I hoped he might give us some advice about finding a house.)

"Aqui," said the girl. Did that mean "here"? Anyhow, she was opening the door to me, so I went in. She showed me into a little room where a table, covered with papers, stood in front of a huge, hooded fireplace. A small, severe woman, erect behind the table, confronted me. She asked me what I wanted. I said that I had called to pay my respects to Mr. Graves, whom I had had the honor of meeting some years before. She said something in Spanish to the maid.

A minute later Robert Graves appeared.

"Robert," said the severe little woman, "here is a young man who *says* he knows you."

Robert looked from me to her, rolled his eyes, grinned and shook his head. "Never saw him before in my life."

I could feel myself turning pale. I was absolutely determined that I would not leave that house before proving that I was not a liar. I began to reconstruct the details of our previous meeting in Islip, eight years before, and desperation gave my memory strength. When I got to the point of the children's row and Robert seizing the stick and breaking it in two, he surrendered: he too had begun to remember. He thawed, the lady thawed. I was introduced to Laura Riding. Two weeks later Robert and Laura moved out of this cottage, Salerosa, so that my wife and I and our two children could move in. (Robert and Laura were building a house on the far side of the village: until it was ready they rented a house in Deya.) In the children's room Laura had hung a small mirror 3 feet from the floor, in case the youngest one wanted to look at himself.

It didn't happen quite as fast as all that, of course. There were preliminary negotiations, and at one point I had to write them a note. Julie and I discussed the proper way of addressing it. We knew they weren't married, but we decided that the correct form would be "Mr. and Mrs. Robert Graves." That brought us our first reprimand. Robert carefully explained that we had not addressed them properly, and that this was an insult, although of course unintentional; the only admissible form of address was "Laura Riding and Robert Graves." Then they invited us to a picnic, the purpose of which seemed to be to find out whom we knew and who our friends were. Robert summed up the inquiry by laughing and saying to Laura, "They seem to know all the wrong people!"

Nevertheless, in spite of our gaffes and our regrettable background, we passed muster; and once they had decided we would do, they couldn't have been kinder. That was just as well for my morale, for at first the primitive conditions in our mountain cottage gave me cold feet. The first night, as I clambered from the frigid stone floor up into the clammy bed, I told myself that I had brought my family 4,000 miles from home to die like rats in a trap. There was no plumbing of any kind, the well water (which we drank) was alive with alien life, the only room in the house which could be made comfortably warm was the kitchen, it rained solidly for the first ten days. And it was January.

Kind and helpful as Robert and Laura had been, Julie and I agreed that it would be as well not to see too much of them. We had come here to be alone: we didn't want to get in their way, or want them to get in ours. Also, as Julie said, they weren't really our kind. In our suburbanite eyes they were an exceedingly odd pair. Robert was gangly-tall, muscular but shambling; with his broken nose and wildly staring eyes, swarthy coloring and frizzy black hair as unruly as the sun's corona, he looked like a bandit from an earlier century. When he was dressed up he sported a brocaded waistcoat with silver buttons and a stock held in place with an antique pin: then he was a squire; but in the nondescript clothes and straw hat of every day he was a distinguished scarecrow.

Laura, who hardly came up to his shoulder, was as primly neat as Robert was gawky. She never had a hair out of place, and her clothes, which were also old-fashioned, never seemed odd. When *she* was in full regalia her dignity matched and enhanced her costume, and I can't remember anyone thinking it laughable or even eccentric that on these occasions she was crowned by a tiara of gold wire that spelled LAURA. She could indeed look regal—a Hittite queen. Was she beautiful? I never thought so; I would have said that sometimes she was handsome and sometimes very nearly ugly, or at least repellent—when her deep-sunk eyes went dead as stone (or a lidded snake's) and her normal pallor faded to the tone of chalk. When she laughed, however (and she did at times), something appealing happened to her face: then she resembled a little girl who has momentarily forgotten that she meant to scare the grownups.

It was Robert who discovered that Laura and I were born on the same day. While we were still settling in, I went to their house to get his help in filling out a form for the police, whose Spanish officialese was beyond me. When he saw what I put down as the date of my birth he called out, "Laura! You and Tom are twins!"

I was amazed: I would have said she was old enough to be my mother. I came so near saying it that I blushed. Laura pursed her lips, gave her slight, omniscient smile, and nodded, as if she acknowledged the fact, now that it was out, but was not yet prepared to commit herself on its significance.

I had thought of them both as "older people"; and since Laura was obviously the senior partner and in charge of Robert, Julie and I had taken it for granted that she was older than he. The discovery that in fact she was six years younger made her apparent domination of him even stranger. We knew they were not married; therefore she was his mistress, wasn't she? And though we had never before actually met anyone's mistress, we had read about them, and in those books the man, although he might have the wool pulled over his eyes, was always the master. It was certainly not so in this case.

The oddest thing about this pair was that they were a pair. I had heard only vague rumors that Robert had left Nancy and his children and had gone off to Mallorca with Laura. That must have been about five years ago. And there was something about Laura having jumped out of a window and broken her back. In

the closing pages of Robert's *Goodbye to All That* there were
veiled references to these violent events. Julie and I were very
curious to know more, but knew enough to hide our curiosity.
The first thing that had struck us about Robert and Laura was
their suspiciousness. They seemed to go out of their way to be
suspicious.

Their exaggerated mistrust of strangers naturally roused
counter-suspicions and gave rise to outrageous rumors. One absurd story, which *Time* got hold of and might have printed if I
hadn't been able to stop it, said that these two eccentric poets
lived in a mountain fastness in Mallorca surrounded by a walled
courtyard; that they sometimes invited unsuspecting guests, who
were then trapped in the courtyard and set upon by a pack of
savage dogs.

One of the apparent gaffes I had made was in even mention-
ing *Goodbye to All That.* Why shouldn't I have mentioned it? For
years I had been an admirer of Graves's poetry, and I also admired this autobiography—which I thought, and still do, one of
the best books written about the First World War. Nevertheless,
Robert had patiently explained that his books were not to be
brought up in conversation; and that if, as sometimes happened,
an ignorant stranger broke this rule, he would either leave the
room or, if necessary, stop such talk by force. This "explanation"
left us completely in the dark. But it obviously had some connection with what had happened to him and Laura. Laura still
showed some effects of her leap from the window. Inside her
house she moved in sudden, short rushes, with something uncertain in her movements. Outside she always walked with a cane,
in small steps that might be rapid but that sometimes tottered.

And there was something besides their suspiciousness that
we couldn't figure out. Their public behavior puzzled us. He was
more than protective of her; he seemed in a constant swivet of
anxiety to please her, to forestall her every wish, like a small boy
dancing attendance on a rich aunt of uncertain temper. And she
treated him—like a dog. There was no prettier way to put it.
Since I admired and looked up to him as a dedicated poet and a

professional writer, his subservience to her and her contemptuous bearing towards him troubled and embarrassed me. The
answer to this puzzling relation finally forced itself on me: she
was not so much his mistress as his master; he was *in statu pupil-
lari* to her—at times he seemed Caliban to her Prospero.

This was hard for me to accept, and not simply because I too
was male. For years Robert had been one of my favorite poets.
He had made himself an honored name by the quality and the
unmistakably original tone of his poetry, the curious variety and
honest value of his prose writing. And he was always beautifully
clear. Shortly before coming to Deya I had read and reviewed his
latest book of poems, and noted a new and rather alarming tendency to unclearness—which at the time I never thought of at-
tributing to Laura's influence; but now I did. Could she really
teach him anything about writing? Privately, I didn't think so.
But we were supposed to believe that she not only knew better
but wrote better than he, and I think he really considered himself
her inferior. Actually, although he was no match for her intellectually—none of us was—he was much the better poet and more
seasoned writer, and much the kinder and more understanding
person. Though Laura demanded and got my awed respect, I
grew to love Robert.

I saw that the price of admission to Laura's circle was the
same for everyone: fealty to her as the acknowledged and absolute monarch of her little kingdom. ("Queendom" it should be;
for in her world the rule was matriarchal, and God herself a
woman.) Then why did I apply for citizenship in this tyranny? I
didn't, consciously: our taking into camp—for it was really more
like that—was a gradual process.

My first chance to sheer off came very soon. Julie and I had
agreed, as I say, not to see much of "them," but Deya was a small
village, and members of the foreign colony had to take elaborate
precautions to avoid each other. Every day we walked in to Deya
to collect our mail, which Castor the postman distributed at the
same afternoon hour; and there "they" were, waiting for us, with
an invitation to come to the café for a drink and read our letters.

As we walked down the road together, Laura tore open a small package and took out a homemade-looking book. From the cover, which was all I saw of it, I thought I recognized a reasonable facsimile of a book of hers, the only one I had ever read, called *Anarchism Is Not Enough.* I had reviewed it for an American magazine, *The Bookman;* the review had been respectful but not reverent, and I hoped that Laura would never see it, as I was pretty sure that she would take offense at it. (Some weeks later a review of the same book in the *Times Literary Supplement* summed it up in much the same way I had, though in more stately language, and sure enough was condemned by Laura and Robert as offensive and inadmissible.)

I never got a closer look at the book Laura had unwrapped and whose pages—were they in fact toilet paper?—she was now riffling through with a frown. She stopped, turned to me, and said,

"Did you send this?"

Why didn't I reply, "Hell, no!", turn and walk away? It was an outrageous question and should have made me angry. Instead, I stammered the feeble truth that I knew nothing about it. I suppose I sounded as guilty as I felt. No apology was forthcoming from Laura. But she seemed to accept my denial, and nothing more was said.

While we were settling in to our life in Deya, Laura and Robert were helpful to us, but we soon discovered that there was a price attached to this help. If we wanted to remain on speaking terms with them, we must not be on speaking terms with a good many other people—in fact, with anyone outside their own circle.

There was one exception to this rule: a youngish couple (unmarried, of course) known as *"los grabadores"* because he made etchings. He was Spanish and she was French—or perhaps it was the other way about. They were not members of our group but they were treated in friendly fashion, and sometimes included in picnics or in a dinner at the hotel in Soller Puerto. But the young American couple who lived in the Casa Blanca a few hundred yards down the road from us were not to be taken into our confidence or friendship; even casual greetings between us were discouraged. Why, for God's sake? Because there was something about them that Laura or Robert or somebody else in our tight little circle didn't cotton to; whereupon the word was passed that they were to be shunned. It was also plainly implied that anyone who did not obey these group orders would also be cast into outer darkness. If Julie and I had been bold as lions or freedom fighters, we might have said, "The hell with you!" But we were newcomers; we were far more intrigued by Laura & Co. than by the couple in the Casa Blanca; we therefore fell into line.

The other members of the inner circle were John Aldridge, Lucie Brown and Norman Cameron. John Aldridge, a young English painter, was an Oxford contemporary and friend of Norman Cameron, a young Scottish poet; and both were devoted dependents of Laura's. John was living with Lucie Brown, a dark beauty; Norman's relations with Elfriede, a German girl whose cheeks flamed with apparent health (but actually with the hectic flush of tuberculosis), were more equivocal. Elfriede had been a member of the community but was so no longer, and mention of her was guarded; but she *was* mentioned, and gradually we pieced the story together—or a version of it. As a member of Laura's household, she had apparently tantalized Robert, and, whether or not this was intentional on Laura's part, Robert had presumably found his way to Elfriede's bed. The result had been an abortion and, as soon afterwards as Elfriede could walk, her expulsion from Canellun and the community (there were several versions of her departure from the house). Where had she gone? Not far, apparently; and she must have remained not only accessible but available, for now it was Norman's name that was linked with hers.

Some time towards the end of our stay in Deya—was it April or May of 1932?—Norman disappeared, and Laura gently and sadly broke the news by saying that he had developed "a kind of horror" of her, and had gone away until he could get over his feeling. He had not gone very far, for when Julie and I and our two boys left in June, by the night boat from Palma, there were Norman and Elfriede on the quay at Barcelona next morning, waiting to greet us.

In 1931, when they first went to Deya, John and Lucie lived for a time in Canellun—where, according to Lucie, Laura insisted that the door of their bedroom remain always open—and later in lodgings of their own. Both John and Lucie struck us as cool customers (both were cat-lovers) and as such, we would have said, not completely under Laura's domination. We discovered later that this quasi-independence was stronger in Lucie than in John. Lucie was deeply skeptical of Laura, who must have been aware of Lucie's feeling but put up with it because she needed John. He was in her continual service, used as a human brush or pencil to turn out drawings and pictures for which she not only supplied the idea but actively directed the making. In the same way she "helped" a sculptor, Dorothy Simmons, with her work, and was overseer (a good deal in the Simon Legree sense) to half a dozen writers, including me.

John was tallish, slim, good-looking in a neat, sparing way, with a small-featured face whose expression might have been called primly alert had not the balance been just tipped against primness by a faintly quizzical air. He still kept (as he did to old age) the lean look of speed he must have shown as a three-quarter in his Oxford days (I don't think he got his blue, but he played rugger for his college, Corpus Christi). You couldn't imagine John giving all his heart to anyone or in any cause: he was far too cautious and controlled for that. But Lucie adored him; and the pictures he painted as a young man had a spooky sort of originality that I think owed as much or more to John's eye (he could see, in those days) as to Laura's peremptory finger. Like the rest of us, he held his own future in contempt: he would never have believed that he would end up, as he did, in the mortuary of the Royal Academy.

The sniggering and giggling in which the English intelligentsia are prone to indulge and which among them passes as an adequate substitute for more robust humor was rampant among

Laura's set, in their lighter moments; she herself was indulgent of these parlor pranks and on occasion even abetted them. One form these mental gambols took was the fitting—or at least the trying on—of nicknames to people of their acquaintance, or to one another. I remember one that was thought to be a good fit for John: Hoof-aloof.

Some special dispensations Julie and I were allowed because we were harmless barbarian innocents. Though we were the only couple—for miles around, apparently, not counting the natives —who were actually married, we were forgiven this old-fashioned deviation from the normal. Walking and mountain-climbing (and swimming in season) were the only tolerated sports, and then only as an occasional aberration, a permitted joke. I liked to play tennis, and used to go in to Palma every week or ten days for a game at the tennis club, but I kept this sneaky behavior as dark as I could.

We discovered that the Riding-Graves retinue were always making flat, generalized judgments about people. Robert was especially good at it. He once announced at lunch that he had seen a couple of Cambridge men in the village that morning.

"Oh?" said I. "Did you talk to them?"

"No, certainly not."

"Then how do you know they were Cambridge men?"

"Oh, I could tell."

"How?"

"Cambridge men are bloody."

If we had known, when we first came to Deya, that we would soon be expected to join a hermetic community, I think we would have moved on, or at any rate sheered off. We would as soon have cast in our lot with a witches' coven. And there were some similarities: there was something occult about Laura and her gradually revealed, gradually acknowledged domination over her circle.

No one but Laura ever spoke *ex cathedra* on any important question, but on minor matters Robert was permitted to join her in small flat statements. These magisterial remarks were some-times uttered on a subject neither one of them knew the first thing about, such as driving a car. Gelat Marroig (pronounced Jel-ot Mar-*otch*), the factotum of Deya, who owned and drove the daily bus to Palma, was occasionally relieved by his son Juan. It was Laura and Robert's joint judgment that Juan drove in such a way as to get the best out of the bus, whereas his father's technique guaranteed the comfort of the passengers. Complete poppycock.

My tennis-playing was very soon discovered and reported. At a bar in Palma where I went for a glass of beer after my game I ran into Norman Cameron and John Aldridge, and remarked to them that we felt much beholden to Laura and Robert for all they had done for us. Next day at the café in Deya I was greeted with a grin as Ben Beholden, and for some days we were referred to as "the Beholdens." What startled me was not the ribbing on my American use of an archaic English word but the evidence that anything you said to one of the circle was immediately reported to headquarters. I never got used to this, and as I never remem-bered to seal the door of my lips, especially on a night off, I sometimes got into trouble.

Once in a while Laura would decree an evening of relaxation as a reward for several weeks of hard work; and then we would charter the Deya bus and all drive together to Soller Puerto or Palma for a bang-up dinner. On one of these evenings, after quite a lot of wine, Robert and I were standing side by side in the men's room, and I spoke to him with great enthusiasm about a story Laura had just written. It was a kind of fairy story, called *The Playground,* and some of my pleasure in it came from the fact that its characters were my two little sons, Julie, myself and Laura. I said to Robert that I wished Laura would write some more fairy tales; why not a whole book of them? Next day I was called on the carpet by Laura.

"What did you mean by telling Robert that I should write more fairy stories?"

When Laura and Robert left Salerosa for us in January 1932, they moved into a rented house, Canpebo, in the village, until Canellun, the house they were building (where Robert still lives) half a mile beyond Deya, was finished. Next to Canellun, Norman Cameron was building a smaller house, C'an Torrent. When he went back to England, Laura said he had given the house to her. Lucie Brown denied this; she said Laura simply commandeered the house.

It was in Deya that I met Maisie Somerville again. She came for a fortnight's visit in the spring. She remembered me, greeted me coolly, and expressed surprise that I was paid $50 a week for writing the kind of book reviews for *Time* that the *Times Literary Supplement* (or so she said) got for nothing. She was now working for the BBC, something to do with education, and I dare say was not being paid as much as $50 a week.

Gelat was the biggest frog in the small pond of Deya: he owned and operated the generator that was the sole source of Deya's flickering and part-time electric light; he owned and drove the only bus that ran to Palma, where he would do shopping errands or carry out small commissions. (He never wrote down the list of these chores but carried them all in his head; perhaps he was illiterate.) He was also, or had been, the Mayor of Deya.

When I knew him he was, I suppose, in his fifties: a short, heavy-set, dark-complexioned man, partly bald, with a saturnine expression and a shrewd and beady eye. He almost invariably wore a soft black hat and a gold collar-button in his collarless shirt. Like everyone else in Deya, Julie and I had frequent dealings with him, and we also regarded him, through Robert and Laura, as a friend. We had perforce to use the electric light his *fábrica* supplied (our only other light was candles and one kerosene lamp, our most prized possession) but we never got used to its vagaries. The current was so feeble that the light bulbs gave out only a dim and flickering glow, impossible to read by. In any case the electricity went off in the evening, at an irregular hour—usually somewhere between eight-thirty and ten—came on again, briefly, just before sunrise; and then blacked out for the rest of the day. Before the lights went off at night you would get a warning signal, a couple of emphatic blinks. Soon thereafter, but no telling when—perhaps immediately, perhaps ten minutes later—the lights went out.

Gelat had only a few words of English; our Mallorquin was nonexistent and we were lost in Spanish without a dictionary, but we managed to communicate after a fashion. Sometimes Gelat would join us all in a card game of *siete y media* (a Spanish form of *vingt-et-un* known among us as "city midge"); or he would drive us to dinner in Palma or Soller.

The only time I ever saw Gelat visibly embarrassed was at one of these dinners, at Soller Puerto. On that occasion his wife was with us: a good-natured, laughter-shrieking woman who stood in awe of Laura but instinctively responded to Julie, though their conversation was confined mainly to gestures and understanding smiles. Julie, who loved to talk to everybody, tried to say something to Gelat, and in Spanish. What she meant to say was, "Are you hungry?" But she mixed up *hambre* and *hombre,* so she asked Gelat, "Are you a man?" His wife screamed with laughter and Gelat turned a dull red.

He got a bit of his own back later, at my expense. He was driving the bus back from Palma, late one afternoon, and I was sitting beside him, in a state of almost complete exhaustion. I had just finished playing a five-set tennis match in the singles final of the Mallorcan "championship." I had won, but it had been a near thing. Somehow Gelat, of course, knew all about it—including, probably, the fact that I had taken this match so lightly that I had stayed up till all hours the night before at a bar, drinking *fundador;* a fact which partly accounted for my difficulty in winning the match and for my present state of exhaustion. Gelat eyed me from time to time with an amused look, and at last said, "Did you win?"

I muttered, *"Sí."*

"How much?" said Gelat, and laughed for at least a mile.

137

In Deya it was a community life, and gradually, gradually, I learned the rules: work, have no traffic with the enemy (everyone outside the community was an enemy), report and justify all your doings. I reported my own, in self-defense, but I drew the line at reporting other people's.

How did we get involved in all this, and after our firm decision not to? It was really my fault, and I can remember the very evening it happened, or began to happen. A couple of weeks after we had moved into our little house, Salerosa, we felt we should have Laura and Robert (we now spoke of them quite naturally in that order) to dinner. By this time I had discovered that Laura had published several books of poems, and I had borrowed one; I couldn't make head or tail of it. Some time in the course of that evening I asked her to explain a poem called *What to Say When the Spider*. She looked at me intently and said, "Do you really want me to explain it?" I said I did. In that case, she said, I could come to see her next day, and she would.

Did she ever say later, in so many words, that she had given me a warning? Or is this my own way of putting it? In any case, this was what it amounted to: as long as I was content simply to live in Deya, keeping to "the courtesies of good morning and good evening," she herself would do nothing to intensify the situation; but if I voluntarily trespassed on her web (and my expressed desire to understand her poetry was definitely trespassing), I was thereby inviting her attention and would have to take the consequences. And that was the way it worked. We soon found ourselves novitiates and then full members of Laura's little group. We saw them nearly every day.

Laura began to take an interest in my writing. She read my very short, hastily written, first novel, the only book I had published as yet, and wrote me a devastating review of it. When she learned that I admired Stephen Crane, she undertook to cure me in one sharp lesson—by getting me to choose one of his pages at random and underline the rubber-stamp words and phrases. When I did, nothing was left but *the, but* and *and;* and most of the *buts* and *ands* should have been interchanged. Laura showed a sympathetic interest in the novel I was working on, and offered to be of any help she could. I thanked her, but said that for the time being, at least, I must just struggle along by myself.

I had never met anyone who worked as she did. She wrote for most of the day and often late into the night—stories, poems, criticism, letters. She always had two or three books going at a time. Besides her own work, and collaborations with Robert, she had a hand in many other pies, helping, advising, "straightening out the muddle" in somebody else's poem, picture, sculpture, novel. When the mood was on her she painted pictures herself: strange abstract whorls and asymmetrical patterns; sometimes she called them psychological portraits. She did one of me, which I kept for years, rolled up in a corner (partly from its size and partly from my own embarrassment) and have now lost. It embarrassed me because, although no one could have guessed it was a picture of me unless he was told, she had written into it, in jagged, fiery letters, two words which she said were my principal characteristics: LUST and FURY.*

I read, or tried to read, Laura's books, and though I thought them oddly impressive, I never more than partly succeeded in understanding them. What I had written in my one review of her still held true: "Miss Riding talks at length, with what may be wisdom (for it is certainly incomprehensible) about a great many subjects which all of us, and not merely artists, are vitally interested in. To read her book is like listening to a man who is passionately anxious to be heard, but who has such an impediment in his speech that he cannot be understood."

The gravest impediment, for me, in Laura's writing, was

---

*Laura may have read Erasmus but I hadn't. When I did read his *Praise of Folly* I was pleased to come on this passage: "So Jupiter, not wanting man's life to be wholly gloomy and grim, has bestowed far more passion than reason—you could reckon the ratio as twenty-four to one. Moreover, he confined reason to a cramped corner of the head and left all the rest of the body to the passions. Then he set up two raging tyrants in opposition to reason's solitary power: anger which holds sway in the breast and so controls the heart, the very source of life, and lust whose empire spreads far and wide, right down to the genitals."

139

something I knew better than to mention: a cousinship, a blood relation, to the tone of Gertrude Stein. I was sure that this would be an inadmissible observation, for, quite apart from the fact that no serious writer is willing to admit a striking likeness to any other, Gertrude Stein was often hootingly comic, and Laura was invariably dead-serious. The tantalizing thing about both of them was that, though they were obviously talking about *something*—and often something very interesting—you couldn't be sure what it was, unless you knew it beforehand.

In the euphemism much employed by writers, my novel "bogged down." I scrapped two painful beginnings; and the next time Laura asked me how I was getting along, I told her the shameful truth. She then suggested that I might help her with a piece of her own unfinished writing (she described it as "a masque"): it might get me out of the doldrums. I couldn't imagine being of any help to *her*, but I was flattered by her offer, bemused and drawn by her extraordinary mind ("the strong pulling of her bladed mind," Robert had called it) and hopeful of learning something from her. I said I would like to.

Every morning I walked the mountain mile from Salerosa to Canpebo, where Laura would be waiting for me. I felt a certain curious aversion to Laura. The texture of her skin was waxy to dead-dull, and her hands were surprisingly large and coarse for a woman's. It may have been partly her eerily brilliant brain, which I felt as an almost tangible force and which seemed to me to render her asexual, sibylline.

Our sessions began at ten in the morning, for Laura usually worked late at night and was not an early riser. She would be looking pale, scrubbed and intense; and her brusque nod, dispensing with the usual civilities, served notice that the workday had now begun and that I had arrived not a moment too soon. "The work" was there on the table; two neat piles of foolscap, stacked with meticulous symmetry on the otherwise bare tabletop in a small whitewashed room as pale, scrubbed and intense as she. We sat down on the two heavy wooden chairs, the only other furniture in the room, that stood side by side in front of the table, and the day began.

By my watch, these sessions lasted only three hours, but by my truer internal sense of time they took the whole of a long day. Our method of work was as follows: some twenty foolscap pages, covered by Laura's ugly-tidy, widely spaced handwriting, made up the unfinished masque. Before another syllable could be added we had to go over this beginning, word by word and phrase by phrase, partly to satisfy Laura that the foundation was solid and partly to acquaint me with the nature and meaning of the work. As far as I could tell, neither of these purposes was successfully accomplished.

I never strained so hard to understand anything in my life, and to so little purpose. Laura was adamant in her resolve not to proceed one millimeter further until she was satisfied that I had mastered what she had already put down. Our progress was understandably slow, in fact almost imperceptible. On my part, the effort of continuous concentration was so intense that at times I experienced an almost physical sensation that my head was actually splitting. Laura was a patient but not a sympathetic partner in my struggles: she drove me relentlessly, remorselessly, to the limit of my mental endurance. Each morning I came with dragging steps to this ordeal, and each afternoon I thankfully took my exhausted way home.

One morning when Laura let me in she did not come with me into her workroom. She stood in the doorway and pointed at the table.

"Read that! I'll be back in fifteen minutes."

She shut the door behind her. At my place on the work table lay an envelope with my name on it. I sat down to read the letter. There were several pages of it, and it was couched in such complex language and my head was in such an apprehensive whirl that I had to read the letter twice to be sure of its meaning. As I read, my alarm deepened. The gist of it was that she knew the effect she made on me; that if I could master my feelings I was

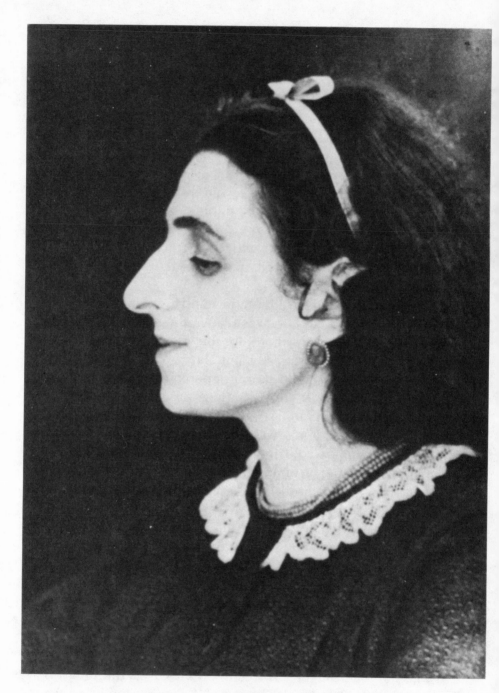

LAURA

to remain in this room, she would come back and we would go on with our work as before; if, however, I could not be sure of controlling myself I was to get up and go, now; she would understand, she would not hold it against me, but we must not continue to work together. She would return to the room in fifteen minutes (five had already elapsed) for my answer. Meantime, if I wanted to leave, the coast was clear.

Why didn't I immediately get up and walk out? What possessed me to stay? I have asked myself that question a hundred times since. But no matter what I did, I said to myself despairingly, she would still think I was in love with her! Of the two hopeless alternatives, it would be better to stay. I'd be damned if I'd give her the impression that I was so mad about her I couldn't trust myself in her presence. Of course I should have gone, and let her think what she liked. And, if I'd had a vestige of humor left in me about the situation, I'd be laughing all the way home. But I didn't; I stayed where I was.

On the dot of fifteen minutes the door opened and Laura reappeared. I had pocketed the letter, and I couldn't bring myself to look at her. Out of the corner of my eye I saw her quick, satisfied nod. She pulled out her chair, sat down, and we went on with our work.

According to the calendar, this "collaboration" lasted for only twelve days—twelve days in a row, for Laura was no respecter of Sundays, and never took a day off. But they seemed to me literally a lifetime. I was at the end of my tether; I felt that I couldn't go on any longer. I had a long talk with Julie, who was also worried about my state of mind, although I don't think she suspected how near I was to collapse. The upshot was that I would somehow beg off, resign, or if necessary just quit. The failure, I felt, had been entirely mine: I simply wasn't up to it, my mind wasn't in the same league with Laura's. I had presumptuously dared to bite off much more than I could chew. At least I had learned one useful, if humiliating, fact: that I was stupid.

I managed to say most of this to Laura. She couldn't have been kinder. In my abasement I even offered, for Julie and myself, the sacrifice of our friendship: of course, I said, we wouldn't expect that to continue. Not at all, said Laura gently; we mustn't dream of removing ourselves, we were her friends and she valued us, and everything must go on as usual, as if nothing had happened—as indeed nothing had, that is to say, nothing *bad*. She dismissed me like a wise and merciful queen, and I took the great good news back to Julie.

This intense time with Laura did leave its mark on me, however (or should I say, her mark?), like a bruise. For a month I was impotent.

Only once did Laura turn her fury on me: I am not likely to forget it. One Sunday evening she proposed herself for supper with us at Salerosa. She did not include Robert, and I got the distinct impression that it was to be an all-female evening, between her and Julie. If I had known a safe or graceful way of absenting myself, I would have. I made myself as inconspicuous as possible and never once opened my mouth; after supper was over I sat as far away as I could, at the side of the small room. Laura's purpose soon became clear: she was trying to get Julie to admit that never once in her life, in anything of any importance, had she ever been in the slightest degree influenced or led by me.

Julie, who was an essentially innocent person but no fool, felt that she was being invited—and more and more challengingly— to enter some sort of trap; she not only wouldn't enter but she acted (it must have been maddening) as if she wasn't even aware that the trap existed. It was like listening to a brilliant and bullying prosecutor trying in vain to snare a witness whose simplicity was more than a match for brilliance and bullying. I continued, tensely and grimly, to say nothing; but I applauded with all my heart.

Suddenly Laura shifted her attack to me: she whirled halfway round in her chair and cried, "Stop sitting there saying nothing—and *lying!*" The next moment she had flounced up and whirled out of the door. All I could think was, "I'm glad it's over."

Then Julie thrust a flashlight in my hand and pushed me after her. Laura had rushed out with no light, not even her stick, and it was a dark night on the mountain. I ran after her, calling "Laura!" but she was nowhere to be seen. I ran down the road for a hundred yards, and flashed my light to the corner. Nobody there. She must have taken the precipitous path, a short-cut, down through the valley.

I found her at the bottom: in Robert's arms. To get there at that speed she must have half-run, half-fallen. He had felt that something was wrong and that she needed him, and had dashed headlong out into the dark, taking the quickest way. He said something reassuring; I breathed a sigh of relief, and went home. Strangely enough, I can't remember that there were any repercussions from this scene.

When an idea that pleased him occurred to Robert, he never stopped to consider whether it might please or displease the public, although his livelihood and his family's depended on the sale of his books. Some of his books sold very well, but I think he was always surprised when some turned out to be failures. He told me once that he had no imagination—a startling statement for any poet to make, especially a poet of his caliber. I suppose he meant that when he was writing fiction he couldn't invent the kind of characters that readers found believable—although that wasn't always quite true, either: as witness the continuing popularity of *I, Claudius* and *Claudius the God.*

Very early in my acquaintance with Robert and Laura I noticed that they lacked the common touch which brought fame and fortune to writers obviously their inferiors. Once they deliberately stooped (or so they thought) to conquer a wider public; they even had hopes of Hollywood. A British publisher had proposed a best-selling title for a novel which he thought so surefire that he guaranteed (or so they said) a minimum sale of 20,000 copies if they agreed to use it: *No Decency Left.* Robert and Laura wrote the novel together, covering their tracks by using a pseudonym, Barbara Rich. The book had just been published, with a dust jacket designed by John Aldridge, when we arrived in Deya. They swore us to secrecy before telling us of this free-booting venture, and gave us a copy to read.

In other hands (or perhaps if Laura had had nothing to do with it) the book might indeed have been a best-seller, and even ended up in the movies. This was the story as I remember it: a pretty girl with no money, no beaux and no prospects, lies in her morning bath before traipsing off to her boring office job in London. As she lies there she decides that before the day is over she will lead a revolution, marry a prince and make a million pounds. And she does. The trouble is (I thought to myself as I read it) all the details are so ingeniously worked out and so meticulously explained that what might have been a rousing romp of a fairy tale becomes an over-elaborate and boring blueprint. I was in much too great awe of the authors to say this; but I did go so far as to intimate that it seemed to me not *quite* Hollywood's cup of tea: much too good for the movie-makers to appreciate.

Another job that Robert had just finished when we came to Deya was, I think, the least successful—as well as the most execrated—book he ever published: *The Real David Copperfield*, a shortened version of Dickens's great novel. It was actually an improvement on the original but was generally received in England as a desecration of a national monument; and this labor of love sold only a few hundred copies. I am sure that Robert did not consider *Count Belisarius, Hercules, My Shipmate, Homer's Daughter* or *Watch the North Wind Rise* inferior in any way to the *Claudius* books, and would have been as much at a loss to explain the great popularity of the one as the small popularity of the others. I realize that most writers, and publishers as well, unless they specialize in producing best-sellers, deliberately cultivating the technique of giving the public what it wants, are apt to be as much surprised by success as by failure. I can only say that Robert was more hit-or-miss than most. Until he became a famous author, and then nothing he did could be altogether a failure.

But for a long time he was well known rather than famous.

These two prolific and indefatigable writers, Laura and Robert, not content with pushing more manuscripts on their publisher than he was willing to bring out in a year, had launched their own private publishing house, the Seizin Press. Under this imprint they set up and printed, on an old hand press, half a dozen books, mainly poetry and mainly their own.* Most of the Seizin Press books were published before we came to Deya, and I can't remember that any were printed while we were there, so I suppose this venture lasted only a few years. Its name outlived its function, however: the novel I wrote under Laura's guidance (or, more accurately, which Laura wrote, using me as a pencil), entitled *The Moon's No Fool,* was published in London under the joint imprint of the Seizin Press and Constable—as were several others in which Laura had a hand.

The Seizin Press books proper (i.e., those printed at Hammersmith, St. Peter's Square, and Deya) were printed on handmade paper with good type; I should think they are all collectors' items by now. Particularly Robert's *To Whom Else?*—whose title poem, one of abject dedication to Laura, no longer appears in his collected verse and every copy of which I am sure he would like to destroy.

Why the name "Seizin Press"? What does it mean? You'll have to ask them; all I can tell you is that the word *seizin* does not appear, except by implication, in the great Oxford Dictionary itself. It's arcane, with a slightly lifted lip; the kind of in-joke that Laura and her familiars used to love to bandy about. As near as I can make out, *seizin* has something to do with *freehold,* and it

---

*The Seizin Press started in 1928 in London, when Laura and Robert were living in St. Peter's Square. The six Seizin Press books I have, in order of publication, are *Love as Love, Death as Death,* by Laura Riding (Hammersmith, 1928); *Poems 1929,* by Robert Graves (St. Peter's Square, 1929); *No Trouble,* by Len Lye (Deya, 1930); *Though Gently,* by Laura Riding (Deya, 1930); *To Whom Else?,* by Robert Graves (Deya, 1931); and *Laura and Francisca,* by Laura Riding (Deya, 1931). Each of these books is numbered (Seizin One, Two, etc.). No. Two, which I never had, was *An Acquaintance with Description,* by Gertrude Stein.

also has a connotation of the right to possession—also, perhaps, of capture by superior force. All those meanings would be consonant with their ideas of themselves.

After my failure at "helping" Laura with her masque, I went back to my novel. It was a pretentious muddle. I was so ashamed of the pretense and so mixed up by the muddle that I could make no headway with it. The next time Laura asked me how it was coming, and would I like her to help me, I said Yes. By now I had some idea of how overpowering her help might prove; I also had some idea that if I could survive the clutch of that octopus brain, the struggle would be worth it.

This was how she "helped" me. First I outlined my plan for the book. She suggested a new character—who naturally brought in another new character, and these additions changed the whole plan. I wrote, in the mornings, what amounted to a first draft; in the afternoons I took what I had written to Canellun—the new house on the far side of the village, where Laura and Robert were now settling in. Though I wrote slowly, her editing was infinitely slower: it would often take three hours to refine one of my paragraphs into a form that satisfied Laura, and in the fiery process my original work largely melted or was burnt away. It was almost but not quite as painful as working on the masque.

This time *I* was the corpse being dissected; I watched with dismay and helpless resentment while not only the anatomical details but the whole visage and body of my book changed out of all knowledge. I put up what resistance I could, but my mind was no match for Laura's, and I think I lost every argument. Once a whole paragraph of mine came through her scrutiny with no word changed; I felt as if I had won the Nobel Prize.

Laura's workroom was on the second floor of Canellun (first floor, in British usage), directly over Robert's. One morning I remember Robert suddenly flinging open the door, white-faced and shaking, and saying in a furious voice: "Will you *please* stop shuffling your feet!" We hadn't been conscious of it, but apparently our mental efforts had been accompanied by tappings and draggings of the feet ("It sounded as though you were *dancing!*" said the indignant Robert), and it had driven him wild. *He* was trying to work too. Laura took the outburst in surprisingly good part and even apologized—anything that furthered work was sacred, anything that hindered it indefensible—and we went back to our task, being careful to keep our feet still. Later I wondered whether mere irritation was enough to explain Robert's vehemence, or whether he had actually thought we were dancing. Dancing, or making love? Dancing as a preliminary to making love? Could it be that Robert was jealous?

The result of these labors was a kind of fairy story novel that was later published, but should never have had my name signed to it. I wanted to put Laura's name with mine on the title page, or at least some sort of acknowledgment, but she wouldn't hear of it. Not only the writing of the book was largely hers or strongly tinged with her, but the scheme also: she had whittled and re-shaped my plan, an old-fashioned picaresque novel, into a moral-istic fantasy, in which both she and I appeared as principal char-acters. Her purpose, which I dimly perceived at the time, was to show me that I was incapable of an equal encounter with her, and to teach me my proper place, a modest resignation to material success, which must always be second-best to her world, and far below it. Though never openly declared to me in those terms, I knew that the book was a private exercise, between ourselves.

Well before my six-month leave was up, I had finished my small part of it: the first draft. Laura's editing was so meticulous —and she had so many other pots on the stove—that her finished version didn't reach me until some time after we had returned to America. There was a moment—perhaps it was only one moon-drenched, nightingale-echoing night—when it seemed to me that I would be a fool to go back so soon, perhaps to return at all, and at the very last, at a farewell feast at Canellun, with only Laura and Robert, Julie and me present, Laura showed that she was thinking something of the same sort. She made an ex-traordinary proposition.

It was couched in such delicate and diplomatic language that

I knew Julie didn't understand it—which was just as well, for it would have shocked her profoundly, and she would have said so, being much more courageous than I. I understood all too well what Laura was proposing; but I didn't want a scene, or a quarrel that would end our friendship; I simply wanted, above all, to get away. How I managed to reply without offending Laura or without letting Julie know what was up, I don't know, but somehow I must have. Laura's proposition was that we should not go back to America but stay on in Deya: she and I would work together, Robert and Julie would live together.

Nevertheless, we left, according to plan, and parted on good terms. In the last weeks I had been feeling increasingly short-tempered, and had been having bad pains, like a fist unclenching, spreading through my belly. In Paris, where the duodenal ulcer floored me, the doctor told me severely that I could not attribute it to the past six months, although mental strain and food fried in olive oil might have helped it along. I had started making the ulcer for myself long before Laura had entered my life. She had only unclenched the fist.

When we took the train from Barcelona to Paris—where I looked forward to a fortnight's glorious vacation from the high tension of our six months in Deya—Norman and John came with us. They seemed in no hurry to get anywhere in particular. When we arrived in Paris, and the pain in my belly, which had begun in earnest the evening before, grew steadily worse, Norman said, "Poor Tom, have a brandy." The calm assurance, both of sound and sense, with which the British generally voice their bromidic comments on daily life has always impressed me, more than it should—and sometimes to my bane.

John nodded. "Brandy never hurt anybody."

We were sitting at a café. I ordered brandy. It was the very worst thing I could have chosen. The brandy quickly made the pain so much worse that I couldn't get up from my chair.

"Have another!" urged the omniscient British accents.

I did. Though it didn't kill me, it was the last drop of alcohol I had for a long, long time.

When we got back to New York, Schuyler met us at the dock. He was shocked at my appearance: I had lost 25 pounds and was still weak from the starvation diet and the treatment in Paris. Perhaps he thought my apprenticeship to Laura was the cause of my illness, and that made him discount my reverent talk about her. At any rate, his only response to my lengthy descriptions of her was a noncommittal silence, and when I gave him her poems to read he returned the book with the comment, "This isn't poetry; it's philosophy." I went to see my old mentor, Edmund Wilson, and after hearing my report on Laura and the life in Deya he said dryly, "I think you got away just in time."

But I hadn't got away. Long letters went back and forth between Deya and Princeton. Laura and Robert printed several numbers of a private little magazine called *Focus,* to which we all contributed letters, to keep us in touch with one another. *Focus* developed into *Epilogue,* a much more ambitious semi-annual, bound in hard covers and published in London. Laura wrote such a large part of these miscellanies that she signed many of her contributions with a pen name, Madeleine Vara. I remember *Epilogue* for two reasons: the first number opened with an argument between Laura and me about God—but it wasn't so much an argument as an occasion for Laura to proclaim the final truth of the matter, using my naïve questions, and equally simple demurrers to her first replies, as easy but useful targets. And in the same number she printed fourteen of my poems, under the heading *Simplicities of Despair*—and edited almost all of them with a very free hand. I don't remember her asking my permission, but I'm sure she would have done it anyway. As a result, the poems were no more mine than the novel she had "unmuddled."

Yet, even though I knew she had done the same sort of thing with other people's books, not to mention paintings and sculpture, and had perhaps even had a finger in Robert's poetry—at some point in that brew she surely stirred the cauldron—I could not deny my shame for submitting to this treatment and my resentment at being expected to. But I kept these feelings from

151

everyone but Julie, and tried to remind myself that we were all Laura's pupils and that I, for one, had learned much from her and still had much to learn.

Laura didn't believe in history, though her disbelief was subtler than Henry Ford's skepticism: she thought history was over—which was a statement I never understood—but at the same time she seemed to acknowledge that the concept of history, at any rate, existed, for she also said, "History is the most depressing word I know." And whatever she might call it, most people would say it was history that uprooted her from Mallorca. When the Spanish Civil War reached the island in July 1936, a British destroyer evacuated Laura and Robert to France at twenty-four hours' notice. Laura never saw Canellun again, and it was ten years before Robert did.

Later that year Julie and I met them in London, where we spent a month. Maisie Somerville found us a "service flatlet" (a bed-sitting room whose landlady supplied breakfast) near Regents Park, not far from where she lived. Laura held court in London very much as she had in Deya: there was a great amount of coming and going, of fidgety bustle, of turning inches into leagues, but here she was not quite so much the absolute monarch: her rule was more extensive yet less sharply defined. Certain relaxations were not only permitted but encouraged.

For example, Robert's latest potboiler, a novel called *Antigua Penny Puce,* had just been published. He gave us a copy and invited our opinions—very different from the Deya days when not even friends had been allowed to refer to his journeyman work. I didn't like the book, but instead of saying so directly I told him that I didn't think it would please the public, as all the characters in it were unpleasant. Robert was rather miffed at this, but explained away my gloomy prediction as the result of reading the book when I was in bed with flu.

And another example: one night Laura, Robert, Julie and I all got dressed up and went to the night club at the Dorchester, where his oldest daughter Jenny was in the chorus. Laura appeared in a long, full, heavy silk gown with a lace collar, and her golden-wire tiara that spelled LAURA; Robert wore a kind of eighteenth-century evening dress, with a ruffled shirt and a stock. Jenny had just had a promotion in the show: she came on stage by herself, doing a cartwheel. This was considered next-best to being given a line to speak. Afterwards she joined us at our table. I hadn't seen her since she was little, that day when I had gone to Islip to tea and helped the children with their galoshes. She was grown up now, with a good figure, like all Cochrane's Young Ladies. Her face was pert, snub-nosed and far from pretty, and her complexion was pitted. That evening she made rather a disagreeable impression on me: partly because of the openness with which she wheedled money from her father and partly because when I danced with her she was shaking and distraught, constantly looking over my shoulder to watch for the arrival of someone she either longed or dreaded to see. In later years Jenny and I became good friends and remained so till the day of her death; but that night I didn't find her likable.

Another night Julie and I went to Oxford with Laura and Robert to have dinner with Alan Hodge, then in his last undergraduate year. He was a small blond boy with a cherubic soprano's face, an incongruously deep and hollow voice, and a deliberate, sententious manner; he seemed about sixteen. I think he was an officer of the Union; I remember that he was in white tie and tails, and that he took Robert off to the Union after dinner.

There were several other indications that Laura's authority might be relaxing, at least in this interregnum in London. She spoke with mild, almost forgiving sadness of various defections from the group; and the arrangements for our meetings and other activities—which sometimes, like the evening at the Dorchester, were unabashed outings, occasions of mere pleasure—were not, as they had been in Deya, peremptory announcements but more in the nature of kindly inquiries or tentative suggestions.

Robert too was driven with a looser rein: he even dined out occasionally without Laura. The morning after one of these evenings he telephoned me in considerable excitement. The host at his dinner had been Alexander Korda, the film producer, who told Robert a tremendous piece of gossip which he had just heard from a reliable source in Buckingham Palace: that the King's mistress, Mrs. Simpson, for whose divorce from her husband the whole British press was watching and waiting, had in fact been granted her divorce a few days before, secretly, in Ipswich. The reason for Robert's excitement was the hope of selling this piping-hot gobbet of news to *Time* (which presumably would pay more for it than any British paper, especially since the British press was still keeping an unbroken front of silence on the whole subject of the King and Mrs. Simpson).

Since I was only a minor figure on *Time's* editorial staff and on leave to boot, I couldn't tell Robert what *Time* would pay for this information, but I thought they would certainly pay something. But how to cable the news to New York without letting everyone else in on it? Robert's ingenuity quickly found an answer: we must concoct a cable in American slang that would fly right over British heads. This was the cable we devised: KINGS-MOLL RENOED MUMLY WOLSEYS HOMEBURG ILYA PEEWEE. I protested in vain that only one American in a million would know that Ipswich was Cardinal Wolsey's home town; Robert overrode me, saying, *"Everyone* knows that!" My only contribution was the two final words: ILYA PEEWEE. Their dark meaning was "a short time ago"—ILYA, which I hoped would be mistaken for a Russian word, was really three words in French—*il y a*—in the idiom of time past; PEEWEE, as every American knows, means *little.*

As soon as we had finished this small masterpiece of cablese I dashed off with it to the *Time* office, which was then in a grubby building in Soho, in Dean Street. Before I could get the cable on the wire came another urgent telephone call from Robert to say that the report was unfounded!*

---

*In 1974—thirty-nine years later—as I was reading Lady Donaldson's excellent biography *Edward VIII,* this passage startled me (p. 247): "The following morning the British Press kept the gentleman's agreement and reported the divorce only in the most formal way. Not so in America, however, where the Press had a field-day even by their own standards, the palm being awarded to the oft-quoted headline KING'S MOLL RENO'D IN WOLSEY'S HOME TOWN." I straightway wrote to Lady Donaldson to inquire which Ameri-

Before coming to London we had spent a week in Berlin with my younger sister Peggy, who lived in Dahlem with her German husband and two little daughters. Germany was in an entranced, catatonic state, and anyone (except the pundits and the bigwigs) could see that the nation was already at war. Paris, where we went for a week after that, was shrilly gay, in jittery despair at the oncoming tide; the French knew they could not save themselves but, since they were the admiration of the civilized world, and the finest flower of human culture, they expected to be rescued. London in those prewar days seemed to be tinged by the same rosy putrescence, the same gaiety of expectant defeat as Paris was. Many of the best people were open admirers of the Nazis and the Fascists; it was generally conceded that the upper classes were honeycombed by craven homosexuals and the lower classes stunted and stupefied by malnutrition and rotting teeth; Oxford's undergraduates had taken an oath never to fight for King and Country under any circumstances. The difference was that in France the decay went to the bone and in England was no worse than German measles.

When we were young married men, Schuyler and I had sometimes talked, not very seriously, about fulfilling the Lake Poets' dream of "a pan-Socratic community on the banks of the Susquehanna." That phrase—was it De Quincey's?—had stuck in our minds, and we liked to roll it on our tongues. And that was about all. Did Laura entertain the same notion, but more seriously? (She was always more serious than anyone else.) Wherever she was, in Deya, France or London, a small community formed around her; but it was too small, too temporary, too centrifugal. "The strong pulling of her bladed mind" needed a more constant element and a larger reluctance to work on. The purpose of *Focus* was to rally us and keep us from straggling; *Epilogue* was

can newspaper had run this headline, giving her the correct version and its origin. In her reply she admitted that she had never been able to find the actual headline but that "it is in almost every book on the Abdication and seemed to me a 'must' as it is a part of history." Shades of Henry Ford!

a discreet advertisement for recruits. Now, with her growing forces amorphous and scattered, she had drawn up a plan for her New Model Army. (She had not yet bent her attention to the impending war or how to deal with it—that would come later.)

The gist of the Protocol was that we "inside people" understood and carried on the true purposes of life that were hidden from the "outside people"—at best useful, at worst dangerous extroverts whose whole concern was with the superficial aspects of living. We were the Marys, they the Marthas.

The Protocol (afterwards known as the First Protocol) was a manifesto proclaiming that the only genuine salt of the earth, the only hope of mankind, were "the inside people." All of Laura's circle were "inside people," though the degrees of their insideness varied in the most complicated fashion. Laura herself, by common consent, was as inside as you could get. I was inside but with some outside characteristics, and in an outside job. Et cetera. This Protocol was printed and sent to all who proclaimed themselves or were presumed to be insiders.*

And now that we had declared ourselves and knew who we were, what was this conspiracy of "inside people" going to do? Our goal was not explicitly named, but our aim was pretty clearly implied: we were going to change the world. How? Mainly by our example but partly through our influence. History was raising its ugly hydra heads all over the place, and I suppose Laura might have said (I can't remember that she did) that our job was to stop history cold. The human equivalent of the Bomb!

How seriously did I take all this? Well, I knew damn well that *Time* in particular and journalism in general were no "inside" activity, but I knew which side my career was buttered on; on the other hand, I was a parson's son, I believed in higher authorities (I still do) and I was not prepared to deny the power of the Word, though I was only fitfully aware of its manifestations. And I thought then, as I do now, that Laura's was the most brilliant

*It also appeared in one of Laura Riding's books, *The World and Ourselves* (London: Constable, 1938).

mind I had ever encountered. Her brilliance, or mental force, was so dazzling and lightning-like that there was something frightening about it. Julie and I agreed that Laura's mind was supernormal but that she used her extraordinary powers for good, not evil. The way we put it was: "She's a witch, but a good witch." We *believed* that. It might seem odd that I, a father, a married man and a suburban commuter, should acknowledge the spiritual supremacy of a witch, even a good witch; but I did.

Schuyler, who had refused to answer her questionnaire, also refused to acknowledge her supremacy or even to admit her into the ranks of genuine poets. Nevertheless he did write to her. Something in one of his early letters must have seemed to Laura lacking in respect, for she wrote him a peremptory rebuke, and their acquaintance began with a quarrel.

After London, Laura and Robert moved to France, where they rented a house in Brittany. Here they embarked on another ambitious project: a "dictionary of related meanings." It was to be a kind of etymological dictionary, like Skeat's—but with a fundamental difference that would make it unique in its field. Instead of depending on the harmless drudgery of lexicographers to dig up the root definitions of key words, Laura's poetic intelligence would illuminate and irradiate these nuggets of scholarship: she would supply the key definitions, making them not only exact but poetic. (This, at least, is as near as I ever came to understanding the scheme.) Although her role was all-important, a great deal of plain digging was also required. Robert was to be head drudge, with three assistant drudges to help him. A contract for this dictionary was signed with an American publisher, Little, Brown & Co. of Boston.

THE MARQUIS OF CARABAS

1

Although Schuyler and I had each been the other's best man at our weddings, for some time afterwards the relationship between our two families had not been an equation but a triangle: it was Schuyler and Julie and me, with Kit pretty much out of it. Not that we deliberately left her out: we just took her for granted. The three sides of our triangle, however, were taut with tension —as if an equilateral triangle were straining to turn itself into an isosceles; and maybe it was.

It's hard for me to explain, even now. I think I understand it, as far as such things can ever be understood. But it's embarrassing to explain because it puts me in a bad light. The fact was, I think, that Schuyler and Julie were jealous of each other. Both of them felt a proprietary interest in me; Julie possessed me as a wife, Schuyler as an almost equally exclusive friend. I knew but didn't like to admit that they were friends only through me and on my account. I knew, or almost knew, that they didn't really approve of each other and that there was antagonism between them. I wouldn't say even now that it was antipathy. They didn't dislike each other, but in a sense they were enemies.

I could never forget that, before Julie and I were married, Schuyler as good as told me I was marrying the wrong girl (the way he had put it was that I shouldn't marry till "there was a point in my life"). But after Julie and I were married, it was I who had insisted on seeing the Jacksons, frequently and regularly. We lived only 20 miles apart, and it was mostly my doing that we had dinner together once a week, alternating between their house and ours. I can remember many a time when Julie was in tears either on the way over or on the way back.

Why? I don't remember that we ever argued the case—
though it may well have started quarrels—but it was her way of
protesting: she didn't want Schuyler to take up such a large part
of my life; I think she would have been happier if he had had no
part in it at all. In spite of my knowing how she felt, I was
determined not to give him up. She considered Schuyler bad for
me, and thought there was something unhealthy (she wouldn't
have used a more specific term) in our friendship. I think she
might have said that Schuyler himself was "unsound"; and that
the bond that linked us was an answering "unsoundness" in myself. She thought me a weak character, helplessly attracted to
other weak characters. Her unspoken case against him was diminished, however, by the fact that Schuyler was generally considered not merely a strong but a wild, proud, Luciferian person
—and no one but God (and not Milton's God) would say that
Lucifer was a weakling.

In those days when the four of us were such intimate friends,
Julie wouldn't willingly have added to the strains of our marriage
by forcing me to choose between Schuyler and herself. But,
being Julie, she couldn't help showing me that she resented and
feared the situation, though she couldn't or wouldn't put her
resentment and fear into words. Any outsider would have said
that the Jacksons and ourselves were like a closed corporation. In
fact, however, we were more like four people shut up together
in a small room: our feelings about one another were unequal and
complicated, not to say ambiguous.

Schuyler and I both continued to take it for granted that he
was my superior, in almost every way that counted. And we both
agreed that money didn't count. We laughed at the same things
in those days, and one of the things we laughed at was money,
and "what it could bring." We were too inexperienced to know
that money is like dynamite: useful and dangerous and not essentially funny. Nevertheless, on this subject our jokes gradually got
rarer and our laughter more forced. We both fancied ourselves
as collectors and connoisseurs of popular humor, but for some
unacknowledged reason I never told Schuyler about the sign I

had seen in a New York bar—it must have been old hat even then, but it was new to me: "If you're so smart, why ain't you rich?"

Schuyler was liable to a particular premonition and to symptoms that, in a lesser man, I might have considered hypochondriac. He was sure that he would die before he was thirty, and this foreboding stimulated in him a heightened sense, often almost frantic, of the little time he had in which to fulfill his life. Consequently he did everything at full tilt, and drove himself so hard that he strained even his robust constitution to the point of collapse.

But for some Schuylerian reason he would never admit that these prostrations were the result of exhaustion: they always had to have a more mysterious cause. When the Jacksons were living on their farm he once took to his bed and was extremely ill for several days. He said he had been bitten by a snake, but there were no marks to show for it, and no one else ever laid eyes on the snake. He had been getting in a soybean crop almost single-handed, and I think he had simply worked himself too hard. When he had one of these seizures (he sometimes called them that himself) he would never see a doctor, perhaps because he knew the doctor's diagnosis would not agree with his.

Our ideas about money were very different. When he was in funds, or thought he was or pretended to be, Schuyler was the most generous man alive; he would even give away money that I knew he had borrowed. I wasn't generous. I had been brought up to believe that money was not to be squandered but saved, and my budgets were always based on a future of rainy days. I felt an almost physical horror of being in debt, and on the rare occasions when I had taken out a note at the bank the remembrance of it, and of the interest that was constantly accruing, hung over me night and day until I could pay off the whole amount. I doubt whether Schuyler was ever out of debt in his life, but he seldom gave it a thought and certainly never worried about it. In his way he was so ingenious about money, pyramiding loans and mortgages and borrowing from patient creditor Peter to pay importunate creditor Paul, that I used to think it was a pity he didn't have millions to play with instead of hundreds. But in that case I suppose the delicately balanced financial structure would have soared so high that the inevitable crash would have been ruinous, and to many others besides himself; whereas he could manipulate his intricate but comparatively flexible cat's cradle so that it never actually collapsed.

He hadn't the faintest hesitation in borrowing money from any source, but preferred to get it from private individuals rather than from banks because he objected on principle to paying interest, which he called usury; besides, he soon exhausted his credit and no bank would lend him any more. But, as I discovered, he had a rooted objection to taking money as a gift: the only exception to this rule was Kit's money (she had a little capital when they were married, but it didn't last long). But of course she was a special case, being his wife. Nevertheless, I think the fact that he did make this exception indicates a certain blurring in his mind on the subject of money. He seemed to me to draw a smudged line between a loan and an outright gift. He intended, or thought he intended, to repay all his debts—some sooner than others; and my position, as his friend and almost-brother, was toward the bottom of the list, just above the banks.

A. R. Orage (pronounced in the French manner, although he was British) was a journalist who had had an erratically brilliant career in London, had fallen under the spell of an esoteric religious teacher named Gurdjieff, and was now expounding the word to New Yorkers. I heard about him from the Jacksons, and Julie and I went with them to our first meeting. Gurdjieff was a man of obscurely Russian origins whose headquarters were in France, in a large house called Le Prieuré, in Fontainebleau. Here for a while he had conducted his "Institute for the Harmonious Development of Man"—I had heard of it because my admired Katherine Mansfield had died there, of tuberculosis. The Institute was no longer officially in being, but Gurdjieff continued to live there with a handful of disciples, traveling from time to time in Oriental style with his retinue (he came to New York every year for at least a month). Meanwhile his teachings were presented in London by P. D. Ouspensky and in New York by Orage.

Most of the Orage meetings I went to were held in bookshops or in barnlike lecture rooms, and I thought the people who came to hear him a pretty job lot. One of my friends who was also a regular attendant described us as "the 100 neediest cases." There were a few notables among us: I remember Muriel Draper, Mabel Dodge, and her fourth and final husband, Tony Luhan, a Hopi Indian. Tony was a massive man who wore his greasy black hair in long pigtails, wrapped himself in a striped blanket and never spoke. It was also a question whether he understood anything Orage said. Nevertheless, Tony was taken as a kind of barometer: if it was an interesting evening he sat erect and watchful; if not, his head sagged and he slept, quietly and solidly as a weathered rock. Perhaps what really affected him was the air.

Orage was a compulsive smoker, lighting one cigarette, with slightly trembling hands, from the butt of another. We often discussed his smoking habits and wondered whether he was completely conscious of them. For consciousness was the lock that Gurdjieff's key was supposed to open. It was Gurdjieff's claim that he had discovered, or rediscovered, a secret known to Pythagoras and handed down to the elect of all later generations: the only possible method of escape from man's doom of "eternal recurrence" and of attaining a real, conscious and lasting identity. This was the method: "self-observation with non-identification." As a slogan it would not have appealed to an advertising man. According to Orage, Buddha perfected this same method.

It was admittedly a laborious process. Buddha had begun by observing his breathing; when he was completely and continuously conscious of that, he went on to muscular tensions, posture, heartbeat and so on. By the time you had finished the course (so we gathered, at least) your complete and objective awareness of

165

your body had not only put you in absolute control of it but had summoned into wakeful being your hitherto nonexistent or sleeping self. The trick was, we thought, to get over the first hurdle. Orage gave us some helpful rules of thumb. One was: be more so—the more like yourself you behave, the more likely you are to catch a glimpse of yourself. "He that is filthy let him be filthy still"—but a damn sight filthier. We discussed this notion with enthusiasm and at length, and when the bolder spirits among us, like Schuyler, broke into abrupt eccentricities of speech or action, we knew they were practicing.

It remained a constant question, however, whether anyone was actually "able to do it." We eventually decided that no one we knew had quite got the hang of it yet, not even Orage; but that Gurdjieff himself must have mastered the method, if anybody had. Our own attempts grew more and more sporadic and finally ceased, but we kept on going to the meetings. Orage was an extremely interesting and lucid lecturer, and there were other aspects of Gurdjieff's teaching which were not so forbidding as the method.

That is, when Orage himself was expounding them. There were other evenings of an unspeakable dreariness when we got it straight from the horse's mouth, in readings from "The Book." This was the Bible of the cult; it was referred to as The Book not only out of reverence but because the full title took too long to say: *Tales Told by Beelzebub to His Grandson.** A literal translation into English of Gurdjieff's Russian original, it was a masterpiece of long-windedness and boring repetitions. Even so, it had its points, its occasional phrases (one I remember is "to go the whole hog, including the postage"), and some of the made-up names were memorable (the Very Saintly Ashiata Shiemash, the Law of Heptaparaparshinokh). Buried under the middens of pretentious verbiage were sly, peasant-shrewd sayings and some pointed fables.

*The Book was later published in New York (Harcourt, Brace) with the more modest title of *All and Everything*.

When Gurdjieff visited New York, I noticed that everyone, including Orage, was afraid of him, didn't understand him, and never knew what he would do next. I neither trusted nor worshipped him. He was a massive, bald, heavily mustachioed man in his sixties, with liquid, bull-like, hypnotic eyes. His manner said more clearly than his never-clearly-understood pidgin-talk that he regarded all people as different classes of idiot; his bearing and manner towards them were those of a pasha. His women followers obviously adored him, and some of those who had found favor in his sight had visible mementos: swarthy and liquid-eyed children.

I can't remember exactly when or why we quit the Gurdjieff cult. I suppose it must have been when Orage did. He had a row with Gurdjieff and was fired, in effect; I believe much the same thing happened to Ouspensky. Orage, a great man for causes, went back to crusading for Social Credit. He once told me that he had never been able to make up his mind about Gurdjieff— whether he was a completely cynical charlatan, an inspired religious teacher, or a bit of both. Though Gurdjieff, Orage and Ouspensky are all dead, the cult still goes on.

Julie went happily back to the Church, which she had missed and where she felt at home. I sometimes went to services with her, but only for the sake of propriety and to please her, as her father had done with her mother. Like many of my generation I felt that the mythic figure of Christ, whoever he was (it was hard, if not impossible, to make out, through all that ritual, interpretation and stained glass which the Church had interposed), was incredible and compelling, but that "the Church," at the same time fragmented and exclusive, was beyond belief. Beyond belief in its claims for itself and repellent in many of its practices.

One of its most repulsive practices was the putting down of heresies and the waging of "holy" wars. It seemed to me that the Christian frenzy to kill, horribly evident throughout the history of the Church, could be only partly explained by the natural human need to be reassured of the correctness of one's own belief, and that there must be something essentially bloody-minded in the nature of Christianity itself—at least in its militant, proselytizing, "missionary" aspects. Short of the absolute, world-wide domination of Christianity, a consummation which could be brought about only by the extermination of all other religions, this murderous ambition was shown to be nonsensical if not insane by the continued and flourishing existence of other gods—Buddha, Mahomet, the God of Israel, to mention three principal rivals.

The one flirtation of Julie's that worried me was not, I think, a flirtation at all. I know he was in love with her. Since he also lived in Princeton and had no job to take him away, as most of us did, he had time and opportunity to court her. Were they lovers? I would swear they were not. But the strain—of resisting him?—went on so long that I think it sapped Julie's health and was the main cause of her nervous breakdown in 1934. At the time I didn't know what was wrong, I only had an uneasy feeling that Julie was deeply unhappy and either couldn't or wouldn't tell me why. I finally got her to see a doctor—not a psychiatrist but the kind of mental doctor who in those days was called an "alienist"—and he strongly advised a change of scene. I told my managing editor, John Billings, that I had to have a month off, because my wife was ill and the doctor said I should take her away somewhere. Billings saw that I was desperate (I would have gone whether or not he gave me permission) and, being a kindly man, said only, "When do you want to go?"

It was midwinter. I had decided to take Julie to Jamaica, and was told January was a good month there, so I said, "January." We went to Jamaica and back by ship—five days each way—and had two weeks at Montego Bay. That was before Jamaica had become easily accessible and overrun by tourists. We stayed at an old-fashioned, strictly managed little hotel, the Ethelhart, where we were so much younger than the other guests that we were thought to be on our honeymoon. (As we had then been married nine years we considered ourselves old married people.)

We read *Emma* to each other aloud, we ate delicious food (I remember particularly the papaya and ackee—and the Planter's Punch, made with the dark, nearly black Jamaica rum), we swam at Doctor's Cave, where on a cool morning the water would be 79, on a warm morning 80. Julie began to feel a little better, but I had pains in my belly and half the time felt poorly. When we got back (we arrived in New York Bay in a blizzard, and I remember the pilot clambering up the rope ladder to the deck of our ship, wearing a coonskin cap and looking more like a frontiersman than a pilot), Julie went on seeing the doctor for at least a year and a half. I don't remember what medicine he gave her, if any, but she saw him often—about once a week—and they talked. When I asked what they talked about, she said, "Oh, everything." He was a froglike little man, kindly and sensible. Eventually, imperceptibly, Julie was all right again.

Or have I got it wrong? Was it only that the wound healed and a scar grew over it? Looking back at that time through the diminishing tunnel of all those years, I see now how little I must have seen then. In 1934 I was puzzled and worried and apprehensive about her—but, as I think now, not nearly enough: I think, now, that the quandary in which she was struggling and that made her ill was that she was in love with Tom Frelinghuysen and was struggling to decide whether or not to leave me.

Tom Frelinghuysen was a proud, reckless, arrogant young bachelor (four years younger than I—which would make him a year younger than Julie) with more money than was good for him and some, but not quite enough, artistic talent. He couldn't be bothered to go to art school but taught himself to draw and model in clay. The subjects that most attracted him were unusual: a dead horse, a Doberman pinscher shitting. He was also a self-taught portrait painter, and some of his portraits I liked. He also tried his hand at writing, though I don't think he ever published anything. Julie was much impressed by a play he had written, and got him to show it to me. I thought it had some good things in it, but could see many others that needed amending, and made the mistake of pointing them out to him. He did not take my

criticism kindly, and I never saw any more of his writing. He and
I had nothing to say to each other, except for those things that
could not be said, so I never really got to know him. But there
was one story about him which I am sure was true and which
made me dislike him more than ever, for it showed that he was
brave to foolhardiness, much braver than I was.

He was at Lake Placid one Christmas holiday when the winter Olympic Games were being held there. He watched some of
the ski jumping and it fascinated him. He himself had never been
on skis in his life. He thought and brooded, and at last made up
his mind that he would try the Olympic ski jump when no one
was around. That night, a night of brilliant moon, he got a pair
of skis, went to the silent, deserted ski jump, climbed it, fastened
his skis, and started down the precipitous run. As he got to the
takeoff he tried to lean forward, as he had seen the champion ski
jumpers do. Though he might have been killed he landed in
more or less good order; he fell and slid for some distance and was
badly bruised, but broke no bones. He never made a ski jump
again. But the point of the story for me was that I never made
a ski jump at all!

What happened to the affair between him and Julie? I know
it ended but I don't know how; I'm not sure that it ever began.
Yes, I'm *morally* sure it began, though I never knew how far it
went. And I don't think Julie broke it off, exactly—it was more
that she gradually smothered it. If there is anything at all to this
surmise of mine, these years must have been the unhappiest of
her life. And one of the worst things about it must have been that
there was no one she could talk to, no one to whom she could go
for help. Perhaps the doctor was a kind of surrogate? In any case,
the upshot was that she reconciled herself to making do with me.
(Eight years later she had to do it all over again, when she could
have divorced me for adultery but decided against it.)

This affair, or whatever it was, with Tom Frelinghuysen must
have been one of the painful refinements that matured Julie (in
my negative way, I may have been another), a kind of rehearsal
for the education of death. She graduated from life (I am not

trying to be euphemistic but metaphorically exact) when she was only forty-six. A short life but a shining one. Everyone who was near her during her incandescent close saw the light she gave out and took some illumination from her.

I come back again and again to Julie, as I must. She always escapes me. She left me forever, twenty-five years ago, and my increasingly feeble memories of her are only a mockery of the living woman she was. She who was my life is now dead. I never had much identity without her, and in her long absence I—the person I was with her—have gradually ceased to exist.

If I grew more critical of Schuyler over the years, I also felt more protective about him. And whatever he did or didn't do, I tried to tell myself that he was headed in the right direction. Even when he was apparently at a standstill he never seemed to be at a loss but rather as if he was carrying out a deliberate plan; and he welcomed neither criticism nor defense, however well it was meant.

When Schuyler renounced poetry, which had been the whole purpose of his life, I tried to believe (and thought I succeeded in believing) that he was right: it was not so much that he had failed to become a poet as that poetry had somehow failed him, that it was not good enough for him. And that he had not yet found the form of great endeavor proper to him, which he was born to find, fated to find. Even now I can't reconcile myself to the fact that the most radiantly promising person I ever knew, who still stands in my eyes as the very picture of all youthful promise, should have missed the mark completely.

In some hopeful ways, Schuyler's new chapter was the best of the lot. He became a farmer—and a real one, with horny hands, dirt under his fingernails, and a sardonic stance toward acts of God and government. Whatever he did he did it with his might, which meant among other things that he always acted like a professional. Although other professionals might see through the act, he never regarded himself as a dilettante; and neither did I. To me he was neither professional nor gifted amateur but a genius, and everything he touched turned for a while to gold. Not, alas, in the literal sense: in hard fact, just the opposite was true. It was lucky for his wife and children that the small capital his father had left him had been made Schuyler-proof by being locked up in a trust.

It was exhilarating to watch that derelict farm come to life under his hands. And it was almost all Schuyler's own work. It took money too, of course. As I saw electrified fences going up (they were to keep the sheep from straying) and a shiny new tractor and a combine in the barnyard, and a plantation of 250 black walnut saplings (they would be, said Schuyler with a large grin, his daughters' dowry) set out in one of the pastures, and 25 acres sown to soy beans, I wondered where the money for all this was coming from. I knew and admired, though at the same time it scared me, Schuyler's expertness at financial sleight-of-hand: his ability to move a mountain of debt (a small one, at any rate) from one range to another, or to poise a loan on top of a second mortgage and somehow keep the pile in trembling balance. And there must also have been, for a while, some unexpended remnants of Kit's money to help out.

Though Schuyler worked like ten men, in this first period of centrifugal expansion even he had to have some help, and for a few weeks he did have a hired hand and the occasional assistance of a neighboring farmer. His evenings were given over to book-keeping: he was determined to show that he could farm not merely for a living but at a profit, and for hours every night he pored over forms and pamphlets of instruction he got from the Farm Bureau, translating officialese into plain English and totting up immense columns of figures. The results didn't always come out the same, he admitted, but in general they did seem to indicate that the farm was either paying for itself already or about to show a profit. His only reading in those days was a weekly farm paper, *The Rural New Yorker,* with which he slapped his thigh and quoted frequently, swearing that it was the only worthwhile paper in the country.

The first lambing season at the farm was an exhausting time

for both Schuyler and Kit. Schuyler was out and about at all hours, delivering balky ewes, and the punier lambs he brought in to Kit, who would bed them down in the kitchen and try to feed them with a baby's bottle: when she had several to look after, she would be up most of the night. Sometimes the lambs were too far gone or she had no luck; but between them they saved about a dozen.

When I visited the farm in lambing time it seemed to me like a primitive hospital, full of the sights and smells of blood and birth and death. I was altogether too squeamish for animal husbandry, and my obvious distaste amused Schuyler and Kit, whose talk would get even earthier for my benefit. One balmy spring day I found Kit working in her garden. She waved a grimy hand.

"Schuyler wants to see you. He's in the barn."

He was sitting on the sill of the barn door, a baa-ing lamb gripped between his knees, while he struggled to get a purchase on its wooly tail with an instrument that looked like a clumsy pair of iron pinchers.

"Give me a hand, Tom, will you?"

"What do I do?"

"I'll show you. Here, you little bugger, stand still!"

He dropped the iron pinchers and seized the lamb by its hindquarters.

"Now get his tail between the choppers—further up—about three inches from the root. There. Now bear down on the handles."

I bore down, but gingerly. I could feel the tough gristle of the lamb's tail through the heavy iron.

"Harder. *Much* harder."

I used all my strength; there was a rending crunch; the lamb uttered a wailing cry and tried to leap, but Schuyler held it. The chewed-off tail, only a little bloody, dropped to the ground. I felt sick.

Schuyler dipped a stick in a pot and smeared some black stuff that looked like tar on the lamb's raw stump. It wailed again. Schuyler let it go, with a whack on the rump.

"Do you have to do this? To all of them?"

"They get all fouled up with shit if you don't."

He fetched another lamb from the pen. I absolutely refused to do any more tail-cutting.

"O.K., you hold him."

That wasn't much better. I could feel the lamb's shuddering fear and the grinding stab of pain, and then the agonizing crunch. The job took about an hour. Afterwards I washed my hands (but Schuyler didn't) and we had a cup of coffee with Kit in the kitchen.

When did I realize that the farm was a failure? The realization came slowly, as perhaps it also did to Schuyler; but I might have read the signs much earlier than I did. First the sheep went. Schuyler had a complicated explanation of why sheep-raising on his scale was uneconomic. I couldn't altogether follow the argument but I understood the wisdom of cutting your losses—and in Schuyler's case I was more impressed by the wisdom than by the losses. The electrified fences stayed, because they couldn't be sold. They were no longer electrified, however.

The pasture land reverted to wild meadow. Schuyler planned to raise a hay crop and sell it to a nearby dairy farmer, and until this scheme came to nothing he kept his tractor and its mowing attachment. He hung on to the combine too, because it might come in handy.

His next five-year plan was built around soy beans. The great advantage of soy beans, he told me, was that they were the most concentrated form of food known to man, and could be eaten with profit by human beings and cattle alike. This was going to be a cash crop: every bean was as good as money in the bank. With unremitting and superhuman labor he sowed, cultivated and reaped 25 acres of soy beans the first year—but found no market for them. He was ahead of his time: people thereabouts simply didn't know about soy beans and in their invincible ignorance preferred to eat other things; they wouldn't even give it to their cattle. Whereas in China soy beans had been highly

174

prized for untold centuries. He showed me the bins stored with dully glittering beans, dipping his hands in them and letting them run through his fingers like freshly minted coins. The Jackson family ate more than their fill of soy beans that year.

Shortly afterwards Schuyler sold his remaining farm machinery and declared himself no longer a farmer. At that late date I remembered one of my father-in-law's favorite sayings: that farming is "the most unostentatious way of losing money in the world." I wouldn't have said that Schuyler's way was unostentatious, exactly; but the rest applied.

How did he make the great sideways leap from farming to antiques? I'm blest if I know, but he did it. It was like an electron jumping from one orbit to another, a feat that scientists accept without being able to explain: one moment Schuyler was pursuing the depressing daily round of a failing farmer, and the next he was a busy and apparently prospering dealer in early American antiques. He roamed far and wide, as far as western Pennsylvania and upper New York State, to buy his stuff, mainly from farmers or at country auctions—chests, samplers, woven blankets, pottery, tables and chairs and chests of drawers. He had a natural taste for such things, and he learned fast; but it remained a mystery to me how he ever knew enough to get started. The odd bits of knowledge his mind was stocked with never ceased to amaze me.

For once he seemed to have timed his venture right. There was a growing market for American antiques, and during the first year or so that he was in business he could hardly keep up with the demand. Being Schuyler, he would sometimes, if he liked the customer, sell at cost or for less than he had paid; but on other pieces he made a handsome profit. Perhaps if he had gone into partnership with an established dealer he might have had a successful career in antiques, but he could never run in harness. And after a while, for various other reasons, this new undertaking began to slow down and even show signs of petering out. The demand for early American furniture seemed to dwindle, he had to go further and further afield to buy his wares, and haggle with shrewder or more reluctant sellers. Sometimes he came back empty-handed from a three-day expedition. And not unnaturally he found these tiring trips and diminishing returns discouraging; the whole affair began to bore him. He decided to finish the business in a grand climax: an auction, to be held at the farm, of all his unsold pieces.

He advertised this sale by handbills and by notices in the local newspapers, and engaged the services of an experienced auctioneer. The crowd that turned up on the day was disappointingly small, and the total sales, which would have been larger if he hadn't bid on several of the best pieces himself, amounted to less than $1,000.

What next?

"Damned if I know."

He sounded cheerful, but that might have been the drinks he'd had.

"Would you consider a job?"

"What sort of job?"

"Oh—maybe something on *Time.*"

"Maybe."

It was impossible for a man of Schuyler's intensity to be idle. For a time, after the collapse of his antique business, he tried to keep himself busy making repairs to the house and relieving Kit of her heavier chores (except gardening: he couldn't bear gardening), but these stopgaps were not enough for him. He told me he was thinking of returning to an old idea of his: editing the epic poems of C. M. Doughty, with notes and a glossary. For once, I couldn't share his enthusiasm for the idea. I didn't doubt his ability to do the job but I questioned whether it chimed with his talents, and I didn't see it as a cash crop.

"Better get a publisher to back you."

Tell a man like Schuyler that there's no money in the scheme he intends to carry out, and you merely harden his resolve. He launched a characteristic all-out frontal attack on Doughty and for the next couple of months I hardly saw him. At some point, however, he must have taken to heart my mild suggestion that it would be as well to get a publisher's backing. He wrote to several, and when none of them so much as nibbled, much to my relief he dropped the project. Although by that time he had made a beginning, he would never show me what he had done.

But he did show me some verses which, though they bore no apparent relation to Doughty, may have resulted from his brief grappling. One odd thing about the first was that he never actually admitted that he had written it. It sounded like someone else —but who? It also sounded like Schuyler, or one side of him: a part of him that was ambiguous, uproarious and brutal—his kind of humor, that was apt to crop out during the onset of one of his black moods. But I mustn't read too much into it:

> There was an ugly man named Mudd
> Who fed on baby's bones and blood;
> His bureau drawers were quite congested
> With little boys he'd half-digested.
>
> For girls he kept an uglier fate:
> To feed not hunger but his hate
> He pressed them into little cheeses
> And hung them out to spoil the breezes.

The other poem was more characteristic. It was addressed to me:

DOUBTING-THOMAS MATTHEWS

> "I sing of damage," Matthews sings;
> "Of hollow queens and hunted kings;
> Of pathways founden by the lost;
> Of every man who's his own ghost.
> Through the earth's orchard I do go
> Where apples dapple every bough,
> And eat the harvest, to my teen,
> Of trees so ripe, and fruit so green.
>
> Green is my heart, and grey my brow!
> I am a little child, I trow.

177

O Sprite of Life! whose tireless breath
Makes rhythmical the dance of death,
I would not bate my note of love—
The carping of a wingless dove—
To fly to an another shore
Where there's no conscience any more:

I'll stay where home and heaven's stations
Are kindred (like men's poor relations),
And break the bread that starves the nations."

This one too I thought ambiguous—although I did understand that Schuyler was summing up my character and the verses I sometimes wrote (which very few besides himself ever saw. Julie, of course, was one of the few, and they troubled her: she still thought them "morbid"). And I could see that it was not a favorable summing up: it made me out either a determined hypocrite or obstinately stupid. But I thought I detected in it also a note of affection—though somewhat jeering affection—and I clung to that.

2

I had learned by that time that if you worked for any sort of organization you were always a square peg in a round hole; but that with practice, luck and cunning you might gradually whittle yourself a better fit. Schuyler didn't have that kind of patience and he would have been too proud to put up with the continual friction; I knew he would consent to do only a job that was fit for him, that fitted him. I doubted if any company could supply that, but my hope was to find him a place in which he could put at least some of his abilities to good use, to get him on the payroll of a company that would make allowances for him, and where he would have only part-time duties.

Puss-in-boots and the Marquis of Carabas: that was what it seemed like at the time, except that my Marquis didn't live up to my advance billing, or else I was a less persuasive agent than that sweet-talking cat. I did get him a job on *Time,* as an "editor." He lasted more than two years. He was attached to the Books department, though his name didn't appear on the mast-head and he came to the office so seldom that very few on the staff knew him by sight: I think only the managing editor and myself. The Books page of *Time* reviewed about five books a week, and as the managing editor was convinced that the readers, like himself, never read poetry and wouldn't understand it or like it if they did, one of the unwritten laws governing the Books page was: no poetry reviews. Once in a blue moon, when someone like Yeats or T. S. Eliot was awarded the Nobel Prize, there would be a hurried reappraisal of this policy, the upshot of the conference always being: "Hell, it's too late now, he hasn't written a line for five years" — and the news would be shuffled on to some other department.

Nevertheless *Time* continued to receive review copies of all the new books of verse, and these were always wrapped up and mailed to Schuyler, who conscientiously read them through and painstakingly sent in a report on each one. The reports were never printed. Then he had an idea: that in the Christmas issue the whole Books page should be given over to a round-up of the year's poetry, and that he should write it.

Traditionally the Books page in that issue, the thinnest of the year, contained no reviews at all but a list of the "best" books (according to *Time*'s middlebrow taste) of the past year. It was known that the managing editor considered this list a waste of space and had questioned whether any of the paper's readers ever bothered to look at it. But no one had an alternative suggestion. It looked as if Schuyler's might be tried.

And so it turned out.

That year (1938) Laura Riding's *Collected Poems* had been published in America. And there were enough others to shake a stick at. That was just what Schuyler proceeded to do. The writing of the page came hard, as it always did with him; and to make sure of getting his copy on time I spent my two-day weekend with him, sitting at the same table—goading him on by making suggestions or proposing phrases, all of which he invariably rejected but some of which brought out ideas and sentences of his own. It was a slow and laborious process reminiscent of my sessions with Laura, but this time it worked.

At the end of the two days we had a comprehensive report on current poetry, couched in downright, not to say authoritarian terms. Schuyler had divided the poets under inspection into three classes: poets, poetasters and poeticules. Laura and Rainer Maria Rilke (who was dead) were awarded the high title of poet. The rest were all poetasters or poeticules. Naturally they didn't like it, and some of them protested. But I think Laura must have been pleased.

The manifesto (that was really what it was) started like this:

During the last three months, to the almost complete indifference of 130 million Americans, some 25 books of poems have been published in the U.S.

Time takes these books seriously. As *Time* sees it, poets acknowledge a responsibility which sooner or later every human being must acknowledge. That responsibility, stated in its humblest form, is to make words make sense: stated in its most ambitious form, it is to make words make complete sense. Twentieth-Century poets have had a hard time trying to make their 20th-Century words make sense, but that was their responsibility. Either they could live up to it, and be poets; or pretend to live up to it, and be poetasters; or ignore it, and be poeticules. . . .

The publication of this manifesto—in *Time*, of all places—went a little to Schuyler's head. He confidently expected that his review would cause a public sensation and would bring in a flood of letters from *Time*'s readers. He demanded that all these letters, instead of being sent to the Letters department, as they normally would be, should be handed over to him; he would answer them all himself. The next two weeks brought a grand total of three letters and two postcards: one letter commented favorably on the review and one postcard was obscene as well as jeering.

But Schuyler by this time had the bit between his teeth. He went to see the managing editor and proposed that *Time* should publish a special supplement, to consist of a reprint of the poetry review, with the ensuing correspondence and Schuyler's answers. He was quite serious, and when the managing editor in astonishment asked him why the hell they should, he replied firmly that his poetry review and its repercussions were a milestone in journalism. The managing editor was speechless but managed to shake his head. Schuyler then appealed to Caesar, to the Editor-in-Chief, Henry R. Luce himself. Luce, who was impressed and puzzled by Schuyler's intensity, countered by asking Schuyler and me to dinner at the Links Club—to discuss the possibilities. I was there, I suppose, as a kind of interpreter; but my services weren't needed and I don't remember saying a word. Schuyler made his speech: Luce seemed sympathetic and said he would think it over. Nothing happened, of course. Schuyler thereupon resigned, and this time it was final: nothing I could do or say would change his mind—or for that matter get him reinstated.

That was the end of Schuyler's career in journalism. A year or so later, however, when we were still friends although I had become a doubting disciple, he proposed himself for another kind of position on *Time*. By then I was Executive Editor, and one of my jobs was to give all the copy a final reading and brush-up before the paper went to press. Schuyler's suggestion was that I should put him on the payroll, at $25 a week, and give him an office where he could be in residence on Mondays only: that was the day the last sections went to press. A sign on his office door would indicate that any writer who was dissatisfied with the way his copy had been edited was invited to bring it to Schuyler to deal with.

I explained that I did this myself, with all the copy.

"You correct it," he said. "I would perfect it."

181

He had no conception of the quantity of copy that went into one issue, or of the amount of "overset" (the copy put into type but for various reasons dropped out in make-up), or that a third of each issue had already gone to the printer by Sunday night, or of the inexorable steady speed of the flow of copy on Monday, the final press day, which only an emergency was allowed to interrupt, and then with costly multiplying consequences: late closing, overtime press charges, trains and planes missed, lower newsstand sales, angry subscribers. I thought of trying to explain all that to him, and then thought better of it.

"No," I said. "I'm sorry, but it wouldn't work."

I was not a successful promoter of Schuyler as a wage earner, and it was not only in journalism that I failed to find him a niche. I made two abortive attempts to get him a teaching job. The first was at a boy's boarding school, Lawrenceville, whose headmaster I had met at a dinner party. He was newly appointed, and talked with enthusiasm of his plans for the school and his ideas of education. His first objective, he said, would be to improve the teaching staff. It would take a little time "to get rid of the dead wood"; in the meantime he would be enlisting men of his own choice, and the kind of man he particularly wanted was the nonconformist, the free spirit, the awkward customer. I listened and said nothing, but the next day I wrote to him to say that I knew a man who would be just the sort of teacher he was after. He asked me to come and see him.

When I described Schuyler and his qualifications he seemed interested at first but then began to hedge: at the moment his hands were tied, he must make haste slowly, etc., etc.

I reminded him of his winged words on the evening we had met, and said, "If you give this man a free hand and start him off with the pick of your Fourth Formers, I'll guarantee that by the time they get to the Sixth Form a few of them will flunk their College Boards and one may try to commit suicide, but two or three will graduate brilliantly and be an everlasting credit to the school."

He agreed, a little nervously, I thought, to have a talk with Schuyler; but nothing came of their interview.

My other attempt, equally vain, was to get Princeton, my old university, to take Schuyler on as an instructor in English. This venture, about which I never told Schuyler, fell flat after a cold interview between me and the dean of the faculty.

Did these failures, which were mine, not Schuyler's, weaken the foundations of our friendship? As the disparity widened between my kind of success and his kind of non-success, the differences between us necessarily grew; and yet, at least for a while, our intimacy did not lessen, it even seemed enhanced. Schuyler was more than ever the senior partner in our friendship, and the more I went up in the world the more I acknowledged his moral authority. Nevertheless, in our private world as well, subtle changes were setting in, though as yet I refused to recognize them.

Julie and I had dinner with the Jacksons once a week, alternating between their house and ours, and no one else was ever invited to these evenings. I knew that Julie, though she never said so, much preferred to have the Jacksons come to our house rather than go to theirs; I thought it was because Schuyler's temperament was less controlled under his own roof. Sometimes for very small cause or for no observable reason he would turn on Kit, half-humorously and half-savagely, and though she suffered these attacks in silence, he gave us all a bad quarter of an hour.

Julie thought it was the drink that set him off; but as I pointed out to her, he usually had more to drink at our house than at home; and since this was a sensitive subject for me (it was drink that had brought him and me together and was still a great cementer of our friendship, and I knew I liked to drink more than was good for me), I always defended him against this charge. I did admit to her, however, that he sometimes drank too much: by admitting this I thought, ostrich-like, to divert attention from my own case. But when Kit asked me privately not to give Schuyler so much to drink when they came to dinner with us, I promised to do what I could.

The first opportunity came unpleasantly soon: the very next week. It was early May, one of those spring days when the afternoon light lingers on and on, and the light itself has a quality almost audible, like the last repetition of a ringing echo; the effect of this light is incredibly exciting, making you laugh out loud for no reason, or feel like cutting a caper or bursting into song, especially if you are tone-deaf. On a day like this everything goes to your head, and you don't need a drink to be slightly tipsy. But if you do take one it affects you more than usual.

The evening began happily, with the four of us looking fondly at one another and wishing we could put our affectionate feelings into forthright words—at least, that's how I felt. Schuyler must have been in the same mood, for in the middle of dinner he got up from the table and went out into the garden. A few minutes later we heard him running up the stairs; then he reappeared, his eyes shining. He had gone out to pick a branch of white dogwood, which was just in flower, and had put it in our youngest son's crib as a loving gesture and a sign of spring.

A minute later bawls and screams cascaded from the nursery. Julie flew upstairs. When she reappeared, some twenty minutes later, the look she gave Schuyler was not fond. He might have known better, she said, than to put a prickly branch of dogwood into a sleeping child's cot: the baby had obviously been terrified, and might have hurt himself into the bargain. Schuyler was remorseful and wanted to go straight up to the nursery to make amends, but Julie wouldn't let him. This awkward little incident put a damper on our effervescent spirits, so I made our after-dinner drinks stronger, hoping that might rescue the evening. It didn't.

Julie, who never had much to drink, was quieter than usual, and got into a low-voiced woman's conversation with Kit. Schuyler, after accepting her rebuke and then putting it aside almost

in the same motion, grew boisterous, but his gaiety had a bluster-
ing tinge that was not agreeable. Kit had taken out her knitting:
her inaudible colloquy with Julie had died into silence. Schuyler,
who was now, as we all knew, quite drunk although his speech
was clear, was talking with brilliant inconsequence and emphatic
repetitiousness, and had the floor to himself. The two women sat
tight-lipped. I wondered uneasily what I would do when things
came to a head. I hadn't long to wait.

Schuyler raised his glass to show it was empty, and turned to
me with a look of hard cheerfulness. When I made no move, he
said,

"I'd like another drink, Tom. If you don't mind."

"You've had enough."

It was the first time I had ever said such a thing to him. He
stared at me without speaking and then got slowly to his feet. He
swayed a little and caught the back of his chair to steady himself.
Then his face contorted with anger and he crashed the glass into
the fireplace. He turned and stalked out of the room. We heard
the front door slam.

Kit stood up, stuffing the knitting into her bag.

"I'll go after him. When he's like this—"

"We'll all go."

"No, better not. I'll find him."

We knew he had set off in a fury to walk the 20 miles back
to the farm, and that he would probably go cross-country, knowing that Kit in their car would have to keep to the roads. Something like this had happened once before; she hadn't found him,
but he got home eventually. She drove off into the night with a
sad face and her eyes full of angry tears.

I was angry too. Before I went to bed that night I wrote
Schuyler a letter, defending what I had done, and saying that as
his closest friend I had to tell him that drink was becoming a
danger to him. But as always he was too quick for me. Just after
I mailed my letter I had one from him. As I opened it I wondered
whether it might possibly be an apology for his wild behavior.
This was the letter:

185

Dear Tom—I'm worried about your drinking, and I think you should be too. My drinking is destructive; yours is disgusting.

Schuyler.

My job at *Time* was going well. One Thursday, I was summoned to the Managing Editor's office and heard the glad news that I was being given a raise—a whopping raise: $1,500 a year. That put my salary up to $6,000. It was all I could do to keep from calling up Julie and telling her, but I saved the good news till I got home that night.

"Why, we're rich!" she said.

"Well—*rich.*"

We really were quite well off. On my twenty-first birthday my parents had given me stock which paid dividends amounting now to almost $7,000 a year, and now I was earning nearly as much again. Julie and I sat up late discussing what we might do with my raise.

I never understood why, except that *Time* had its favorites and just then I was one of them, but six months later I got another raise—this time $1,000. Meantime the stock my family had given me was split, two shares for one, and the dividends doubled. All of a sudden my income had shot up to nearly $21,000 a year. This was really too much. I was quite convinced that no man on earth was worth a salary of more than $10,000, and I was getting within shooting distance of that figure. And besides my pay I had an unearned income of nearly $14,000.

We didn't need all this money. We owned our house in Princeton: it had been a gift from my parents, so there was no mortgage to pay off. All our small sons had been given stock by their grandparents which would pretty well pay for their schooling. We had a nursemaid who slept in, a cook who came in by the day and a cleaning woman twice a week. We didn't belong to the country club, but none of our friends in Princeton could afford to, so we didn't care. We had a car and didn't want another.

There was nothing more we needed. So the latest windfall was really embarrassing.

It was Julie who put the idea in my mind.

"Why not give it away?"

I thought she meant, give it to the Church. I didn't want to give it to the Church. Then I thought: Schuyler!

"What about the Jacksons?"

"They wouldn't take it."

"Why not? We're *friends.* We've got more than we need, they haven't got enough. Simple as that."

Julie didn't seem to agree that it was quite that simple. And I could tell she wasn't very enthusiastic about the idea. But she admitted that we didn't need the money, and she didn't actually object to my giving some to Schuyler and Kit—if they'd take it. By the time I had won her around, or thought I had, I'd convinced myself that sharing this surplus money with the Jacksons was the only possible solution, and the most natural thing in the world. I was sure they'd see it that way too.

On the way over to their farm some of my conviction began to trickle out of the heels of my boots. Julie had said it would be better if I went alone, but I wished now she had come with me. I went over my sales talk and couldn't see anything wrong with it; just the same, I could imagine Schuyler balking. It depended on what mood he was in: if I caught him at the right time I was sure I could persuade him.

I hadn't started till after dinner, and by the time I got to the farm it was nearly nine, and dark. But there was a light in the living room. Schuyler was reading and Kit was knitting. Schuyler seemed glad to see me but surprised I had come at that late hour, and without Julie. I explained that she hadn't wanted to leave the children.

We sat down, and Schuyler looked at me. He didn't offer me a drink, so I guessed there was nothing in the house, or else he was in one of his puritanical moods. Maybe both. That wasn't going to make things any easier.

187

"Well, I've got some news," I said, trying to sound offhand and hearty. And I told them about the raise. They thought that was fine but I could tell by the way they said it that they were wondering why I had come 20 miles just to tell them that. After I'd told them, there was a silence, tenser than it should have been. I could see that Schuyler was in a mood, all right; he wasn't going to help me at all. He sat there like a wall, and I had to get over it. I was sure now I'd make a mess of it, but I started scrambling.

It was a hell of a poor sales talk, I admit, but I finally got it all said. I remember using the phrase "spoiling the Egyptians"—and I was trying to make Schuyler see that "these people" were paying me more than I wanted or needed, and what could be more sensible (and satisfactory: that's where the Egyptians came in) than sharing the extra with him? He never said a word until I'd got it all out, but he stopped looking at me and just stared at the floor, with a tight mouth.

After I'd finished nobody said anything. Kit went on knitting, without looking up. Schuyler sucked his pipe, took it out of his mouth—I thought he was about to speak—then put it back again. He stood up, and walked up and down the room. He was frowning. He went over to the door and turned with his hand on the knob. In a high, light, unnatural voice he said,

"Don't forget to say good night to your hostess, Tom," and went out, closing the door behind him.

The only sound was the clacking of Kit's knitting needles. I sat there feeling like a condemned man, on whom an unjust but unalterable sentence had just been passed. At the same time I felt guilty. Why? What had I done? Something apparently unforgivable, that was evident. Schuyler was offended. But there was something more. Why had he said that I wasn't to forget to say good night to Kit? What did he mean?

The silence in the room was uncomfortable, embarrassing, finally unbearable. I waited, hoping Schuyler would come back, but it became obvious that he was not coming back. I looked questioningly at Kit, and she shook her head; she knew him. So I got up and said: "Well, I'm sorry."

There didn't seem to be anything more to do. I said good night to Kit and left. As I walked to my car, there was no sign of Schuyler.

3

Schuyler's feelings about Kit seemed to me a strange mixture of contempt and reverence; but it was clear that he was getting tired of her. In fact, it couldn't have been very long after that scene at the farm when he told me he was going to leave her. And for whom!

"You wouldn't know her."

"Well, what's her name?"

"Maribel Vinson."

I didn't know her but I'd heard of her: there had recently been a piece about her in *Life*, so I also knew what she looked like: a sulky-looking girl with a small snaky head.

She spent hours of every day on skates; she was a figure-skater, practically a professional, and had just won the national figure-skating championship. Schuyler had met her on a transatlantic crossing when he went to England to see Mrs. Doughty. Apparently he had been seeing a lot of her since then. And he was sure he was in love with her and she with him.

I was dismayed. In spite of all the quarrels, the hand-to-mouth life and the threat of poverty in their household, I still regarded Schuyler and Kit as an ideal couple; their break-up would have affected me like the parting of married gods.

Julie was just as concerned as I was.

"I just can't believe it."

"Oh, I don't *believe* it, either. He's infatuated and she's—"

"What?"

"How do *I* know? Tired of her racket. Or getting a kick out of being the Other Woman."

And perhaps, though Schuyler would never have agreed to those crude terms, that was about it. Julie and I didn't believe for a minute that either of them was being swept away by a grand passion; more likely they were desperately bored and looking for excitement. In any case, we agreed that something should be done about it, if possible. Besides the prospect of Kit being left high and dry, there were the children to consider.

Julie's first impulse was to tell Schuyler that he simply couldn't be so completely selfish and cruel, but I was sure that wouldn't work: he would only get angry and harden his heart. Especially if it was Julie who attacked him. I thought if I could get Schuyler to go away with me for ten days I might be able to talk him out of his crazy resolve, or that perhaps he would talk himself out of it. When I suggested this to him I put it in rather different terms, giving as my main reason the alarming speed with which time was passing and my fear that we were growing apart. He grudgingly consented, as if he were doing me a final favor. My managing editor was equally reluctant to give me a leave of absence on such apparently flimsy grounds—at first I told him I was getting stale and needed a change of air—but he was a kind man, and when I took the risk of confessing to him the real reason why I thought the trip was necessary, he let me go.

Neither Julie nor Kit could be left without a car, and my father had two, so I borrowed one of his. We headed south. My father owned a house in the mountains of North Carolina which was empty at this time of year (it was nearly winter); the caretaker would open it for us, and it was the only place I could think of where we could be alone and quiet. We drove for two days. Schuyler was in a difficult mood; he criticized my driving, talked incessantly about Kit (contemptuously) and the other girl (sentimentally), and showed no gratitude whatever for my having dropped everything and come away with him.

Looking back on it, it seems to me that that trip with Schuyler was ten days of unrelieved encircling gloom; but of course it couldn't have been as bad as that. It must have had a few bright intervals. We were still friends, even if our friendship was getting badly strained, and we had a great many memories and tastes in common. One bright interval I do remember was our collection of Burma Shave signs. These particular roadside advertisements have now been crowded out by bigger and worse billboards, or perhaps the company has gone out of business; but in those days they were a cheerful feature of the motoring landscape.

A Burma Shave ad was a series of low signboards—four or five, as I remember—set far enough apart so they could be read comfortably from a speeding car; each one carried a line printed in capital letters, and the lines rhymed. Their quality varied considerably, and it was Schuyler's theory that you could always tell which of them were written by "the Master" and which were turned out by hired hands. We were sure that the ones we liked were the Master's work:

> Grandpa's beard
>> Was stiff and coarse
>>> That's what caused
>>>> His fifth divorce

> If you wonder why
>> She doesn't like your bristles
>>> Try walking barefoot
>>>> Through a field of thistles

> He had a car
>> And no b.o.
>>> She felt his chin
>>>> And let him go.

But on the whole our time together was a constant strain, and I got small pleasure from it. I was determined to keep my mouth shut as much as possible, in the hope that Schuyler would do the talking and finally talk himself around. If I saw an opportu-

191

nity to put in a word for Kit or for the necessity of keeping his family together, I would say something, but not otherwise. As it turned out, I hardly got a word in: the resentments that Schuyler had built up were astonishingly bitter and widespread. Before the trip was over I came in for my share of criticism; he up-braided me for meting out a mingy ten days and no more, and when I showed signs of being homesick for Julie, chided me for my selfishness. When I dropped him at the farm and joyfully headed home, his goodbye had no hint of thanks in it. I thought my attempt to preserve his marriage was a complete failure; but it may have had some effect after all. At any rate he didn't leave Kit for the figure-skater, and their patched-up marriage lasted another year.

And Kit's feelings about Schuyler? I think she loved him—whatever meanings are clouded in that word "love." She knew him as a wife knows a husband, as he knew her; and I think she bore the knowledge more tranquilly than he did. Julie and I were married for twenty-four years, and the graph of our relations would have looked like a very active stock market. Yet I know that we ended by loving each other—although very differently from the way we had begun. If there is something touching or even tragic about young love, always fated and always ignorant of its fate, there is something more heartbreaking about the en-during love of a long-married couple who know what will hap-pen: that death will separate them although they are bound to-gether.

For years after I met her, I never thought of Kit as a person in her own right. She was Schuyler's wife, and that, in my eyes, was her entire and sufficient role as a human being. To be his wife and the mother of his four children was, it seemed to me, her whole life.

She was not femininely pretty, like Julie, nor obviously desir-able, like Jo. She was rangy and raw-boned, with large hands and feet, a big nose, rather prominent front teeth and not quite enough chin. She had fine, brandy-colored eyes. Her voice, deep for a woman's, was hoarse and, in anger, strident: she had a hot temper. There was nothing dainty about her, though when she was dressed up she looked handsome. She could keep her mouth shut, but she was more apt to blurt out what she thought. When something amused her she would collapse into caws and squawks of laughter. I used to wonder that Schuyler, with his impatient way, should be so patient with her; though on the occasions when he was not, his roughness to her sometimes shocked me.

I suppose I thought of Kit, and might have described her, as a backwoods aristocrat—what the British would call "county." Yes, before I really got to know her I would have said that Kit was a lady; after we became friends I recognized her as that rarity among women, a gentleman. However anti-feminist or uncomplimentary this may sound, I mean it as high praise.

Julie, feminine to the marrow and far more perceptive than I, was quicker to fathom Kit's true quality, and they became friendly allies without my noticing it, although not the kind of intimate friends who had sought each other out. If it hadn't been for Schuyler and me, I question whether they would have been friends at all. As for me, I took Kit for granted as a necessary part of Schuyler's life about which I didn't have to concern myself.

I think the first time I really noticed her was on that uncomfortable evening at the Jackson's farm when I failed to persuade Schuyler to go shares on my salary. And then something Julie said when I was telling her what had happened.

"I think they're having a bad time."

"You mean they're hard up?"

"*No.* With each other."

She was right, of course. I'd never noticed it, or thought I hadn't. But now I remembered the harsh, almost brutal tone Schuyler sometimes used to Kit, and the way Kit, without answering back, would look at him with narrowed eyes and the corners of her mouth pulled down. She never quarreled with him if anyone else was present, but no doubt they had their scenes.

"I hate to think of it."

I knew my feeling was more superstitious than rational, but

I felt that the safety of our own marriage was somehow bound up with theirs. Julie's distress was simply over the threat to a settled family, and especially the future of the Jackson children.

Soon after I became an editor on *Time*, I found that my job would not fit itself into a regular commuter's schedule. As the week wore on I had to catch later and later trains home; and by Saturday, which was my longest day at the office, I often missed the last train and had to spend the night in town. This meant the expense of a hotel room or the mutual inconvenience of staying with friends, so eventually I rented the smallest possible apartment in a brownstone house in the East 30s, not far from the boardinghouse in which I had begun my life in New York. Julie furnished my one and a half rooms (bedroom, tiny bathroom with shower, and an even tinier kitchenette which I never used) with second-hand furniture, and for the next few years I spent at least one night a week there.

The house had seen better days, when it was occupied by a single family. My landlady, its present owner, shared the faded gentility of her property. She was a widow of more than middle age who looked as if she had always been a spinster. Her face was careworn and defeated; on the rare occasions when we met she always wore the same long black, high-necked dress, with a double string of beads round her neck like a badge of office. She lived in rooms on the ground floor. I ended by becoming her favorite tenant, for the simple reason that I paid my rent promptly, always had my latchkey, didn't smoke in bed, and never bothered her with what she regarded as unreasonable requests. When at last I gave her notice that I was ending my tenancy she flattered me by suggesting that I buy the house!

She ran her establishment with the help of an old Irishman named Pat, who was supposed to make the beds and clean the rooms. Often the only sign that he had been there was a filthy dustcloth abandoned in the unmade bed, or a mop leaning against the wall. If I ever succeeded in cornering him, and pointed out such shortcomings, he wouldn't deny that he had scamped that particular chore but he had an overall defense.

194

"Ah, wud you believe it, Mr. Matches, I been workin' like a mad thing since dawn. Since *dawn!*"

Once in a long time Julie would share my night in town, and then it was a delight to trudge up the three flights of stairs and find her asleep in my bed, which was just big enough for two. But these comforting visits were infrequent, and in a week when I had to stay two nights in town I felt as lonely as a widower.

I was in charge of a "cover story" that week at *Time:* a big Art story that was coming very slowly. As midwife, there was really nothing I could do at this point: it was now up to the writer to produce the copy; but by the rules of the game I was supposed to be on call. One foggy Saturday in November I was facing the prospect of two such evenings, and feeling sorry for myself. The phone rang. It was Kit. She had come to town to do some shopping and was staying overnight. When I asked "Where?" and she said, "The Murray Hill," we both laughed.

I agreed to meet Kit in the lobby of the Murray Hill at seven-thirty. Just before I left the office I looked in on the travailing writer. He glared at me, a terrible look of mingled agony, appeal and accusation. His hair was over his eyes, his cubbyhole office was foul with cigarette smoke, but his hands were poised over the keyboard of his typewriter. I gave him a cheery wave and softly closed the door. A moment later I heard his typewriter clacking. He was coming along nicely. All I had to do now was to leave him alone in his torment—and clear up the inevitable mess in the morning. But I was as full of confidence in my ability to do that as any young second-year intern.

Kit looked very handsome and aristocratic, also countrified: she was wearing a round fur hat, an unstylishly long overcoat, and galoshes. We went into the dimly lit bar, an 1890 version of an Oriental seraglio. The Murray Hill was then the most old-fashioned hotel in New York—so old-fashioned that it had a distinction all its own. Its style was Victorian-Moorish, with a fountain in the lobby, and the dining room full of enormous pots of ferns and noisy canaries in big cages. The hotel was soon to be demolished to make way for something bigger and more up to date; so

it was already regarded as "historic" as well as endearingly quaint
—and it was cheap, as New York hotels went.

It was a wonderful evening. It seemed to me we never
stopped laughing, we always had a drink in our hands, and we
were always going on to some spur-of-the-moment place that
turned out to be a temporary but huge success. Kit wanted to go
dancing: I can't remember where we went, only that the room
was rather dark and had a low ceiling and a crashing band with
just the right kind of compelling beat. We had a late dinner at
an Italian restaurant: lashings of spaghetti and a bottle of Chianti,
then a half-bottle. I noticed that Kit was still wearing her
galoshes: she must have danced in them! That made us laugh
some more; everything that evening made us laugh.

After dinner we walked; we were so full of high spirits we
must have walked for miles. Kit said she had never ridden on the
"El," so we walked to the nearest station on Ninth Avenue and
clambered up the rickety stairs. When the train came along,
everyone aboard seemed to have been on a party; they were all
singing. The cars were crowded, so we stood arm-in-arm on the
windy platform, and we sang too, all the songs we could remember. We rode all the way to the Battery, where I expected the
train would head north again, but we were told that was the last
stop: we had been on the final run of the Ninth Avenue El. It was
a long walk from the Battery to 42nd Street, but there wasn't a
taxi in sight and by that time the buses had stopped running; it
never occurred to us to take the subway, we didn't want to go
underground. So we walked. By the time we reached the Murray
Hill it was beginning to get light, and we were sober but still
exhilarated.

The Murray Hill was shut. I rang the bell for the night watch-
man but he must have been asleep; nobody came to the door.

Kit said, "Damn! What am I going to do?"

"You'd better come to my place."

It was nearly four o'clock. Kit said she wanted to get into the
Murray Hill when it opened, and we guessed that would be about
seven-thirty. I was due at the office around ten. There wasn't

much left of the night. When we got to my brownstone and were climbing softly up the stairs, I wondered what my landlady would think of her star tenant if she heard us and opened her door. The evening no longer seemed quite so innocent.

In my room, Kit and I had a whispered argument about who should have the bed. I insisted that she should, and she gave in. She took off her galoshes—that was all she took off—and lay down. I put a blanket over her, and she seemed to fall asleep instantly. I arranged myself as well as I could in the only arm-chair. But I couldn't sleep. I tried not to look at Kit. She lay with her back towards me, so I couldn't see whether her eyes were open; she never moved.

At last my watch said 7:15, so I woke her. We tiptoed down the stairs. No sign of the landlady. The Murray Hill's doors were open. I kissed Kit goodbye, on the cheek. We both said it had been a wonderful evening. We said "evening," not "night."

But when I next saw Schuyler, I took good care to relate all the events of what I called Kit's and my "white night." I tried to make it as uproarious a story as it had been in fact, but for some reason it didn't sound uproarious, and obviously it didn't amuse him. Julie, when I made my report to her, only said, "Goodness, you did stay up late"—and then changed the subject.

As for Kit, things between us were never quite the same again. I no longer thought of her only as Schuyler's wife, or as a friend I was fond of: I thought of her as a woman I had seen lying on my bed.

YEAR OF THE BIG WIND

1

Would Laura and Robert have come to America in 1939 if I hadn't put the idea into their heads—if I hadn't urged them? I'm afraid the answer must be: No, probably not. I wanted Laura to meet Schuyler; I tried to bring about their meeting. In Deya I had talked to them often about Schuyler; again and again I had said to Laura: "Schuyler is the one who should be here, not me." Her only response then, as far as I can remember, was a cryptic silence.

If it hadn't been for me . . . Without meaning to, I made the match; I was the principal pimp.

I had suggested several times that Laura and Robert should come to America for a visit. Early in 1939 they wrote that they had decided to come; could we find them a place to stay? The Jacksons and ourselves scoured the countryside—it was understood that the house must be in our joint neighborhood. In several weeks' search we found nothing that would do. Then Schuyler had an idea. On his farm stood the ruin of an eighteenth-century farmhouse; why not rebuild it? It would be quite a job, as nothing remained but a stone shell; the builder's estimate for the reconstruction was $25,000. I took out a note at the bank for that amount and Schuyler and the builder between them drew up the plans.

How was I to get my money back—or would I? Well, the scheme was that Schuyler or Laura or somebody would pay me $50 a month rent until the whole amount was repaid. I didn't stop to consider that this would take more than forty years! Schuyler pointed out that the house would outlast our time and could always be rented. As it turned out, I recovered less than $200 from my "investment."

As the date of their arrival drew near, it was obvious that the house would not be ready in time, so we arranged that Laura and Robert would stay with us in Princeton and the rest of the party —David Reeves, Alan and Beryl Hodge—would be put up in a boardinghouse nearby; later they would all move to the Jacksons' farm. It was a tight fit: we had one spare room, which of course Laura got, and we put a cot for Robert in my study.

Rack my memory as I may, I cannot recall the great day of their arrival, or any of the circumstances of our meeting. I think I drove alone to New York to fetch them. And I think Laura and Robert came ahead of the other three, for I remember being in New York later with Robert and going with him into a bar near the docks. Was it St. Patrick's Day? Anyhow, there must have been some sort of parade in New York that day, for there was a soldier at the bar in the uniform of some Scottish regiment which Robert immediately recognized.

"If you want to start a fight," he said, "just go and stand near him and order a half-pint of broken squares."

"Why?"

"He'd have his belt off in a minute."

"? ? ?"

"Those are fighting words to any man in that regiment. The Gordon Highlanders [if that was the regiment] had one of their squares broken at Omdurman, and they don't like to be reminded of it."

The three we were meeting were David Reeves and Alan and Beryl Hodge. Beryl looked like a small, thin cat or a baby mouse. They didn't seem nearly old enough to be married. David Reeves, who looked to be in his late twenties, had a plump, round face, dark eyebrows and hair, and wore glasses: he had a pouting, semi-frowning, self-satisfied expression.

We found their British complacency, but especially David's, rather hard to take. Their birdlike cries to each other, expressing scornful comparison or—much more rarely—a shocked surprise

202

were suffered in silence by me, but not always by Julie.

"O look, David, it's a proper beech!"

"Well, not *really.*"

Robert didn't seem to mind having to sleep on a cot in my study. The first thing he did was to inspect my book shelves, after which he said to me severely,

"You have some very dirty books there."

It turned out that he meant my half-dozen copies of D. H. Lawrence—which didn't include *Lady Chatterley's Lover.* This Lawrence, but not the other, stood high on Laura and Robert's lengthy black list of bad and harmful writers.

It was decided (and the decision must have been Laura's) that the appropriate time to meet the Jacksons was the day after she and Robert arrived, when they had had a night's sleep to repair the effects of their journey, and that the appropriate place would be the Jacksons' farm. We drove over the next day. It was sunny and pleasantly warm, and Kit had made a picnic lunch which we had outdoors, sitting in chairs and on rugs on the ragged lawn.

That first meeting was tense with subdued response. It wasn't so much that they all took to each other on sight (they had done that already, sight unseen) as that everyone was intent on engaging gears smoothly. Laura took charge right away, and Schuyler seemed to accept that: he said very little but his lowered eyelids and continual slight smile looked receptive. Kit was friendly and open, as she was with everybody except the few people who put her teeth on edge. I wished Laura would stop calling her "Katharine"; it sounded all wrong: it was like putting a stiff, unbecoming hat on Kit and made Laura seem governessy. Robert gamboled awkwardly about Laura, like a benignant bear, on the watch for something to fetch or carry, and getting the kind of reward from Laura he often did: "Robert, stop *fussing!*"

Presently Laura made an announcement, almost a sort of speech. This was when we heard about the Second Protocol. Besides the Dictionary, she said, which was a daily task that concerned only herself and Robert and their assistants, there would be other work to do in which we would all have a hand; and it was this work which had been the primary cause for their coming to America. The First Protocol, to which we had all (except Schuyler) subscribed, declared our solidarity as "inside" people and our general purposes. This new Protocol would be more specific: it would be in effect a program for "inside" action —a program and at the same time an instrument. We all knew, as the so-called leaders of the outside world did not know, how helpless they were to prevent the war that everyone but themselves and their "expert" advisers could see was impending and which no "outside" effort could much longer possibly prevent. The only hope of averting this war lay in the force of our concerted behavior and effort as "inside" people. This, then, would be the purpose of the Second Protocol: by declaring ourselves with effective intensity, to save the world from war.

Quite an assignment! But in Laura's Alexandrian empire all assignments were worldwide.

The next weeks were one of the most disagreeable periods in my life. I think several of the others involved would say the same. At first everything went well, if a little self-consciously: Laura and Robert and the Jacksons immediately hit it off, everyone first-named everyone else, and Julie and I felt that very soon now we could relax from the anxious feeling that afflicts hosts at the start of a party.

But we couldn't and didn't relax—on the contrary. In the first weeks after Laura's arrival most of the meetings were held at our house in Princeton. I had arranged to take a couple of weeks of my vacation then, so I was able to be there the whole time. Laura kept us all busy: running errands, writing letters, protecting her privacy, rearranging our daily lives to conform to her pattern. There was no time for tennis or the movies or seeing our friends, or any such nonsense. In theory we were all engaged in working out the Second Protocol. Work on the Dictionary had been temporarily sidetracked for this urgent matter. I remember seemingly interminable meetings, in our living room and at the Jacksons' farm, when we sat around the sides of the room in a brooding circle, trying to discuss—or keeping silent: and the silences were the worst. They not only weighed more than they should have but they stopped the clock.

While these sessions were going on in our house, once or twice some innocent friend of ours would drop in, and be met with such stony stares and monosyllabic replies that he would soon leave in a hurry. I was ashamed of allowing friends to be treated so in my own house—but it was no longer my house, it was Laura's headquarters. Our visitors dwindled to none as word got about that something was going on at our house—something that felt like sitting up with a dead body. It was worse than that, really; we were waiting for the dead body to turn into something else.

When my two weeks' vacation was over, I got a daily respite from this continual strain, as I had to go to my job in New York, and I could temporarily forget the coiled and smoldering inquest at home. And there was the day when I went to town with twenty Picassos in the pocket of my coat.

They were genuine Picassos, small pen-and-ink sketches the size of a wedding invitation; some of them were on the backs of advertisement cards. They were handed to me by Laura, who told me that they really belonged to a friend, who had given them to Laura for safekeeping—and to sell, if she ever needed the money. Her instructions to me were to peddle them piecemeal in New York, to whatever gallery would give a good price. I knew no one in the art world except Alfred Barr, whom I used to see, when we were undergraduates, at tea at the Marquands, and who was now Director of the Museum of Modern Art.

When I showed the Picassos to him, Barr was not as impressed as I had hoped he would be. He strongly advised me not to sell the sketches separately but as one package, and politely regretted the fact that his Museum had all the Picassos it wanted. I tried some other galleries, but with no better luck; and at the end of the day brought the Picassos back to Laura with considera-

ble relief: the responsibility of carrying such valuables in my
pocket all day had weighed on me. Whatever became of them—
whether Laura succeeded in selling them or eventually returned
them to their rightful owners—I never knew.

Every morning I left the house with alacrity, and came back
in the evening with dragging steps. I always dreaded to know
what had happened while I had been away. Usually it was nothing much, and that was the worst of it; whatever was happening
was taking a tormenting, fiendishly slow time to happen. *What
were we waiting for?* During one of these racking sessions, it
suddenly dawned on me that this long-drawn-out torture, which
had brought everything to a standstill and all of us to the tautness
of hysteria, was for a purpose: we were being put to the question,
and one of us must sooner or later break. I think we all knew that
the pressure was coming from Laura; but who would be the one
to go under?

In a stab of unreasoning fear I thought: it might be Julie!
Without stopping to think, I burst out: "If it's Julie you're after,
it's me as well, because we're together!" It must have been funny,
for they all laughed, and the tension was temporarily broken. But
soon it tightened down again.

The power and the weight of silence, especially the silence
of a group, grow as it grows. In the Society of Friends, they say,
the stillness hovers and soars until someone bursts out like a
happy bird above the clouds. We were supposed to be a society
of friends, but our silence, imposed and directed by Laura, took
us down, not up; we sank through sunless levels into a darkness
where we were each alone, isolated in the blind dark, hearing
only the thudding of the blood in our ears, straining to catch one
saving syllable of the silent and terrible colloquy through which
we continued slowly to sink.

If this attempt to describe the quality of that silence seems
hysterical, I cannot help it: the state of mind—but it was less and
more than that—induced by this ordeal verged on the hysterical.
I couldn't of course tell about the others, but as for me, I felt sure
that some sort of dialogue of the depths was taking place, like

monosyllabic stones sinking slowly past me. I began to feel more and more excluded, more and more laggard, more and more to blame.

It was stupid of me not to see which one of us would go under; but I don't think any of us was sure, until it happened. One evening we were all, or most of us, having dinner at our house. Kit leaned forward and laid her head on the table. If she was weeping, it was very quietly; but there was something dreadful, hopeless, defeated in her gesture. I think Schuyler and Laura took her back to the farm. It was the last I saw of her for months.

I had come to dread the weekends most, when for two full days there was no getting away from the situation. A late closing at *Time* had kept me in town for the night, and as I walked home from the station next morning I almost felt that nothing could wither this lovely spring day. No one was at home except Julie and David Reeves. They were waiting for me, to tell me what had happened. It was soon told, though it was a guarded report, as much of our conversation was in those portentous days: Kit had been taken to hospital; Laura was rearranging the farm. And "they wanted to see me." No one had to tell me that "they" no longer meant Laura and Robert; "they" were now Laura and Schuyler.

I drove over to the farm, alone. (David and Julie had been through whatever it was to which I had now been summoned, and were obviously in no hurry to go back for more.) I found the farm seething with activity and the kind of fussy bustle that Laura induced when she was directing household work; Robert, Alan and Beryl were running up and down stairs, carrying small pieces of furniture, calling to each other and asking Laura for instructions. It looked like a spring cleaning. The Jackson children were nowhere to be seen, neither was Schuyler. Laura summoned me to the study.

In the first three minutes, although I don't think that on that occasion she ever used the word "witch," I understood what it was she wanted me to agree to. She was telling me that "Katharine" was a witch, that she had been unmasked and her sorceries brought to nothing; that the house was now being purified of her cabalistic relics and of all her associations with it. There had been terrible scenes with Kit (which Laura described) before she had finally dropped her mask and confessed her evil practices. The others, who had also been witnesses of these scenes, were in perfect accord with Laura (Julie too? I doubted it very much). Was I? And would I now show my solidarity with the rest by doing my share of the purifying chores? Everything "she" had touched or might have used for her spells, all her private possessions were being burnt, destroyed or otherwise got rid of.

Laura, as usual, called Kit "Katharine," a name which no one else ever used. Perhaps it was this small thing, this ridiculously pompous misnomer, that saved me now. "Katharine" might have been—oh, anything Laura could conjure up; but Kit was Kit, someone I knew better than my own sisters. It was horrifying to hear this crazy charge solemnly leveled against her; horrifying, yes, but not in the slightest degree convincing. I suddenly realized who it was who had been casting the spell we had all been living under. I clung to the one thing I was certain of: that Laura was wrong about Kit, that Laura was wrong . . .

I don't know what answer I made to Laura, except that it was not the answer she wanted. And I refused to have anything to do with "purifying" the house. Above everything I wanted to get away, to go home and talk to Julie, to try to find an answer to these crazily whirling questions. Laura didn't want me to leave yet. I still hadn't seen Schuyler, and I didn't want to see him. In order to get away, I compromised—I am still ashamed of it: I agreed to take a little china figure that belonged to Kit, and get rid of it. (Later, when I told Kit about this, and apologized, she roared with laughter.) Well, I took it, and left. All the way home I felt worse and worse about throwing it away, but I had promised. On the last bridge before Princeton I stopped the car and flung the little china figure into the creek.

As soon as I talked to Julie I felt reassured of my sanity. Of course she didn't agree with Laura. Furthermore, we began to see now what had been going on: why all pretense at work on the Protocol had been stopped; why everything had come to a standstill and hung suspended by a tauter and tauter thread. Schuyler and Laura were falling in love. What a way to do it!—in front of our fascinated, wincing but unseeing eyes. I thought of two basilisks, motionless and staring, the rest of us like little lizards, waiting, immobilized into cramped stone until the predetermined affair was ready. The reason we had all had to wait so long was that Kit stood in their way.

Now Kit was out of the way, and there remained only Robert. He was more tractable, for he was still, as he had been for thirteen years, following orders. All the same, it must have seemed to him like being forced to connive at his own murder. Perhaps, if he hadn't had the sympathy and understanding of Beryl, he too might have been carried off to hospital. It was a near thing, I think. Some weeks later he went back to England alone. At the dockside in New York I went aboard the ship with him to see him off, and wondered if we would ever meet again: he was desperate and wretched, near the end of his tether.

2

Schuyler had supplanted Robert but he had not taken Robert's subordinate place: he was to be not Laura's servant but her equal, and the signs of this dual monarchy were soon evident to us all. The orders and manifestoes, written and verbal, no longer issued from Laura but from the two of them; I'm not sure that in the signatures Schuyler's name didn't precede hers. One odd incident of this time stands out in my memory: of taking a walk with Schuyler and receiving a pretty severe talking-to about my "loose attitude towards women." Neither of us apparently saw anything funny in Schuyler's preaching me a sermon on this subject while he was living with Laura.

And both Schuyler and Laura continued to grill me on the subject of Kit, like the balky witness I was. They returned to it again and again. In June Julie took our children to the seashore, and until I could join them for my vacation in August, I dutifully spent one night a week at the farm, being given the works by these stern interrogators. Sometimes Laura would take me on alone, sometimes both of them. In the first sessions I was asked to agree that Kit was "a witch" (the word was then brought out for the first time); later the indictment was changed to "wicked woman," finally softened merely to "bad woman." I don't think I could ever stand up against a real brainwashing, for these interrogations shook me, though I never quite gave in.

When Julie and I got back from the seashore in September we found ourselves in the unenviable position of being Schuyler and Laura's only remaining subjects. The work that had been done on the Dictionary so far—nearly three years' worth—was all scrapped. Schuyler had a different scheme for the book, and he and Laura had decided that they could dispense with drudges and would both function as equal poetic intelligences.

To these intense grownups, blinded by preoccupation with their own affairs, Griselda, the eldest of the Jackson children, was only partially and intermittently visible, but she watched them with a tireless eye. One of her vantage-points was the front stairway. There, half-hidden by the stair-rails and perfectly still, she witnessed the scene between Schuyler and me in which he "disowned" me (a scene my *amour-propre* has completely erased from my memory, though I don't doubt that it occurred).

Griselda had started a family magazine, *The Jackson's Quarterly,* and some of the surface events of that time, couched in her twelve-year-old language, appeared in its pages:

The old ruin across the road which is on Jackson's Farm has been rebuilt to a lovely little stone house in which shall live Miss Laura

Riding, Mr. Robert Graves, Mr. David Reeves, Mr. Allan Hodge and Mrs. Bearal Hodge. All famous writers from England.

Mrs. Jackson is in the hospital, sick, in Philadelphia.

Miss Riding's sister is here also.

Mr. Jackson is harvesting his soy bean.

Miss Laura Riding and Mr. Frank Baisden are new subscribers to this magazine.

Some of the English People had to leave the farm and return to fight in the war.

Children are realists who do not (until they learn to ape their elders) think in such grown-up concepts as *good* and *evil;* to their wide-open eyes their world is ruled by strength, which they fear and placate, and complicated by weakness, which they despise and share. How much did the children know of what was going on in that house? They must have seen a great deal more than they could take in or interpret. But how little we understand of the unuttered, unutterable complications inside children's heads! Twelve-year-old Griselda saw and felt more than the others: she could feel wrongness in the house, like bad air that everyone had to breathe—a wrongness not concentrated in Laura but surrounding her.

The climax came one night when the whole household was at dinner, Laura at the head of the table. Kit got up and announced that she was going for a walk and taking the children with her. Laura said that Robert would go along too. Kit flared up: they were her children and she would not have Robert with her, or anyone. And off they went down the marshy path to Nimrod's Rise and the woods beyond. Robert came running along after them; Kit screamed at him to go back. Laura dispatched other messenger-guardians—David, Beryl, finally Schuyler. Just before Schuyler appeared Griselda had been quizzing her mother: "Something is wrong with you. What's the matter with you?" and Kit had persisted in denying that anything was wrong. Griselda kept after her, plaguing her for the answer. Kit lost the last of her control; as Schuyler came racing up she had Griselda by the throat.

When Kit had been taken off to hospital, Laura immediately took over the running of the household. At first she slept in the guest room and had her breakfast in bed, a custom not unknown in that house, but Laura's usurpation of the practice was deeply resented by Griselda. One morning, told by Laura to let the cook know that she was ready for breakfast, Griselda stood at the far end of the dining room and yelled: "Laura wants her breakfast!" The next moment, like a quick slap in the face, Laura was out of bed and hissing at Griselda: "Never call me 'Laura' to the servants!"

Did Schuyler himself feel remorse for what he had done? Had he no qualms about leaving his wife and children for Laura? I think he must have had more than one bad hour before abandoning them. There is one piece of evidence to back up this probability: a poem he wrote and left at the farm; Griselda found it among his papers there and sent me a copy:

DISCORD

All this day my youth has fallen from me
Until suddenly I am old, and yet not old;
But rot away in the full strength of my flesh,
Poisoning beauty like a worm in a nut.

I have dreamed beauty, and beauty has failed me.
Friends, and the one or two whom I love,
Infected with my mind, have failed me.
All these, with the mind that poisons, fail me.

Shall the heart perish because it has loved flowers?
And die of unrest until it shall find flowers?
And poison these flowers with its own death?
My heart has done this, God save my soul.

Am I reading too much into this if I say that it sounds like the final broken bubble of despair from a drowning man? No, not final, for it took him nearly thirty more years to drown.

When Kit was taken to hospital for the first time she stayed there only a few weeks. (It would be twenty years before she recovered completely, and in that time she outwitted almost all her doctors. She soon persuaded her first one that she was well enough to go home and would be better off there.) When the news reached the farm that she was returning, Laura made the children tidy up the lawn, under Robert's direction, to a ridiculously immaculate degree. Why? To show the children how much less than tidy their mother's state was? To tire them out, so that their tension should not add to the travail of the occasion? Laura always had her reasons, however far she fetched them. When Kit arrived, looking ghastly and obviously far from well, there were strained greetings and a few stilted exchanges. Soon the children were sent to their rooms and Kit, after a horrible struggle, was taken back to hospital in a straitjacket. From her third-floor window Griselda watched the scene.

That summer saw a great shakeout and shifting of the farm's inhabitants. Robert was the first to go. Then David Reeves went off with Robin Hale, a handsome creature who couldn't seem to make up her mind whether to be a boy or a girl; she was a member of the Forbes-Robertson clan, the famous family of actors. She and David eventually returned to England, where they married, divorced and remarried other partners. Alan and Beryl also went back to England, but their odd little music-box marriage, which looked like Babes in Toyland, had ceased to tinkle, and they separated.

3

I remember going to the hospital with Julie to see Kit, some weeks after she had been committed. It was in Philadelphia—not in the city itself but somewhere in its voluminous outskirts. And I remember that the building looked polished and expensive, more like a hotel than a hospital. Kit had been under "shock treatment," not electric shock but insulin, and seemed lethargic, quiet and not much interested in anything. She made no reference to Laura or to anything that had happened to her. Her face was terribly changed, I suppose on account of the insulin: she had great black circles under her eyes, almost like two black eyes, and her face was puffy. She looked completely unlike herself. She had said once, with a caw of laughter, that her brother Jimmy had said she was getting to be "an old farm crow." The Kit we knew was lively and sharp-faced, almost haggard, not this morose, fat-cheeked stranger.

When she went back to the hospital she was given another shock treatment (this time electric shock) and I remember talking to her doctor about the probable result. He told me that shock treatment was administered only as a last resort, when medical art had to acknowledge defeat; and that a cure, or some improvement, could be claimed only in a very small percentage of cases. In short, a desperate remedy, a gamble that rarely paid off, and never more than the return of your stake money. To my own skeptical, layman's view, shock treatment was no different from the eighteenth-century inquisition of the insane, when mad people in Bedlam were beaten or plunged into icy baths. I knew two other people besides Kit who were subjected to this barbarous torture, and I regarded all of them as survivors—but survivors whose minds ever after bore the scars of their punishment.

In Kit's case, the scar seemed to blot out or distort all memory of what had happened to her in her last weeks at the farm.
More than that, her feelings about Laura, far from being resent-
ful or hurt, were affectionate and admiring, not to say worshipful.
She revered Laura with the same fervor as Robert's in the days
of his humble discipleship. She either could not remember or
angrily brushed aside all evidence that Laura's presence had
contributed to her collapse. Of Schuyler, Laura's partner in this
attempt, she spoke with a disdain almost impersonal; but of
Laura herself as of someone unique, extraordinary, more than
human.

Laura continued to govern the household at the Jackson
farm fussily and by fits and starts. As always, her life was brim-full
—with affairs of state as well as with domestic duties: the Dictionary, her correspondence, and us. For the everyday chores of
housekeeping and child-minding she needed assistants. The first
of them was her younger sister Isabel, whom she summoned from
California, where she had a husband and children of her own.
Isabel looked remarkably like Laura, though her expression was
open and cheerful and her nature warm. She was not at all an
intellectual, like Laura, just a nice woman.

But she was only a temporary stand-in; after a few weeks the
demands of her family called her home. Then the Jackson children were packed off to their grandmother in Cooperstown till
the end of August. By that time Laura had summoned up two
more obedient spirits, old retainers from Deya days: an English
couple named Dorothy and Montague Simmons. Montague ran
an "approved school" (Americans would call it "a state school for
delinquent boys") near London, and Dorothy was a sculptor who
had been under Laura's tutelage. In the autumn Montague had
to get back to his school, but Dorothy stayed at the farm all
winter, to everyone's relief.

The volcanic explosion, which blew apart Kit and Robert
and the Dictionary and its drudges, and the Second Protocol
(thus removing the last bastion against the now inevitable Second

World War) had erupted in the early summer of 1939. For the rest of that year Schuyler and Laura held court at the farm. Since Nimrod's Rise had been intended for Robert and herself, and since Robert was no longer there, Laura now regarded the house as her property. Since I had contributed the $25,000 it cost and had got back less than $200 in rent, it was quite a bargain. The house was later sold, I think separately from the rest of the property. I hope Kit got the money, but I was never told.

The following year, 1940, Kit was enjoying such a lucid interval of health that she came back to the farm. Her younger brother Jimmy came with her and kept her company for nearly a year. Jimmy, earthy scion of an earthy family, made short work of both Gurdjieff and Laura, dismissing the first with the contemptuous pronunciation "*Gore*jeef!" and always referring to Laura with a mocking phrase.

4

The first book Robert wrote after his lonely return to England in 1939 was *The Long Weekend,* with Alan Hodge: a social and cultural history of England between the two world wars. It was a useful, unpretentious and competently written report—more journalism than history, but the kind of journalism that future historians will have to read and that a small section of the contemporary public finds entertaining. I was a reader with a particular interest; I searched it for a mention of Laura, and found this:

It was in 1927 that Laura Riding, a young American who had recently come to Europe, first published her poems and critical work in England. Wiping her slate clean of literary and domestic affiliations with America, she became for the next twelve years the best of "good Europeans"; the Americans only knew her as "the highest apple on the British intellectual tree." . . . None of her books sold more than a few dozen copies, nor did she ever . . . consent to give the larger public what it really wanted. She was the one poet of the time who spun, like Arachne, from her own vitals without any discoverable philosophical or literary derivations: and the only one who achieved an unshakable synthesis. Unshakable, that is, if the premise of her unique personal authority were granted, and another more startling one—that historic Time had effectively come to an end. . . .

The literary *avant-gardistes* could do nothing with her: she was interested in value, not in post-temporal fashion, she had a better head than any of them and a better heart than most, she was accessible but not clubbable, and she resented the constant unacknowledged borrowing from her work by the ambitious and the insincere. This made everyone uncomfortable: they would have liked to make a Great Woman of her, but to do so would have meant changing their own unsynthesized habits. They did their best to ignore her. Laura Riding was remarkable as being in the period but not of the period, and the only woman who spoke with authority in the name of Woman (as so many men in the name of Man) without either deference to the male tradition or feministic equalitarianism: a perfect original. At the very end of the period she returned to the United States, surprisingly rediscovered her American self, and wiped the slate clean again.

I thought these parting respects mighty civil and handsome. No hint here that she and Robert had lived together for nearly thirteen years as lovers, as master and pupil. He spoke of her with respectful gratitude as if she were one of the great dead with whom it had been his good fortune to be slightly acquainted. And for some time after their parting I think this was how he felt about her; his resentment was almost completely concentrated on Schuyler.

It may seem odd that Robert's collaborator on *The Long Weekend* was Alan Hodge, since by that time Robert was living with Alan's wife, Beryl. Not only the three people chiefly concerned but apparently their close friends, such as Norman Cameron and John and Lucie Aldridge, seemed to accept this change of partners as perfectly natural and nothing to make a fuss about.

In America, where there was still a widespread belief in the sanctity of divorce, Schuyler and Laura raised no objections to

Kit's divorcing Schuyler—mainly, it appeared, because they wanted to get married themselves! In New York, where they lived for some months after leaving the farm, in a walk-up flat in a brownstone house on the West Side, a card beside the doorbell gave the false information that "Mr. and Mrs. Jackson" lived there. Why these two absolutists found it expedient to shelter behind such a pretense is one of those heartening questions that demand an answer unflattering to mankind.

I remember those divorce proceedings, because I took part in them, as a witness for Kit. The only other witness present was Haven Page, whose friendship with Schuyler antedated mine: they had been schoolmates at Pomfret. The case was heard in Doylestown, in the judge's chambers at the Court House. It would have been much worse if we had had to testify in open court, before the eyes and ears of all those officials and perhaps of some gawping sightseers. The judge and his clerk were as discreet and brief as could have been expected, and the ugly ceremony was soon over.

While the suit was still in process Laura wrote one of her massive manifestoes to Kit. Griselda, although she was then only fourteen, had power of attorney for her mother; she intercepted the letter and read it. She had not lost her fear of Laura—she never altogether lost it—and she felt Laura's power in this letter, which she thought, as it was written in the knowledge that Kit was already ill, was "beyond anything one could describe." She showed the letter to Paula Chapin, a neighbor and old friend of the family, and it made her literally sick at her stomach. "Imagine the doughty Paula rushing to vomit. I then took it to Ma's doctor, who could not get over it, and Ma read it in his and my presence—and laughed."

Robert must have brought out half a dozen different editions of his *Collected Poems* (I have four of them); he was always changing his mind about which poems should be included, and tending to favor the latest. In the Foreword to the 1938 edition he had written:

In 1925 I first became acquainted with the poems and critical work of Laura Riding, and in 1926 with herself; and slowly began to revise my whole attitude to poetry. (The change begins half-way through Part II.)

That the proportion of what would be called "unpleasant poems" is so high in this twenty-three-year sequence surprised me on first looking it over. But I see this now not as a furious reaction against the anodynic tradition of poetry in which I was educated but as the blurted confession of a naturally sanguine temperament: that the age into which I was born, in spite of its enjoyable lavishness of entertainment, has been intellectually and morally in perfect confusion. . . . I should say that my health as a poet lies in my mistrust of the comfortable point-of-rest. Certainly, this suspicious habit, this dwelling upon discomfort and terror, has brought me good luck: for in the midst of my obstinate stumblings there have come sudden flashes of grace and knowledge—

> As to the common brute it falls
> To see real miracles
> And howl with irksome joy.

I have to thank Laura Riding for her constructive and detailed criticism of my poems in various stages of composition—a generosity from which so many contemporary poets besides myself have benefited.

And on page 179 a poem appears, beginning:

TO WHOM ELSE?

> To whom else other than,
> To whom else not of man
> Yet in human state,
> Standing neither in stead
> Of self nor idle godhead,
> Should I, man in man bounded,
> Myself dedicate?

This poem was never reprinted. And in the revised edition (1957) of *Goodbye to All That,* every mention of Laura was expunged.

Julie and I were beginning to grow restive; we were getting tired of having to read grandiose, inflated pronunciamentos, like much-too-frequent speeches from the throne, of equally lengthy telephone conferences and peremptory summonses to meetings. We wished we didn't take up so much of their time. And, since we were the only privates left in the army, the drill and the discipline became more and more onerous.

The way things were going, sooner or later we were bound to give offense, and sure enough we did. One fine day a lengthy letter from Laura took us severely to task for daring to call ourselves their *friends;* this was inadmissible talk from disciples, who should be more respectful. With a sigh of relief I wrote out our letter of resignation—and made sure that it would be accepted by respectfully pointing out that Laura was wrong (she had tried to make out that our relationship with her had never been more than a kind of casual, tea-table acquaintance; and I quoted her a passage from one of her own letters that amply disproved this nonsense).

There followed a telephone call from Schuyler, who seemed anxious not to lose us and wanted further negotiations. I said, No, we'd had enough; more than enough. Nevertheless he came to Princeton to see us, and to tell us that as far as he was concerned there had been no quarrel. Laura came with him but didn't get out of the car. My last sight of her was her Hittite profile, dimly seen behind the car window, staring grimly straight ahead.

When Julie and I realized that we were safely excommunicated, that we were free, we shouted with laughter, and hugged each other.

WHERE TRUTH BEGINS

1

In spite of Laura's contempt for marriage, she married Schuyler after Kit divorced him, and became plain Mrs. Schuyler Jackson. Laura Riding disappeared. The little news I ever heard of them was roundabout, second-hand, almost rumor. Apparently they still went on working at the Dictionary, though the publisher had long since cut his losses and canceled the contract. Schuyler had nearly run down as a writer years before; but I found it hard to believe that Laura had ended her career so abruptly. Was she still writing but unable to find a publisher, having lost Robert, that excellent and most professional potboiler, as bait?

One happy memory I have of Kit from those days. It was some time after she got out of the hospital, and Julie and I were visiting her at Cooperstown—not at Brookwood, the big house on the lake where we had first known her and where she had been married; her mother had had to sell Brookwood and move into a much smaller, featureless frame house well back from the lake. Her mother and stepfather were off somewhere, and Kit was alone when we visited her.

It was winter, or at any rate there was a lot of snow on the ground. When Kit suggested that I come skiing with her I protested that I had never been on skis in my life. Time I began, she retorted, and before I knew it the skis were fetched and I was buckled into them. We set off down the lane towards a nearby hill which Kit thought should be suitable for a beginner.

I shuffled along, breathing hard but keeping my balance, till we came to a fence that had to be crossed. "How do we get over this?" I said. It was not a tall fence, and the snow had further lowered its height, but we couldn't just step over it.

Kit told me to put my left ski parallel to the fence and as close to it as I could, then to swing my right leg around and over the fence, pointing it in the opposite direction. I did what I could to carry out these impossible instructions, and found myself straddling the fence, caught in a kind of hammer lock and unable to move a muscle. I shouted to Kit for help, but she was laughing so hard she couldn't speak; in fact, she had to lie down in the snow to laugh; she yelled with laughter.

When at last she recovered, she straightened me out and got me over the fence. She showed me how to climb the hill by making a crude herring-bone pattern with my skis. By the time I got to the top I was sweating and puffing. Climbing the hill was such an effort, in fact, that I think I made only two runs down. They were not very fast runs and I kept my feet till I got to the bottom, where I was confronted by a stone wall. As I didn't know how to stop by shifting my skis, I simply fell down. This set Kit off again. She did a lot of laughing that day.

In the spring of 1941 Schuyler and Laura left New York and went south to Florida, getting married on the way in Elkton, Maryland—a small town famous for giving marriage licenses to runaway couples. On a trip to the east coast of Florida with Kit, three years before, Schuyler had seen a small place named Wabasso, near Vero Beach, where his eye had been caught by a tree-lined road leading from the mainland to the beach; now he decided to settle there with Laura. They were joined by Frank Baisden, a Georgian who adored Schuyler as a great and infallibly wise man. Frank was a gentle soul, small of stature but large of heart, a painter and teacher of painting who was a useful man around the house (he could mend or make almost anything). He was a member of the Jackson household at the time of the break-up. This had greatly distressed him, but in spite of his fondness for Kit and the children he had followed Schuyler and Laura to Florida—Laura worried and puzzled him, but because of his adoration of Schuyler he accepted her. Schuyler also sent for

David Owl, a Cherokee Indian whose family had for years worked for the Jacksons on the farm but who had all now returned to the Cherokee Reservation in eastern Tennessee.

I never saw Schuyler and Laura's house in Wabasso but I have twice driven through the village, and with a fast-beating heart.* That was many years ago, and since then the place has no doubt undergone its share of Florida's "development" (the American euphemism for "ruination"). The impression that remains with me is one of tumbledown dreariness: sand and stagnant water and scraggy Australian pines, submerged in the humid hothouse air of Florida.

The house was described to me by Frank Baisden, who knew it well. It was a small, square, box-shaped dwelling, with a steeply pitched roof of galvanized iron, standing on stilts in a sandy yard. A screen of scrub palmetto intruding between pines surrounded the house on three sides and partly hid the neighboring tracks of the Florida East Coast Railroad. A driveway of soft white sand twisted through the clumps of palmetto. The front door opened on a small porch. From the hall a simple flight of stairs, with no stair-rail, but with a door halfway up, led to the attic. This was the guest room, and contained a cot, a wash stand, a candle and an oil lamp.

The other rooms were all on the ground floor: the bedroom to the left of the hall, Schuyler's office to the right; behind the hall a large room running the full width of the house. At one end of this room, under two windows, was a dining table; at the other end Laura's work table, which faced a single shelf just large enough to hold the ten volumes of the great Oxford English Dictionary. Other works of reference stood neatly on her work table. The table in Schuyler's office held the six volumes of C. M. Doughty's unreadable masterwork, *The Dawn in Britain.*

At the back of the house a very small kitchen gave on to another little porch. An outdoor pit-privy adjoined this porch. To

---

*Another ex-friend of theirs, Henry Chapin, told me that on the one occasion when he drove through Wabasso he had *two* punctures—and he attributed both of them to the house by the railroad tracks.

the right of the stairs in the hall was the bathroom.

Both Schuyler and Laura worked away at their separate tables. Definitions for the never-ending work-in-progress were written in longhand on 3 x 5 inch filing cards. At intervals Laura would carry a small stack of these to Schuyler's office. He would study them, make his own notes on some, then carry them back to Laura's table, his footsteps heavy on the bare floorboards.

When he first came to Wabasso, Frank slept in the attic; later he took a small house near by. For a time there were other resident laborers. Schuyler had bought a grapefruit grove, which was to maintain him and Laura while they finished the Dictionary, and Montague and Dorothy Simmons, Laura's disciples from Deya days, were given a tent to live in and put to work picking grapefruit. (The main packing house in Wabasso was owned and managed by a man named—believe it or not—Robert Graves.) For a while Schuyler advertised his grapefruit in the *Rural New Yorker,* but in spite of low prices and unpaid labor the venture was a failure.

The Simmonses were the first to leave. They were indignant and angry: they said they had come as friends and had been treated like slaves. Somehow they managed to get back to England.* Frank Baisden persevered for at least another year. For some of that time David Owl was his fellow laborer. On the Pennsylvania farm Schuyler had sometimes been a hard master; in Wabasso he and Laura set work standards that were Himalayan. David Owl was a good workman but he went at his own pace—which did not always fit the rigid schedule now required of him. Asked if he had completely picked a certain tree, he replied, "It will be picked"—meaning, "Not yet, but I'll finish it later." This was taken as evidence of gross insubordination; his mild evasion was magnified into a barefaced lie; and he was told, "You are expelled!"† His departure left Frank Baisden the only

---

*They never saw Laura again but—however they felt about Schuyler—thirty-five years later they still, in their own words, "retained for her a deep regard."

†Years later, when Schuyler heard that David Owl was dying, he went to say goodbye

remaining devotee, and the burden of work became so crushing that he ruptured himself. At last he too had enough, and quit.

It was mainly through him that I got my few and second-hand glimpses of the life Schuyler and Laura led at Wabasso. These glimpses were as tantalizing as watching an animated conversation through a glass door, when you can see the gestures and facial expressions but hear not a word that is being said. Their marriage was apparently the very opposite of the unequal partnership between herself and Robert Graves. Robert had been her servant, she his master. Now, it seemed, it was the other way about: it was Laura who anxiously watched over Schuyler's comfort, darting to fetch his slippers, his jars of pills, silently accepting the lordly thanks of his impatience ("Oh, Laura, stop *fussing!*"). She cooked his meals and kept his house and deferred to him as meekly as any Old World housewife to her husband.

In the fall of 1941 I was sent to London for three months, ostensibly to run the *Time* bureau there, but actually because I wanted to see something of the wartime world and because Luce, who loved a double-edged ploy, saw how to grant my wish and at the same time reshuffle *Time*'s editorial board, apparently discarding me but with the secret intention of leading me later on to trump the trick.

It was very much the low point of the war: England had been defeated on almost every front and deserted by all her allies; the United States had not yet been forced into the war by Pearl Harbor, and the Battle of Alamein, the turning point of the war, had not yet been fought. But the RAF had saved England from invasion and London had survived the blitz. During the three months I was there not a bomb dropped on London. I was relieved at the time but have never ceased to regret my luck.

London was pocked, dingy and dented, and its inhabitants

---

and to give him a last chance to confess. David, seeing how passionately Schuyler wanted to be in the right, agreed that he had lied.

were bored with the blackout and bomb shelters, bored with the makeshifts war had forced upon them. There was not enough of anything, and nobody but the Americans, who had pipelines from home, had all they wanted to eat. Oranges had vanished, eggs and ham were almost unobtainable. Everyone licked the platter clean, and because there was not quite enough to go round, the national health had never been so good.

The *Time* office had engaged a room for me at the Savoy, and on my second night there I put out a pair of shoes to be cleaned. They vanished without a trace, and my complaints to the management proved unavailing. "There's a war on, etc.," I was told; I shouldn't have left my shoes outside the door: with so many foreigners (i.e., Americans) in the hotel these days, what could you expect? I was particularly annoyed because these were very special shoes, stout and thick-soled, which I had bought in New York to armor me against the exigencies of the London winter.

Robert, who had tried to enlist but had been turned down for various reasons—his age, the length and excellence of his service in the 1914–18 war, his wounds—had rented a cottage in the Devonshire village of Galmpton, where he and Beryl and their first child, William, spent the war years.

When I went down to Galmpton for the weekend the loss of my shoes was still rankling, and I told Robert about it as we were walking in the garden. He snorted with laughter, said, "There are a lot of Americans at the Savoy now, you know"—and disappeared into the house. He reappeared carrying a pair of shoes exactly like the ones I had lost, which he told me he had bought before coming to America, to armor *him* against the exigencies of the American climate. They fitted me perfectly, and he insisted that I take them, "as a gesture of good will from one ally to another."

For the first twenty-four hours of my visit Beryl kept to her room; she was not well, Robert said, but nothing serious. Besides his writing, an unbreakable daily habit, he did the cooking and all the household chores, as well as minding William, their obstreperously lively child. When he had a spare fifteen minutes

Robert would seize a pair of scissors and a pile of magazines and cut out colored pictures from their illustrations and advertisements, to paste into a scrapbook for William's amusement.

William was "spoiled rotten," and obviously enjoyed bullying his father, who seemed to like acting as his devoted slave. William looked like a miniature John Bull, and behaved like him too, in his Eatanswill, jingo days. On Sunday we were invited to tea by Mrs. Mallowan (better known as Agatha Christie, the detective-story writer), who lived in a handsome Georgian house a couple of miles from Galmpton, overlooking the river Dart. We walked there, Robert pushing a pram (in which William refused to ride) in case William got tired. Whenever William opened his mouth to bawl, which he did at intervals of about 50 yards, Robert scrambled hastily up the bank, clawing the hedgerows for blackberries, and stuffed William's mouth with them. Until he swallowed them he couldn't start bawling again.

Mrs. Mallowan and her daughter received us, and William was temporarily subdued by her cool manner, the imposing silver tea service and the neat prettiness of her sitting room. He soon recovered his lust for uproar, however, and began jumping up and down on the sofa. When he threw a cake at Mrs. Mallowan (his aim was poor), that lady's speculative look and the thinness of her smile calmed him more effectively than Robert's anxious cries of distress and Beryl's feeble chirping. We finished a rather anxious tea with nothing broken and not much spilled.

On the way home William was tired, but he wouldn't get in his pram. He preferred riding on Robert's shoulders and pulling the lobes of Robert's ears. Once he pulled so hard that Robert told him sharply to stop it. This hurt William's feelings and he burst into an outraged bellow. Robert, beside himself with contrition, begged William to forgive him, placated him with more blackberries, and at last won him back to precarious good humor.

I found Beryl considerably changed from the retiring little creature she had been in America. Not in her appearance: she still looked more like a child than a grown woman—a child-mother now instead of a child-bride—but in her manner. Was she trying to model her behavior on Laura's? Before she had left her room and come downstairs I had heard her voice, querulous and weakly strident, calling to Robert, upbraiding, complaining, impatient. And I had heard his responses, or the tone of them: anxiously conciliatory, humble, apologetic. Exactly the tone he had used to Laura.

When I saw them together this resemblance to Laura was so much less noticeable that I told myself it was imaginary; whatever strain there was between them was due to the disparity in their ages, Beryl's obvious ill health and the natural anxieties that went with it. Yes, all that was probably true; yet it seemed to me that Beryl was making a conscious effort to be or do something that was not natural to her—to rule the roost— and that Robert played his part in this game much more easily than she did. I was not alone in this opinion: other friends of Robert's told me that when he and Beryl first set up house together her treatment of Robert had been strikingly and unexpectedly reminiscent of Laura's. I think, by the time I saw them, this phantasmagoria had begun to fade; and in later years I know that Beryl settled into a role more natural to her as housekeeper, wife and mother.

I had always thought of Robert as a classically English type, though perhaps 100 years or so out of date, which would explain some of his apparent eccentricities of dress and bearing. I think he might well have been a country squire—a Tory, of course, but with a difference; a justice of the peace renowned for his dictums and the odd brilliance of his judgments. And that he would have been happy in such a life.

On my first day at Galmpton I got up early and went with Robert (who had already lighted the stove and taken a cup of tea up to Beryl) to fetch the milk from a neighboring farm, as he did every morning. An old farm laborer gave us good day, addressing Robert as "Captain." On our way back he said to me, with a smile, "All the old boys around here call me Captain."

2

It was in wartime London in 1942 that at last I met Len and Jane Lye. They were pretty much as I had imagined them, although by that time Jane's face had lost its softness of outline and her voice had collected some gravel of asperity.

In 1942 Len was working in Dean Street in Soho, where *Time* had its wartime office, and which was a center for small companies making documentary films. Len had a wide acquaintance in the neighborhood, and knew most of the people in the *Time* office. One of them, Steve Laird, told me how Len always made his entrance: a pork-pie hat would come skimming through the doorway of your office; if you were too busy or didn't want to see him, you were supposed to pick up the hat and skim it back. If you let it lie for as long as ten seconds, Len would roll in after it, grinning archaically from ear to ear.

He had a lizardy look, as if he had just darted in from sunning himself, and his watchful, evasive eyes gave a hint of sudden departure. He was bald as a Buddhist priest.

Len's pleasures were simple, almost childlike; he loved jazz, he loved shooting galleries. On Friday evenings in London, when he had collected his weekly pay packet, he would stop at a shooting gallery on his way home. By the time he got home Jane would be asleep. He always brought back his best targets, as trophies, and these he would prop up at the foot of the bed so that Jane might see them first thing in the morning.

In 1942 he was already a near-legendary figure in the film world, with a widening reputation as an exploring experimenter. Under the economics of British cinema his most experimental films came out in the guise of advertisements or propaganda—

231

for the Post Office, for Shell Oil, for the Ministry of Information. He had made a film entirely of puppets—I believe the first ever produced. The two short films for which he was best known, *Colour Flight* and *Colour Box*, were sound made visible: as you listened to the percussive beat of a jazz record you saw on the screen the sound track that the music produced: a shivery green line down the center was the trumpet, the red blobs exploding on either side of it were the drums, and so on. Len made these films by laboriously painting this sound track directly on to the celluloid film and then hanging the reels up to dry—a process that took literally months.

Either this invention of Len's could not be guarded by copyright or patent, or it never occurred to him to do it. At all events, Walt Disney adopted the same idea for his famous *Fantasia:* in the interval in that film Deems Taylor goes through the motions of introducing the sound track—which turns out to be a polished-up, Hollywood version of Len's invention, conceived and produced years before.

Len was an instinctive, not a reasoning creature, and the thing that did him in was an idea—I always thought of his trouble as a form of intellectual encephalitis. I had noticed the tell-tale furrow in his brow soon after we met in London. The worm in his mind irked him so much that I think he told everyone about it who would listen, and he found a new listener in me. The idea that bothered him was "Individual happiness now." This slogan, as he had persuaded himself that it was, had been contributed by Robert Graves. Len considered it a good enough rallying cry, but it fell far short of explaining his idea. He tried, at various speeds and from various angles, to show me exactly what his idea was. I remained in what T. S. Eliot once called a state of enlightened mystification.

"Why don't you do a film about it?" I said. "You're a man who thinks in images."

"I have!"

He showed me the scenario, if that's the word, for a projected film. The "story line" seemed to me almost too simple: the protagonist, Charlie Chaplin (Len intended to have Charlie himself play this part), makes his way around the world, in each country confronting the head of state with an arresting gesture and the categorical imperative: "Individual happiness *now!*" The monarch, prime minister or president thus addressed scratches his head, looks nonplussed or wary, according to his nature and nation, but sees the point eventually, cries "Yes!" and puts a program in motion to ensure that every citizen of his country shall immediately—not next Tuesday but action this day—become and remain *happy.*

As the outline of a film it seemed to lack drama, for one thing, and I tried to say so, gently, in a way that would be acceptable to Len. It was not acceptable: the idea bothered him, he admitted, and all he wanted to do about it was get rid of it; but he was sure that the only way of getting rid of it was through this film. Like everyone whose bat in the belfry has become a cherished pet, he would brook no criticism of the project that had grown into an obsession with him—nor of his scheme for putting it across. Talking with Len about individual happiness, in fact, degenerated into a gloomy wrangle.

But one event soon occurred that bade fair to restore Len to his natural cheerfulness about his fixed idea. Wendell Willkie, having made a name for himself by campaigning for the U.S. presidency against the paladin, Franklin Roosevelt—a campaign that ended in honorable defeat—was now on his travels, and in Chungking he made a speech that became briefly famous. The speech grew out of an idea as simple as Len's: that we are all inhabitants of one world. For some reason this simplification caught the public imagination, and people went around repeating this phrase ("one world") to themselves and feeling better.

Next time I saw Len he said to me, with barely suppressed excitement: "Do you know Wendell Willkie?" I admitted that I had met him several times, but could claim no more than acquaintance. Len made me promise that when I returned to New York I would get Willkie to read a copy of his scenario.

3

We cannot do without the word, yet who can define it: *love*, the most battered ornament of our vocabulary? All we can truthfully report of the mysterious thing itself is that from time to time, in greater or less degree, according to our capabilities and our natures, we are bowled over by it, illuminated, crushed, burnt or blest by it. And that it is better, both for us and for them, to love people than to be "in love" with them.

But the size of some meanings is too big for words. "In love" is quite often big talk for the ravening appetite most men are born with, and which, from puberty on, sharpens and concentrates into the lust of the flesh. Some men find it possible, and wiser, to insure themselves against this craving by distributing the risk. I once knew a monk who told me that he had been miserable as a young man, always in love with some girl or other, but that now he was happy because he was "in love with everybody."

In the course of my life I have loved several human beings, some of whom I remember, and a few animals, most of whom I have forgotten, and I have been in love with more than one woman. As for Julie, I was always in love with her, and I love her still. Yet while she was alive I was unfaithful to her, and more than once. That doesn't make sense, I know, but it's not nonsense either, though it may make nonsense of any definition I could give of love.

As Hervey Allen once wrote, a young man is a sorry thing, at the mercy of his "three troublesome globes" (I suppose the third is his brain, or what is laughingly called his mind), who never knows peace except for an hour or so after a girl has nearly killed him. And how many times in his life—say, between the

ages of twenty and sixty—does a man perform this "act of love"?
Five hundred? A thousand? A meager estimate would be at least
5,000 times. If he were impeccably monogamous his whole life
long, as the Church requires him to swear that he will be, can
every one of those acts be the exercise of "love"? Will the beast
with two backs never enter his marriage bed? What a rhetorical
question!

But how could I have brought myself to be unfaithful to the
wife I loved, to whom I had sworn and intended lifelong fidelity,
and who was never once unfaithful to me? At the time, this would
have seemed to me an irrelevant point, or at any rate one I
couldn't answer satisfactorily. My lame answer would have been
that I did it, and if that fact seemed to contradict the opposing
fact that I loved her, I would have said angrily that there was no
contradiction. Incredible but true? No, of course there was a
contradiction, and I felt it: the discordance between unselfishness
(which almost exists) and possessiveness (which can almost die).

To say that there was no contradiction is splitting hairs,
which I used to do better than I can now. Looking back, it seems
to me that there was no excuse, however ingenious or plausible,
for hurting Julie as I did. Nevertheless, I did it; and she forgave
me, which proves—I am driven to this shameful and unwanted
conclusion—that she loved me more and better than I loved her.
Worse than that, for she was the person I would have sworn I
loved the most; and yet I failed her.

I got back to New York in January 1943, after a miserable
voyage (zigzagging through mountainous seas to evade subma-
rines) on the *Queen Elizabeth,* which was used during the war
as a troopship and sailed under U.S. Navy orders—which meant
that not a drop of drink could be had aboard her! I was mindful
of my promise to Len Lye to broach the idea of "Individual
happiness now" to Wendell Willkie; and I soon had an opportunity.

I started by saying: "Mr. Willkie, what do you think of crack-
pots?"

"Why, some of them are pretty interesting folks."

"Well, I'm glad you feel that way, because I have a friend who's a bit of a crackpot, and he wants you to read something he's written."

"Send it along."

Two weeks later, not having heard from Willkie, I telephoned his secretary to find out what was up. It turned out that Len's typescript had somehow been lost before Willkie had read a word of it. I relayed this information to Len in England, who cheerfully sent another copy. This time the result was prompt. I had a telephone call from Willkie.

"Say, who is this Len Lye? He's talking about what *I'm* talking about! I'd like to see him."

"Well, Mr. Willkie, he's in England, but I'm sure he'd come over at the drop of a hat."

And shortly thereafter, as luck would have it, Len did arrive in New York to finish a teaching film for Basic English, the hoped-for *lingua franca* put forward by C. K. Ogden and I. A. Richards. It was summer, and I whisked him up to Boothden to let him catch his breath before plunging into the whirlpools of New York. I don't recall the title of this film, if it had one, and I never saw the finished version, only some rushes with sound—including Len's yelping interruptions. The film was intended to be used with a textbook by foreigners who knew no English, so the dialogue was spoken with almost idiotic slowness and distinctness.

The first night Len was there he was working late when my two oldest sons (who had not yet met him) returned in the small hours from a party in Newport to find this bald-headed stranger, who greeted them with an unseeing glare, pointed a finger at himself and uttered in molasses-slow accents: *"I - am - a man,"* with a slow, sorcerer's gesture of pulling the words with difficulty from his pregnant mouth. Then, pointing at one of them: *"You - are - a woman."* They thought he was a madman, and were so alarmed they almost took to their heels.

A telephone call from Boothden to Willkie's office raised the exciting prospect of having Willkie as a weekend guest, but there were too many complications, and that plan fell through. Nevertheless, a few weeks later Len and Willkie met at last. And what happened? Nothing. Apparently there was no meeting of minds, only the brief encounter of two strangers who at first glance had taken each other for a long-lost brother but who soon discovered that they were only strangers after all.

Eventually Len and his plans got to be a bore. After his encounter with Willkie he dropped the scheme of a film and rewrote the scenario into a more abstract thesis. This in turn was transmogrified into further and increasingly abstract—or vague and wooly—attempts to put Len's feelings into words. The gist of the matter remained hopelessly elusive. But each time he had a new idea about the presentation he would bring a new manuscript to my secretary, Miss Stanton, for her to type. Acting as Len's stenographer was no part of her job, and neither she nor I liked her taking on this extra work. Gradually a coolness formed between Len and me; at last he stopped bringing Miss Stanton anything to type, and we ceased to see each other.

4

There was no doubt about it, Kit's attitude towards Laura was neither sensible nor normal. Julie and I worried over it until we came to the conclusion that there were only two possible answers: either Kit was taking an early Christian view of what Laura had done, or else she didn't remember anything about it. When we put these alternatives to Kit, she whooped with laughter at the notion that she could or would emulate an early Christian. Nevertheless she refused to accept the other alternative.

Since Kit persisted in her stubborn admiration for Laura, we came to the painful decision that we could no longer be friends with her. It was doubly painful for me, but Julie insisted.

I come now to a part of the story which I am afraid I cannot be altogether trusted to get right. I cannot even be sure of the chronology. Since I am also ashamed of my behavior, I find it painful even to make the attempt to tell about it, and I may have altered or rearranged some circumstances, without being aware of it, to gloss over my conduct.

Some time—I really can't remember when—after Kit left the hospital she was in New York, staying in a friend's apartment. She telephoned me at the office, to say she was there. It happened to be a day when I would be working late and staying in town overnight. I think we had dinner together, and then I went back to the office. But after I'd finished I went to Kit's apartment. She had a new record called *Bach Goes to Town,* a jazzed-up version of one of Bach's lovelier melodies. We played it over and over, and danced to it. I think we also kissed a little, but not much. But as we danced we clung to each other as if we were drowning. We didn't go to bed together, although we both wanted to, and eventually I said good night and went back to my little flat, only a few streets away. Several times that night I was on the point of going back; perhaps I did telephone but I think not; I can't remember. Anyhow, nothing more happened between us, and while Julie was alive Kit and I never became lovers. But it was a near thing, that night in New York.

Some time later Julie and I went to a concert to hear Kirsten Flagstad—it must have been one of her last appearances. Her voice bowled me over. We had a late supper afterwards, and what with the drink and my excitement over Flagstad's voice (I thought it was what truth would sound like if truth could sing) and some feckless talk about my own untruth, Julie's suspicions were aroused; she began to question me, and soon found out all about my evening with Kit. And *that* was the real reason—or more truly the reason than the alleged one: that Kit would not disavow Laura—why we broke off with Kit. I was given the job of telling her; Julie wouldn't come with me. It was much worse than the time I was told to destroy the little china figure. Kit was living at the farm again, and I drove over alone. I don't remember anything about our meeting but I'm sure she behaved well. I suppose I tried to forget it, and succeeded; but I wrote this:

LAST CALL

Hill water sifted down
And tainted the new river an old brown.
Trees along the bare high road
Collected grackles, talking treason
Against the helpless, the dying season.
Turning into the lane, I silently cried:
This is the way the last time comes again.
How are goodbyes said? Goodbyes are said like greetings.

Our estrangement didn't last forever, although I feared and expected it would. I can't remember now how long it did last; I think it must have been about three years. Then Julie relented; we made overtures; we were friends again.

A novel Robert wrote after his return from America, *Wife to Mr. Milton*, was not a success, although in its way it was well done, and although he worked on it as competently as on any other. It was published in 1943, during the war. I have my own theory about why it failed. The book was a first-person narrative, supposedly told by the young Cavalier girl whose marriage to the scholarly Roundhead poet was such a disaster that it caused him to write his treatise in favor of divorce.

Robert's dislike of Milton was only too obvious throughout the book; he made him a small-minded, vengeful, self-righteous, priggish pedant who would have been quite incapable of writing *L'Allegro, Il Penseroso, Lycidas* or most of the sonnets—to say nothing of *Samson Agonistes* or *Paradise Lost.* I knew that Robert disliked and denigrated Milton as a "great poet"—a category he equated with "great phony"—but the personal animus he showed towards Milton in this book was more than dislike, it was hatred. I believe that he visited on Milton the bitter detestation he felt for Schuyler: that the Milton he was writing about *was* Schuyler.

Though I never voiced my theory to Robert, I did venture to suggest that the Milton he had pictured could not have been the man who wrote Milton's poems; and if we had an argument about it, I am sure he worsted me. But I did catch him, or thought I had caught him, in an anachronism. He had his heroine say, "God will temper the wind to the shorn lamb"—a biblical-sounding statement which in fact comes from Laurence Sterne, in the eighteenth century; it appears in *A Sentimental Journey*. When I pointed this out to Robert, instead of admitting the error, he tried to wriggle out of it. He discovered that much the same sentiment is voiced in one of Corneille's plays, and argued that his heroine, as a well-read young lady, would of course have read Corneille. The weak point in this rejoinder, which neither of us mentioned, was the extraordinary accuracy with which she had translated the French line into the exact words of Sterne.

Robert's prose writing, until he grew to be famous and consequently in demand as a lecturer, was done largely to make money. But even in Laura's time, when these potboilers were not allowed to be mentioned except, as it were, in the bosom of the family, and even there with circumspection, three of them— *Goodbye to All That* and the two *Claudius* books—were so widely acclaimed that Robert must have been affected by the continuing public admiration which kept them in print and, in the case of *I, Claudius* very nearly (missing it only by a series of grotesque mischances) achieved one of his lifetime ambitions: to be translated into a Hollywood super-film.*

He told me once, with a characteristic sigh, "You know, I'm not really erudite." On the scholarly level I don't suppose he was, but he had a working knowledge of Latin and Greek that enabled him to read them without depending on translations, and this ability, combined with his native ingenuity, led him down the tortuous trail to his private oracle that supplied the answer to

*In 1976 it was made into a TV series that won popular if not critical acclaim.

more and more historical riddles; and gradually the trail became a beaten path. At first I think he merely delighted in the dexterity with which he contrived these unorthodox solutions, especially when they undermined or ran counter to received opinion; later he almost came to believe that his oracle was no mere Wizard of Oz but the true voice of a god.

I used to think that Julie's views about the Church, like her feelings about certain people, were inconsistent; now I am not so sure. Like her mother, she was devout but not pious; the Church was part of her life, and a most important part. Why then, when my brilliant older cousin, Stanley Cleveland, an intellectual Anglo-Catholic priest, in 1924 wanted me to join him as a sort of lay brother at the University of Wisconsin, where he was then a chaplain, did Julie declare herself so strongly in opposition? I had not accepted Stanley's offer, I had not faced the possible implications that would arise if I did; but Julie, fearing that if I did go I should end by entering the Church—*her* Church!—had told me flatly that if I became a priest she would not marry me. Was there something about Stanley Cleveland she neither liked nor trusted? Or did she feel in her bones that if I turned priest I would be a false priest? These are guesses that I never voiced; they may be wildly wrong. And yet I think now that if she thought or felt something like this, without being willing or perhaps able to put her thought or feeling into words, she was right on both counts. At the time I resented her feeling but bowed to it with secret relief.

I observed the same sort of apparent inconsistency, more apparent than real, in Julie's attitude towards my father. She loved him but at the same time disapproved of him—not *all* of him, but fairly large parts. She didn't like his bad temper or his dependence on food; she didn't always like his behavior in church. She humored him, up to a point; but she too had a temper, not bad but hot, and he respected it. They were on very good terms.

One thing Julie wholeheartedly liked and admired about my

241

father was his carving. He was a really expert carver—not as great a virtuoso as his father-in-law, old Mr. Procter, who could carve a duck in the air, but as deft and sure as a surgeon. And, like a surgeon, he lectured as he cut, telling the audience just what he was doing; and he didn't mind spattering blood around —in his case, gravy. His performance with a turkey or a duck or any kind of joint fascinated Julie. As his only daughter-in-law she almost invariably sat next to him at the table, so she had a front-row seat, where she could study his technique. Carving was one of the several accomplishments my father had in which he so far outclassed me that I refused to compete with him (public speaking was another; charming strangers was a third), so I was a desperate and miserable carver. At the first dinner party we gave after we were married, I not only signally failed to serve four people from one side of the duck but with a desperate slash pulled the whole bird into my lap. That was the end of my carving; thereafter Julie did it—and thanks to her observation of my father, with increasing skill.

Julie and I had both hoped that our fourth child would be a daughter. I think she thought that I was more disappointed than she was. At any rate, when Sandy was about two, she suggested that we try again. I knew she was suggesting it for my sake, and that it was a characteristically brave and unselfish offer, for in all her four pregnancies she had suffered miseries of sickness at the start, so that she had to go to bed, sometimes in a hospital, for as long as six weeks. She would willingly have gone through all that again, I know, in order to give me a daughter. If we could have been sure that it would be a girl, perhaps I would have said Yes; although I hope not. At any rate, I said No: four sons were enough.

Where did we get the idea that Sandy was like my father? I don't know, but the notion was strongly imbedded in both of us. And, fond of my father as Julie was, she was determined that Sandy should not grow up to be like him. There was a time, when Sandy was five or six, when it looked as if she might be losing the struggle. Julie and I and our four sons had spent Christmas with my father in Florida. The two older boys had returned to college and I to my job in New York; Julie and the two young ones stayed on for another ten days. One morning at breakfast, usually a silent meal in my father's house, even when he was in a good mood, Sandy broke the thunderous hush by announcing, "I never make a mistake."

My father immediately cleared for action: he thumped down his glass of water, pushed his plate away, discarded his napkin, glared down the table at Sandy and cried: "You're making a mistake right now. You have your fork in your left hand!"

Sandy's timing—a slight pause before he answered—was professional: "I'm left-handed."

A few days later Paul, our fourteen-year-old son, asked Julie what a graven image was. She started to explain and then had a better idea. "Ask your grandfather—*at lunch*," she said. Paul did. My father, in fine fettle, launched into an explanation, ending with a list of graven images: the golden calf, Diana of the Ephesians—at this point Sandy interrupted, "And the duckbilled platypus." It says a good deal for my father's midday equanimity that this piece of impertinence only made him laugh. Shortly after my father returned to his house in Princeton, where he spent the spring and summer months, Sandy went to call on him, and was invited to stay for lunch. It takes no great effort of the imagination to conjure up the scene: these two very similar cronies, eyeing each other with the respect of onetime opponents who had taken each other's measure and had tacitly agreed to bar all further contention, nodding agreeably to one another over a good lunch.

We had had a nursemaid for the three older boys, but Sandy was taken care of, from the time of his birth, by Julie alone. Was he her favorite? I never knew. The other boys thought she spoiled him and used to tell her so; she vigorously denied it, saying that she sometimes gave in to him on little things but never on anything important. He was so much younger than his brothers that he was almost like an only child, with some of the only child's quirks and odd sayings. He alarmed us once by saying

243

that the most beautiful sound in the world was the noise of taxi
tires going down Park Avenue on a wet night. He was a city child,
born and brought up in New York, and he and his mother knew
Central Park, where they went for a walk almost every day, like
the back of their hand. On their way to the Park he would often
tease her by pretending to run away; but, being a city child and
knowing the dangers of traffic, he would always stop short at the
curb before crossing a street, and let her catch up with him. Once
in the Park, where he had space to maneuver, it was a different
matter. One day, as they entered the Park hand in hand, Julie
heard one of the park policemen admonishing a small ragamuffin
for breaking some rule, "An' if ya do it again," said the cop, "I'll
cut yer ears off!"

"How *dare* you speak to a child like that!" cried Julie. A
small, grinning crowd began to gather, avid for a row; the cop
sputtered, then launched into a loud defense. Julie was just collecting her breath for another indignant speech when she realized that Sandy had taken advantage of the situation to slip her
hand and run away. So she had to quit the field of battle—and just
when, as she said to me later, she was about to lay the man out!

She once sprang to my defense under similar circumstances
—at least, she thought they were. We had been invited to an
evening gathering at Bruce Bliven's apartment to meet the great
Harold Laski, just returned from Moscow and some straight talk
with Stalin himself. Laski reminded me of our former Princeton
neighbor, Henry van Dyke—a preening, strutting little man with
great respect for his own acumen and importance, but not far
removed from a figure of fun. We got to the party too late to be
introduced but just in time to find seats for what was obviously
to be a lecture. As by that time seats were scarce, we found chairs
out of sight of each other; a lecture hall had been formed out of
two rooms at right angles, with Laski seated in the doorway
where both rooms could see and hear him.

"Before I begin," he said, "is T. S. Matthews here?"

I said I was. He then said he wanted me to realize that what
he was about to say was "off the record." Why had he singled me

out? I suppose because he disliked and distrusted *Time,* of which I was then Managing Editor. As soon as he said this I heard the unmistakable sound of Julie clearing her throat, and waited with some alarm for her words. But she said nothing. Although she was very indignant, and was just preparing to demolish Laski, she was overcome by an attack of hiccups and couldn't speak.

I remember her tone of voice and the look on her face when Julie once said to me: "Have I married a ladies' man?" But I can't remember when it was, or why she said it. We must have been married for some time, and she must have had some cause for thinking that my eye, at least, had wandered towards some other woman. At the same time her tone and her expression told me that she thought there was something ludicrous in the very idea. Shy, blushing Tom, whose chief claim to her own affection had been his year-after-year constancy, his doglike devotion which had enabled him to outlast her other suitors—Tom, a *ladies' man?* Nevertheless, as a jealous and possessive wife, she was alert for danger signals, and she must have seen some. So, although her question demanded the answer "No!" (and got it) it also raised a warning signal ("Perhaps I have!").

I knew this much: that I liked women; but I would not have admitted even to myself in those days that I could possibly be a womanizer or anything like it. Even now, in spite of the record, I find it difficult to reconcile my idea of myself with the contradictory facts that record shows. My record seems to me "unlike me" —but of course it's not. The answer I should have given Julie was "Yes, you have!"

When I say that Julie was a jealous and possessive wife, I mean something much more delicate and imprecise than those rough, crude, blocky words convey. Julie as a girl had been a flirt —it was a tendency she inherited from her father—and just as she never ceased to be attractive to men, she remained latently flirtatious after she was married. But there was a great gulf fixed in her mind between "having fun with men" and being unfaithful to her husband. I was jealous, too; but I can remember only two times when I was seriously worried by Julie's feelings about another man, and perhaps I should say "only one," for one of them—her brief infatuation with Robert—was too contrived and stagey to be convincing, though at the time I remember working myself into a state of mock-despair.

It must have happened about halfway through our six-month stay in Mallorca. Robert was being disciplined by Laura, who, he said glumly, would not admit him to her bed nor permit him to visit anyone else's—and, as he complained to us like a small boy deprived of his daily sweet, he hated to sleep alone. He and Julie went off one afternoon for a mountain walk; and after she came back she told me with bated breath that Robert was in love with her. I don't remember whether she said that *she* was also in love with *him,* but I think we both took that for granted, for some odd reason. I didn't really believe it, but it was a shock, which for about twenty-four hours I mistranslated into despair and misery. Then (isn't it amazing not to remember the details of such an emotional affair? But perhaps that's another indication that nothing really happened) it just blew away, and she and I were together again.

She had another pseudo-affair during our stay in Mallorca, and this one might have bothered me but didn't. There was a young Mallorquin, upper-class or rich (I couldn't tell the difference), whom I had met at the Palma Tennis Club. He was doing his Army service, which did not seem to be very demanding, and he looked very trim in his officer's uniform. He was not particularly good-looking, but he was tall for a Spaniard, and with polished manners. He obviously took a fancy to Julie; when she came to the tennis club he would always try to whisk her away to a café, and though he never introduced us to his family he did go so far as to take us to a country estate, apparently theirs, where we were given a picnic lunch, served by old retainers.

I have carefully forgotten his name, but I think I knew what he wanted. He hoped to seduce Julie. I was sure he wouldn't succeed: anyhow, by the rules of the game as we understood them, if I tried to interfere I would show myself a ridiculously jealous husband. When we left, he came to the Barcelona boat to see us off, and I left him in our cabin with Julie for ten minutes so that he could kiss her goodbye. Ten minutes? Well, perhaps it was only three. I think she prized his "devotion" as a romantic compliment.

Although Laura sometimes seemed inhuman she did in fact share our common humanity. In 1945, when Griselda and her sister Maria made a painful visit to their father in Wabasso, he "disowned" them, as he had disowned me—and made his anathema official and public by ranting and raging at them, with tears streaming down his cheeks, as they were waiting for their train (which was late, of course)—to the grinning delight of lounging Florida crackers. The two girls, drained, numb and speechless, endured his tirade. It was wartime, and they were traveling by day-coach in what was virtually a troop train. When at last the train arrived and they were clambering miserably aboard, Laura "simply and kindly" handed them a basket of food for their journey. For this show of ordinary humanity, Griselda was able, at that point, to like her.

When Laura had cast off Robert, her chief drudge, and had jettisoned the minor drudges, she and Schuyler announced a complete change in the scheme of work: whereas Laura had previously been the sole, Prospero-like poetic intelligence, infusing the base ore of drudged-up scholarship with radioactive insight, henceforth Schuyler and she would be co-equal poetic intelligences, and the drudgery would presumably take care of itself. (The actual result was that over the years, imperceptibly to themselves, both of them turned into drudges who still felt like Prospero but who talked and behaved more like Caliban.)

Since they made no money, and must have lost some on the grapefruit venture, how did they manage to survive? Luckily for them, Schuyler no longer had room for financial maneuver, as in his disastrous Atlantean days of propping up the sky by piling mortgages on bank loans. His father had set up a trust for him so iron-clad that even Schuyler's ingenuity could find no way of breaking it; and this trust enabled them to live. "Living" included not only food (but no drink; neither of them took a drop of alcohol) but medical expenses. It also paid for occasional vacations, spent usually in Watrous, New Mexico, where they owned another small house.

With Frank Baisden no longer there, only rumor or widely spaced reports from the rare visits of Schuyler's children brought me any news from Wabasso. Rumor was more dramatic than dependable. For example, the story, relayed to me by Jenny Nicholson, about her mother Nancy sticking pins in a wax image of Laura. Like Kit, Nancy had been amazingly tolerant of Laura and, like Kit, apparently bore her no ill-will. But now Laura had done something—I don't know what: some piece of seamless dishonesty or high-minded disobligingness—which really annoyed Nancy. She wrote to Jenny about it, and added that she was so fed up with Laura she thought she would make a little wax image of her and stick pins in it—but only down one side. And a few days later Jenny had a letter from me, passing on the latest rumor I had heard: that Laura had suffered a slight paralysis, affecting only one side of her face. I believe there was no truth —or could we say only a grain of "poetic truth"?—in this little ghost story. Of the two, Laura enjoyed—though "enjoy" is not a word that properly applies to either of them—better health than Schuyler, who had often told me he would never see thirty, and whose ailments, mysterious or imperceptible to doctors, struck him like thunderbolts and were constantly propitiated by pills.

Robert was not the most businesslike of men. He trusted anyone whom he considered his friend and, to put it mildly, his taste in people was catholic. He himself was quixotically generous, even when he could not afford to be. Long before he became what he considered "affluent," he owned four houses in Deya: Canellun (which he had built) and C'an Torrent; the Posada, next to the church, and a small house on the path down to the *cala*, both of which he had bought. With these houses went several acres of valuable olive trees. The Posada, a large-ish house, and the one on the path to the *cala* could have been let, but Robert used them instead as guest houses for visiting friends.

In 1945, when the war was over, Robert returned to Mallorca, with Beryl and their three children, William, Lucia and Juan. Everything at Canellun was just as he had left it nearly ten years before. His hat was hanging on the same peg, his stick was leaning in the corner, all his books and papers were in order. On the table in the hall a shallow bowl still held the varicolored pebbles he had put there.

Robert had left all his property and belongings in the care of his trusted Mallorquin friend, Gelat, the factotum of Deya, whom I have described earlier. Robert was touched by this evidence of trustworthiness and at the same time delighted by the vindication of his own judgment—like a gambler who thinks he has won his bet not because he is lucky but because he knows the winning system. To simplify Gelat's stewardship and to put a respectable legal face on the matter, in case the Spanish authorities grew suspicious and perhaps tried to confiscate Robert's possessions, a legal document had been drawn up and signed which declared Gelat the owner of all Robert's property.

Was Gelat really the faithful friend Robert thought him, or did he intend to hang on to this windfall? The possibility may have occurred to him. In any case, at his death the title went to Gelat's son Juan as part of his father's estate. That one was a jovial character, unlike his father: he laughed heartily at the idea of restoring Robert's property, which was now legally his. Juan did not try to turn Robert out of Canellun, but while this unpleasant business was going on, and while three of the children were at school in Palma, Robert rented a dreary flat in the outskirts of Palma, and there he and his family lived for several years.

I visited Robert and Beryl and the children—now four: the baby, Tomas, was my namesake—crammed into their flat (actually two flats) on a characterless street. The household also included a young English couple, Martin Seymour-Smith and a girl whose name I have forgotten; they didn't live in Robert's flat but had a workroom there. Seymour-Smith acted as tutor to the two oldest children, and he and the girl were doing the spadework for Robert's biggest potboiler yet, *The Greek Myths.*

It was on this visit that Robert introduced me to the works of Georges Simenon, a writer he much admired. Before I left on the night boat to Barcelona, we were all having dinner at a restaurant on the waterfront in Palma. The talk was mainly of writing and writers, and not a name was mentioned without being scornfully dismissed as an overrated fake. This began to annoy me, and at last I said, "Who *is* any good?" Robert looked at me in surprise, and then he and the others started to draw up a list of writers of whom they approved. It was a short list: E. E. Cummings and Simenon. Nobody else.

Once in a blue moon Schuyler came north. One of the doctors who presided over Kit's case in the early years must have kept in touch with him; how else could Schuyler have heard in 1947 that Kit had had another breakdown and was again in hospital? Anyhow, he did hear it, and the news brought him north to see whether he could get the divorce agreement changed, giving him custody of the children. He found that this was not possible, and returned to Wabasso without meeting any of his family. He did get a glimpse of Griselda, however: as their cars passed on the river road between Brownsburg and New Hope, they saw each other but made no sign.

The process of Robert's self-delusion (as I thought it) was a gradual one; but I saw it coming, and even made an attempt, halfhearted and too late, to warn him against taking himself too seriously as a solver of historical riddles. I say that "I saw it coming," but of course that's only true in a sense. I couldn't help noticing that whenever he got on the subject of Mediterranean mythology he showed himself violently hostile to the gods of Olympus, whom he characterized as usurpers, and was an equally violent partisan of the Mother Goddess, the head and front of "the old religion," the true faith that, according to him, had been driven underground by the Greek gods. His mystical and reverent attitude towards the Mother Goddess was only explicable, I thought, in the light of his long thraldom to Laura and his worship of her—a thraldom and a worship whose effects on him were permanent.

To Robert the orthodox version of the Greek myths was an attempt to cover up or give a false interpretation to the older myths that lay behind them, and he set himself the task of peeling off the top layer of this palimpsest and restoring the faint traces of the original. Pure scholarship would have been unequal to this job, since too much evidence was lacking. Robert undertook to supply the missing evidence, either by setting the scholars at naught and reinterpreting what they had misunderstood or by imagining the nature or even the form of the missing facts.

As he worked his way around the coasts and islands of the Mediterranean, I asked myself what would happen when he reached the eastern shore. It was too much to expect that he could bear to overlook or refrain from setting straight the myth of Christianity, with all its conjectural facts, wrong guesses and false conclusions. I feared the worst. And I remember the first indication that my fears were well founded.

It was in the summer of 1949; we were having a reunion, the first and last of its kind, at Portofino. Our hosts were Robert's oldest daughter Jenny and her husband Alec Clifford, who owned the Castelletto, surely one of the most beautifully placed houses in the world. The Castelletto stands on the highest point of the headland, 900 feet above the sea, overlooking Portofino's miniature harbor and the hillsides behind it, the Bay of Rapallo and the whole sweep of sea towards Spezia on one side and San Fruttuoso and Genoa on the other. Most of the house itself is carved out of the solid rock, with two turret-like rooms—an octagonal living room and a spare bedroom—emerging from the walled terrace that is also the roof of the house below. The path to the Castelletto is half an hour's climb from the village (twenty minutes for a native), and all luggage and supplies have to be carried up.

Jenny had a room for Julie and me in the Castelletto itself; the boys stayed at the Nazionale, a small hotel on the village square; and Robert and all his family were in a house about halfway up the hill. Jenny was an indefatigable and efficient hostess, and for the three days of our stay there was a continuous round of lunches, cocktail parties and dinners. Robert was in great form. He announced happily that this was the first time he had ever been in Italy—in spite of all he had written about the Romans—and that he liked it.

After one of the lunch parties at the Castelletto Robert produced a typescript which he wanted me to read then and there. I saw by the title that it had something to do with one of the New Testament parables. I took it back to my room to read. I think (but can't be sure) that the parable in question was the one about the unjust steward; I do remember that Robert had recast it so that the moral was just the opposite of what it had been. Robert's assertion was that he had *restored* the parable to its original and proper form; that the reason why it had come down to us in a corrupt version was that some enemy had tampered with the original manuscript and had turned the meaning of Christ's words upside down.

This was the first hint I had of Robert's dawning interest in a new crossword puzzle, the Christian religion, in which he was not only going to fill in all the blank spaces but correct many of the accepted answers. I didn't want to get into a public argument with him that might end in a quarrel or at least bad feeling. So when he asked my opinion all I would say was that I preferred the original version.

We were given a farewell lunch *al fresco,* the whole party sitting at a long table on the piazza in front of the Nazionale. I sat next to Robert, who was not feeling well and had little to say. But at one point he turned to me with his characteristic sigh and said,

"I don't think you could ever do anything I would really mind."

I was surprised and touched. "Why, Robert," I said, "what makes you think that?"

"*I* don't know."

JULIE DIES

1

Eventually Julie found out about my philandering (a word I preferred to "infidelities," which was the term she insisted upon). I won't say how she found out, except that I didn't volunteer to tell her. In any case, with the cats all out of the bag, it was a relief to know that there were no more secrets between us. For some time, of course, she didn't trust me; and in fact we had a bad time, but at last we agreed that we had been through so much that we wanted to go on together to the end of the chapter. Neither of us suspected how soon that would come; I was looking forward to our growing old together. I knew Julie would become a "character," and I expected to enjoy that: listening to her and watching her and being with her. She was going to be an eccentric little old lady. Though I didn't expect to become an eccentric myself, or even a nice old man, I was sure I would be a seasoned connoisseur of Julie and that would do me very well.

But Julie didn't live to be a little old lady. She died just after her forty-sixth birthday. It took her nearly six months to die. This was hard on everybody; what it was like for Julie I can only guess. I sometimes thought the six months might have been the equivalent of twenty years for her.

It was cancer that killed her. I think she knew that was to be her fate; at least, she feared it. Both her father and mother had died of cancer, and she supposed that the disease, or at least a susceptibility to it, is inherited. The doctors assured her that this was not so, and she did her best to believe them. Thanks to these doctors, she was given a brief reprieve from her final sentence —a reprieve which they, in their kindly ignorance, had told her was a complete acquittal.

Julie's gynecologist, Dr. William Studdiford, was an old family friend as well. His father had been Mrs. Cuyler's doctor, and Bill Studdiford had delivered three of our four children. Shortly after Julie's forty-fourth birthday she went to him for a check-up, and he told her she ought to have a minor operation. During this operation he found slight traces of cancer of the cervix and removed them. Afterwards he told Julie and me that there could never be a recurrence of the disease in that part of the body, and that the chances were a thousand to one against its reappearance in any other part.

About a year later I took a three months' leave of absence from *Time,* and that summer Julie and the four boys and I set off on a long-planned trip to Europe. Like most American fathers I had a travel agent arrange every detail of our journey in advance, and I had typed copies of our daily itinerary. One steamy hot July morning we took a taxi to the New York docks and boarded a ship for Marseilles. The ship was an elderly character that had been redecorated and fitted out with new-fangled gadgets, some of which didn't work very well. Our cabins, for instance, were air-conditioned, with windows instead of portholes, and the windows could not be opened. This annoyed Julie very much. What's the use of going to sea, she said, if you can't get fresh sea air? There was something wrong with the air conditioning in our cabin, so we got no air at all. We had the engineers in, and after long struggles they got the air-conditioning system working after a fashion. The air smelled musty and stale.

After several days at sea Julie felt ill. This was not at all like her; she was a better sailor than any of us, and none of us had a qualm; the weather was fine and the sea smooth. After a couple of days in bed Julie said she felt better, but she was not her usual lively self, and spent most of her time lying in a deck chair. This time it was I who told the Mistress of Revels to leave Julie alone —and not nearly as tactfully, I am sure, as Julie had once begged me off. To make up for her defection Julie promised that at the Captain's Dinner, on our last night at sea, we would put on a family act. The idea, which I think was hers, was very simple but we thought sure-fire: at our cue all six of us would rise and give the ship's company a wide-mouthed grin. Since each of us would have a piece of black sticking plaster covering one of our front teeth, the effect would be gap-toothed and irresistibly hilarious. But alas, on the night our fellow passengers' resistance was at its height, and the act was not a success.

The ill-fated trip went on, at first according to plan, but as Julie grew worse and worse I was soon obliged to make changes. In Rome she felt so wretched that I went for a doctor. And again in Florence. The Roman doctor prescribed an ointment, the Florentine a pill; their diagnosis was vague and the treatment useless. In Venice Julie was so miserable that she spent three days in bed. I stayed with her and sent the boys off to the Lido on their own. We drove from Venice to Switzerland, and during that journey Julie seemed to recover; at any rate her spirits rose amazingly. It was partly the prospect of seeing snow-covered mountains and breathing cool mountain air after the hot plains and valleys of Italy in July.

At Stresa, where we stopped for the night before the drive over the Alps, there was a fresh breeze off the lake. Julie felt so much better she even thought of going for a swim, as the boys did. That night we made love for the last time in our lives.

In Switzerland the nightmare (it was beginning to be that) seemed to lift. We had the name of a doctor in Geneva who had studied in New York and knew Bill Studdiford. He came to see Julie and whisked her off to a cheerful and spotless little clinic, surrounded with flowers, where he wanted her to have a complete rest and then an examination. I sent the three older boys on to Paris and our seven-year-old and I were taken in by a friend who lived in Geneva, Victor Stanley.

The Swiss doctor kept Julie in hospital for two weeks. By that time she was definitely feeling better and she and the doctor had become great friends. When he had the results of all his tests he summoned us both to his office and told us that Julie had a tumor that should be removed when we went back to New York, but that it was certainly not malignant (therefore not cancer) and that there was no reason to cut our trip short. He said he would stake his medical reputation on the correctness of his diagnosis. He was most emphatic, and we had great confidence in him: he was that kind of doctor. You felt that he was a good man as well as a good physician. And I could see that he liked and admired Julie.

We went on to Paris and joined the three older boys. By this time, according to our itinerary, we should have been in England. But Julie wanted a week in Paris, so again I sent the three older boys ahead, saying that we would join them in London later. The day after they left Julie had a relapse, so painful and frightening that I lost my nerve and called up a doctor. He refused to come to the hotel to see her, but made an appointment at his office. I took her there in a taxi, he gave her an excruciating examination, confirmed the Swiss doctor's diagnosis and collected 1,000 francs in cash.

That night the nightmare returned in full force. Julie was in bed, pretending to be asleep, so as not to worry me. She had been unable to eat any dinner. Sandy, our youngest son, was asleep in another room. I sat in the faded grandeur of our hotel sitting room, fighting off panic, trying not to think. I no longer had any faith in any doctor. In spite of what they all said, I knew there was something dreadfully wrong with Julie. We must go home at once; we would fly back tomorrow. I would get the air tickets first thing in the morning.

I thought to myself: Julie may die. She may be going to die. I didn't think I could stand it. I wanted a drink, I wanted more than one drink, but I didn't want to call room service because it might disturb Julie. I went out to the nearest zinc bar and bought a bottle of brandy. Then I sat at the round table in the hotel sitting room, and drank, and tried not to think. Whenever my thoughts got too close I had another drink. By the time I went to bed I felt numb. Julie was asleep.

We flew home the next day. It was a horrible trip. Julie was in pain, I knew. The plane was American, a Constellation, but the crew were French and I had no faith in them. Some time between midnight and early morning we put down at the Reyk-javik airport in Iceland, to refuel, and all the passengers had to get off. I told the stewardess my wife was ill and in pain. She was very sorry; Madame would be made quite comfortable in the waiting room.

The waiting room was a bare, harshly lit room with hard wooden benches, and a counter where you could buy weak coffee and stale crackers. There was no place else to go. Julie and Sandy sat on a bench while I tried to find someone or something to make her more comfortable; but there wasn't anyone or any-thing. After we'd waited nearly an hour, our flight was called.

It was steamy hot, hazy sunlight when we landed at Idlewild. I was in such a rage of anxiety about Julie that I didn't care about anything else; I shouted and cursed our way through Immigra-tion and Customs in twenty minutes. And when I discovered that the ambulance I had cabled for wasn't there (the plane had ar-rived half an hour ahead of time), I put on such a scene that they got another ambulance in ten minutes. Julie was driven straight to the hospital, and Sandy and I followed in a taxi.

It had been his first flight. He had slept soundly half the time but denied that he had closed his eyes. I was still in a bad temper from the rows I had been making, and a nearly sleepless night. I said to him, "You know what's the trouble with planes? They go too slow, you might as well be on one of those old prairie schooners."

"Dad, how can you say such a thing? Why, yesterday after-noon we were in Paris, and here we are in New York!"

He was still excited and pleased. He didn't know about his mother.

When we got to the hospital Julie was already in bed, in a quiet room high over the East River Drive. Dr. Studdiford and a nurse were with her. He was as cheerful and confident as ever. He told me to go and get some sleep. Julie said, "Yes, darling. I'll be all right now."

"I'll be back this afternoon, as soon as I can."

Bill Studdiford came out into the hall with me. He said he

261

was sure the Swiss doctor had been right, there was nothing badly wrong with Julie. They would operate as soon as she was strong enough, in a week or so. Nothing to worry about.

It was nearly two weeks, however, before they did operate. By that time I'd taken a room at the hospital so as to be near her. When I knew the date of the operation I telephoned her brother Dick, who was a schoolmaster at South Kent, and asked him to sit it out with me. I hadn't seen much of Dick since we grew up, but we'd known each other well all our lives, and I'd always thought he was the one man I'd want with me in a tight place. This looked like the time. He said he'd come; I knew he would.

Bill Studdiford said the operation would take some time, probably about an hour and three quarters. After they took her to the operating theater, Dick and I sat in the visitors' waiting room. There was nobody else there. We smoked cigarettes and didn't say anything. I had been sure about that too; that he wouldn't say anything.

The time crawled on. We'd been waiting just forty minutes when Bill Studdiford appeared in the doorway, staring at me. He was getting a little deaf, so he always spoke in a louder voice than most people. He said loudly, "It's all over, Tom. It's no good."

"What do you mean?" I knew what he meant.

"It's all through her. No use operating."

That was what I'd thought it would be. But here it was. I said, "You're sure?"

"Yes, I'm sure. I'm sorry, but I thought you'd want to know."

I thought, you poor son of a bitch. I didn't have room to think about the doctor in Switzerland.

"You'll have to tell her, Bill. I promised to tell her."

He said he would, but not till after she came out from "medication." That wouldn't be till tomorrow, he said: she was pretty heavily doped.

I tried to think of the next thing to do. I felt that I had to think slowly and carefully. Call up the boys and tell them to fly home. That was it. I had to figure out where they would be in England. Then put in a transatlantic call. They let me have an empty hospital room, more comfortable than a telephone booth. I asked Dick to stand by, in case I couldn't hear. But the connection was fine, when I got the call. They were in a hotel in Cambridge, and I could hear the clink of glasses and voices in the background. I told my oldest son what had happened and what I wanted them to do.

Then I went back to Julie's room. She was still unconscious, and the nurse had lowered the Venetian blinds, so the room was half-dark. What would I say to her when she woke up? I would have to say everything was all right, and say it as if it were true. Julie could always tell when I was lying. This time she mustn't be able to tell. Bill was right; she mustn't be told until she could really take it in. I never had the slightest doubt that she was right in wanting to be told.

She stirred in her drugged sleep, and groaned. I think she must have been willing herself to wake up. She was very anxious to know the result of the operation. Long before she should have, she opened her eyes. The nurse tut-tutted her and tried to persuade her to go back to sleep, but she was too excited. I guess she must have had some hope, maybe quite a bit of hope. She called me and said, "Well?"

"Everything's fine! You're going to be all right." How could that phony cheerful tone fool anybody, let alone Julie? But maybe she wanted to be fooled, for just a little while longer. She said, "You're sure?"

"Absolutely! Everything's right as rain. Now you go to sleep, and Bill will see you when you wake up."

She sighed, squinted her eyes as if she were trying to focus them, gave up, and in a moment she was asleep again.

The next twenty-four hours were the longest in my life. For all that time I had to keep up the pretense with Julie that the operation had been a success and that she was going to recover. I tried to keep my face in shadow while I answered her questions, but she made me come over where she could see me. She was much more alert now, more than she should have been. It was as if the anesthetic had keyed her up. But if she suspected me, she decided not to show it. One bad mistake I made was in answering her question about how long the operation had lasted: I told her, before I thought, that it had been less than an hour. I could see her thinking that one over. She knew it should have been twice that long.

She slept a bit during the day, and I made various excuses to get out of the room—telegrams to send, phone calls, cigarettes. But there were terribly long stretches when she was awake and I was there. I didn't have to talk much, but she did make me say several times over that it was all right, she was going to get well. I don't think my act improved with repetition. And it wasn't just the tone of my voice—I had to *act* cheerful, and relieved, and happy. Or try to. It must have been a miserable performance. I couldn't be sure how miserable, for Julie never spoke about it afterwards. That meant that at any rate she didn't hold it against me.

Finally it was the next day. I knew Bill Studdiford would be in to see her that morning, so I didn't dare leave the room. I wanted to be there when he told her, to be sure she understood. He must have been dreading it too, because he didn't come till late in the morning. But he put on a much better act than I did. We could hear him whistling as he came down the hall—Julie used to call him "the whistler." And he was smiling, but not too much, when he opened the door.

He went over to the bed and took Julie's hand. She looked up at him and smiled too. She said, "Well, Bill?"

"You won't have to have any more operations."

That's all he said, but I swear she understood him instantly. Her smile didn't fade, it seemed to deepen. They looked at one another without speaking. Then she turned her head on the pillow and shut her eyes.

She didn't speak for two days. I thought she might never speak again. Most of the time she lay perfectly still, with her eyes closed or looking at the ceiling. I think now she was working very hard: she was accepting her death. If it was a lonely time for me, my loneliness was not in the same world as hers. She was only forty-five, and she would have liked to live a good deal longer. But in these two days—God knows how long they were for her —she mastered the fact that she was going to die.

I didn't master it; I never did, I haven't yet. And my problem was nothing to hers, but she solved hers.

Bill Studdiford couldn't tell me how long she had, but he thought it would be a matter of months. It was early August now; he said it was unlikely that she'd live till Christmas. We decided that as soon as she was strong enough I'd take her home, to Princeton where she longed to be. Bill would get a good nurse to come with us, who would stay till the end.

And that's the way it was. Except for the details. Such as what the weather was like and how slow her dying was. Miss McCue, her trained nurse, was quite a detail in herself. She was an old hand at death, in fact a specialist: all her patients died, because that was the kind of case she always took. Miss McCue was a good nurse—just how good you didn't notice at first. Her manner might put you off: she talked a good deal and her voice was loud and cheerful. She barked and yapped like an enthusiastic Pekinese, which she somewhat resembled. Julie liked her, and she adored Julie.

At first I didn't much take to Miss McCue. I thought her bedside manner left a good deal to be desired, and I didn't understand how devoted she was to her patient. It was that word "patient" that finally exploded my resentment of Miss McCue and cleared the air between us. I overheard her telephoning one day—that was easy to do, as she almost never lowered her voice —and heard her referring several times to "the patient." Why should this have made me so angry? It wasn't very much, in fact it was nothing, but I was on edge.

I called Miss McCue into the sitting room and shut the door. In a shaking voice I told her what I had overheard, and informed her that "the patient" was *not* the patient but my wife, who was dying; that if this was an indication of the impersonal way Miss McCue thought of her, she had better leave now, and that if I

265

ever again heard her refer to Julie in these terms I would send her packing.

Miss McCue's reply was to burst into tears—which surprised and shook me. She sobbed that she did *not* think of Julie impersonally; I began to see that I had made a bad mistake. I apologized to Miss McCue, she accepted the apology, and we shook hands. From then on I began to appreciate Miss McCue at her true worth. In a profession that demands hard work and selflessness, but doesn't always attract the tender-hearted, Miss McCue was the hardest-working, most selfless and tender-hearted nurse I ever met. Until a few weeks before Julie died she was on twenty-four-hour duty, and fiercely resisted all my suggestions that we should get another nurse to help her.

Finally the doctor overruled her, on the ground that she was not getting enough rest and would become ill herself if she didn't. One night well after midnight, when she should have been asleep for hours, I found her hard at work cutting and stitching up an "airfoam" pillow she had designed herself to fit under Julie's wasted body and make her more comfortable.

For the first month after we brought her home, Julie was strong enough to be outdoors, in the garden. We would carry her downstairs and she would lie in a long wicker chair, wrapped in blankets. Sometimes she liked to be alone, but until she became too weak the doctor allowed her a few visitors, usually in the afternoon. It was a beautiful fall, warm and mellow, with a long procession of sunny days. She was pitifully thin but she was still pretty. No, more than that: now she had the same look as her mother, the deep sad look of beauty. When I went into the garden to tell her visitors that their time was up and escorted them to the gate, they were usually in tears; but when I returned to Julie I would often find her smiling. It was almost as if she were on holiday.

Time slowed almost to a standstill. The weather worsened; everyone agreed that it was too cold now for Julie in the garden, but it was also because she had grown too weak to be carried downstairs. She could no longer eat much of anything, and the dreadful period of intravenous injections began. The worst part of that was getting the needle into one of her poor wasted veins; the doctor was always having to find a new vein, and these explorations hurt her. Our local doctor was a good man, though gloomy, and he found a colleague who was much defter than he at "finding a vein."

Visitors were reduced to a minimum; two or three of her closest friends. How could politics have found a place at this deathbed? Not in the same sense or to the degree as in the sickroom of a dying monarch, but politics just the same: vying for favor, jockeying for position. I am ashamed to say that I was not only aware of these maneuvers but took part in them. I was jealous of my own children, and I resented anyone who seemed to be more favored by Julie than myself. Once she called me "Darling Number One"—and I took some satisfaction from that, telling myself with relief that she didn't consider me, as she well might have, Darling Number Two. And another time, when she was floating between half-sleep and coma and couldn't open her eyes, and murmured, "Where's Tom? Is Tom here?" my heart leaped with joy (it was *me* she wanted!), and I said, "I'm here." She said, without opening her eyes, "If you're here, I'm all right."

I suppose the only people in that waiting household who were quite free of these tainted feelings—although perhaps I was wrong; perhaps I was the only one who felt them—were Julie herself and Miss McCue. No, there was one other; our seven-year-old son. His mother had been ill so long now that he seemed to take her illness for granted; he probably couldn't remember the time when Julie had been well. He certainly didn't expect that his mother was soon going to leave him forever.

As Julie grew weaker, no one—herself most of all—wanted her life prolonged. The doctors kept reassuring me on that point: they were not keeping her alive by giving her intravenous injections and drugs but only trying "to make her comfortable." They said she was not in pain and I hope they were right, though who could suppose that the slow, interminable-seeming struggle of one's body to die could possibly be "comfortable"?

267

One of the results of her disease was that the space between her back and ribs became filled with liquid. Since this added to her miseries, the doctors decided to drain it. It was a simple and horrible proceeding: you could hardly call it an operation, because not even a local anesthetic was needed. The doctor simply punctured Julie's back below the shoulder blade with a large syringe, and pumped out this gruesome dark stuff. There was a lot of it; two and a half syringes. The doctors made a kind of social occasion of it—besides Miss McCue and themselves, our sons and myself were gathered round Julie's bed. Everybody, including Julie, was very jolly, except me.

The doctors wanted Julie sitting up in bed, and asked me to hold her there; she was too weak to sit up by herself. I was proud and pleased to be able to do something for her at last. Miss McCue and the doctor raised her head and shoulders from the pillow, and I sat on the edge of her bed, with my arms around her and her head on my shoulder. It was the first time for months that she had been in my arms, and it would be the last time, I suddenly thought, until she was dead. She wouldn't be very different then—she was nothing but skin and bone now—except that she would be dead. I began to shake and sweat uncontrollably; the strength went out of me. My trembling shook Julie and made it difficult for the doctor who was working the syringe. I had to give up my place to my second son, who was young and strong, and didn't tremble. At that moment I hated him.

I knew that my state of mind in those days was not what it should have been. I was under a strain, but so was everyone else in that household, and the others seemed to be able to behave better, taking their cue from Julie. She was really long-suffering and serene: the rest of us had to act as if we were. I knew people were making allowances for me, and that didn't help. I had trouble sleeping, and of all things I dreaded lying awake at nights. Before I went to bed I tried to drink enough to make sure I would sleep. I never took a drink until after I had said good night to Julie; after that I would drink with anyone who was there, or by myself. It didn't work very well: I usually fell asleep as soon as I got to bed, but after a while I would wake up in the small hours, and in the mornings I felt rotten.

I was jealous of my own sons. I knew how fiercely Julie loved them, and I wasn't sure now whether she loved me as much. It seemed to me—it may have been my state of mind—that there was a competition among us all for signs of her affection. I knew this was all wrong, but I couldn't help competing. She was old enough now to be the mother of all of us, but she was also my wife; I couldn't forget that. She grew away from us—she certainly grew away from me—in those endless days. No, it would be better to say that she grew beyond me. She was learning something now that I didn't know; she was wiser, much wiser, than she had ever been. I could tell by the way she looked at me. Why couldn't she tell me what it was she had learned?

She had never been very articulate. That was part of the reason. And with all the others to whom she had to give her dwindling time, she hadn't much left for me. Even when I succeeded in being alone with her we weren't really alone, for Miss McCue would be there or the doctor would interrupt us. We had a few times. I knew she wanted to tell me something, but I knew it was hard for her to try and I feared it would be impossible for me to listen. For I knew she wanted to say something about death, and I didn't think I could bear to hear her.

When at last Julie and I had our talk, it was not Julie but me who mentioned death, though I didn't use the word. She was thinking in other terms. As her mother had been, Julie was a naturally religious person. When she had stopped going to church to keep me company as an agnostic, she must have felt like an unwilling expatriate. After we had sheered off from Gurdjieff's pale imitation of a church, she had returned happily to her own, and I went with her; but she knew I had gone with her mainly to keep her company. She had been immune to Laura. She knew I had not been totally immune. Now she must have thought a long time about how to say what she wanted to tell me, because it all came out in only two words:

"Love God."

Hearing this in her hoarse little voice, hardly more than a whisper, was very different from hearing it, as I had many times, from a pulpit.

"I'll try," I said. "But it's you I really love."

"He is in the love between us." She was looking at me very earnestly, and her slow whisper was just audible. "Not in you, or in me, but in the love between us."

"But you're going away."

I couldn't see how she was looking at me because my eyes were full of tears.

"He is always there."

Everyone who went into Julie's room in those final months came away with a strong sense of having been in the presence of something extraordinary—the presence of some lasting certainty. Miss McCue, and she was not the only one, thought Julie was a saint. I thought she had become a heartbreakingly wise person. (Why heartbreakingly? Because I wasn't wise.) Maybe we meant the same thing. My memories of Julie were too human for me to accept willingly the idea that in dying she was becoming a different kind of person. Whatever else she was or might become, she was still my dying wife.

A small measure of Julie's preeminence in the family was the extent to which every one of us, in our different ways, depended on her. This was as true of my father (whose relations with Julie, I thought, were rather like old King Saul's with young David) as of Sandy, our youngest son, who almost succeeded in giving the impression (except when illness turned him into a helpless, demanding and terrified infant) that he was dependent on nobody. Because our children were all sons —how a daughter would have appreciated and cherished Julie!—they were awkward and shy with their mother, and hid their real feelings for her like a guilty secret. But on her deathbed her dominion over us could no longer be denied or hidden. Her spirit filled the room, and our lives; and when she died and left us, it was the end of our world.

And saint or not, she found it hard to die. Once I heard her whisper, "I'm struggling"; and twice I heard her complain. One night she said, "Oh, why does it have to be like this?" And another time, waking from a sleep she must have hoped she wouldn't wake from, she said in a tone of great disappointment: "Oh, I'm not dead *yet.*"

But she was not her father's daughter for nothing. There was a family story about some grandmother or great-aunt who on her deathbed had opened one eye on the circle of relations around her and remarked: "A watched pot never boils." It was in this tradition that Julie, after coming out of a sinking spell, opened her eyes and said to me in a small, clear voice: "First false alarm."

On the few occasions when we were alone together, Julie several times brought up the subject of my marrying again. This was such a painful topic to me that I always tried to divert her from it, but she would not be put off. She said she thought "it would be all right" for me to marry again (knowing Julie, I knew this meant "I want you to marry") "after the suffering is over."

From time to time in our married life, when there was something Julie felt deeply about and was anxious to express as precisely as she could, she would write it down and then show it to me: partly because she had little faith in her own command of words and partly because I made her feel inarticulate. She felt this need for the last time when she was dying. Two weeks before she died, she wrote me a letter. She was so weak by that time that she had to write it lying on her back and holding the paper above her. It must have cost her a tremendous effort.

The letter was written faintly, in pencil, and she had tried to correct it—she wanted to say exactly what she meant—so that one sentence is almost unreadable. This was the letter, as nearly as I could decipher it:

My dearest one in all the world, you will have some suffering to do my darling and do it because it will be your path to God and after that everything will be all right. Please remember [and then comes a bit so written over that I could never make it out] . . . my fault . . . you will

271

be the wonderful man you never could be with me. I love you beyond all telling and always will.

Cuy [That was my pet name for her]

Miss McCue was an expert in her field who knew every signpost along the approach to death. She was also a kindly woman who wanted to make not only her dying patients but their families as comfortable as she could; so it was not until a week before Julie died that she told me it would be any day now. And she told me about "Cheyne-Stokes breathing": the sure sign of the end. This is an unmistakable irregularity of breathing, some breaths rapid and some slow, that gets fainter and fainter until the last held breath is held forever.

One night Miss McCue summoned me, saying that the Cheyne-Stokes breathing had begun. But this turned out to be Julie's second and last false alarm. Three days later she was still alive and seemed still conscious. That morning the publisher of *Time* telephoned me from New York to tell me some "great good news": I had just been promoted to Editor, with a raise. I couldn't have cared less, but I said, "Thanks, that's fine."

"Be sure to tell Julie!"

I whispered the "great good news" into Julie's ear, and she smiled. I think she understood, and I think she was glad for my sake, but she would have said if she could that I mustn't let that kind of thing matter too much.

Next day, a cold and sunny December morning, she was in a coma, and the Cheyne-Stokes breathing started up again. We were all in her room, standing around her bed—the doctor, Miss McCue, the four boys and myself, Julie's favorite brother and his wife. The ragged breathing stopped, went on, fluttered, stopped ... Suddenly I realized that it had stopped for good. Miss McCue gave a great sob.

I said in a loud, false voice: "Thanks be to God!" Then, "Please go away, all of you, and leave me with my wife." They all tiptoed out and shut the door.

I looked at my dead Julie. It wasn't Julie any more. Just a

dead body on Julie's bed. A minute ago she had been there; now she had gone. I knelt down beside the bed and put my arms around that body and laid my head on its breast. Still warm. But not Julie any longer; not Julie ever again.

WHAT BECAME OF THEM

1

In the days when Laura ruled the roost in Deya, she and Robert
were exceptionally suspicious of all outsiders—and under that
head they lumped everyone outside their little circle. When Robert returned to Deya after the war, there was a notable relaxation
of this standing order: the right of entry to Canellun was still
select but no longer nearly so exclusive. And as Robert's fame
spread through the literary world (which really means the world
of readers, not writers), he became a popular local figure as well.

At first I welcomed this change. I imagined Robert becoming
a benign and honored celebrity in his adopted village: a pictur-
esque sage whose hospitable door would be open to *bona fide*
pilgrims. And to a certain extent something like this did happen.
Robert became a familiar and accessible landmark, and visitors
to Mallorca with any sort of introduction found it easy to see him.
When I met some of these visitors and heard about others, I
began to wonder whether he was not letting himself become too
accessible.

Which of these new friends were real friends and which
merely hangers-on? One I was sure was altogether a bad lot.
Derek was a reckless fellow who had more money than was good
for him. He owned two army surplus jeeps, which he drove as if
they were racing cars. He rented a house that was perhaps a mile
or so down the road from Canellun, and imported two Spanish girls from the mainland to do the housework. One day
Robert took me to lunch there, and the girl who waited on the
table was very pert and very pregnant. There were ugly rumors
about the reason for Derek's presence in Mallorca: that he was
wanted by the mainland police for manslaughter. Driving fast, at

night, through a Spanish village, he had hit and killed an old woman—and had driven on without stopping. Some said this had happened more than once. Eventually Derek disappeared from Mallorca—had there been a hit-and-run "accident" there too, or were the police too close on his trail? At all events Robert seemed to find nothing shocking in Derek's reputation or his conduct. He did say that he held no brief for Derek's behavior but that there was something about him he rather liked.

There was another class of visitor, none of whom I ever encountered but whose traces I saw: the journalists who came to Mallorca to interview Robert. There had been a time when not one of these gentry would have been admitted to Canellun, and if they had persisted in pestering him would have been sent off with a stinging flea in their ear; but times had changed. If Robert didn't welcome publicity, he no longer went out of his way to avoid it; and articles about him, illustrated by snapshots and posed "camera studies," appeared in all sorts of newspapers and magazines, from *Vogue* to the *Daily Mail*.

The most embarrassing one, I thought, was published in some glossy journal like *Queen*. It was written by John Davenport, who had never met Robert before, and its title was *Big Man*. The article made Robert out to be a kind of Hemingway hero, an epitome of two-fisted masculinity; and the most striking photograph, which took up a full page, displayed his well-muscled, slightly hairy naked torso, from Adam's apple to navel.

Another one, which explained that he had settled in Mallorca on the advice of Gertrude Stein (and never mentioned Laura Riding), showed him posed in a pseudo-Greek temple and began: "There are those who say he is a Greek god walking the earth thinly disguised as an English poet; others say only a demigod, and nobody is quite certain which one."

The farm at Brownsburg had long since ceased to be a going concern. The only relics of Schuyler's farming days were some rusting tractors, a few sagging lines of once electrified fence (for sheep), and the long rows of black walnut saplings (goodbye, his daughters' dowry!). Now the farm was simply a large, decaying property that brought in nothing and cost more in taxes and upkeep than Schuyler could afford. For technically the farm belonged to him—although Kit had put the last of her money into it, and might therefore have been considered part owner, at least. Some time in the early forties Schuyler began to sell the farm piecemeal, and Kit eventually had to find some other place for her and the children to live.

The place she eventually found was not very far away, on the New Jersey side of the Delaware and up the river, above Lambertville. It was a hamlet called Raven Rock: a dozen frame houses in a line under a sheer cliff a couple of hundred feet high. A stone's throw away, between the cliff and the river, were the tracks of the Delaware and Lackawanna; a dozen times a day a train (almost always a long freight train) screamed and rattled past. The engine drivers always blew their whistles at just this point.

The house at Raven Rock that Kit rented—she couldn't afford to buy one—was only half a house; her landlords, whose names were Sorby and Jeff, lived in the other half. Sorby was a serious, almost solemn young man with a large, sweet face, a bibliophile and local historian who made a paying hobby out of buying up derelict houses, restoring them to good condition and selling them. Jeff was a saturnine, black-haired Englishman, who, when he wanted some extra money, would cash in on his good education and prosperous background by taking a temporary job as a waiter.

Kit herself was in chronic need of money. Schuyler doled her out a regular pittance, but it was not enough to keep her and the children. Her first attempt at making money was a rather social scheme called Townsend Woollens. It was an unmitigated disaster. She bought bolts of expensive wool, traveled expensively to call on her wide, far-flung and increasingly unenthusiastic acquaintances, collected a few orders and lost a lot of money. Needing capital even to start these proceedings, she had to borrow from friends—as Schuyler's ex-wife she knew enough to avoid the banks—and when the money was gone and she tried to raise more, they refused her. At first she was furious and hurt; then she roared with laughter and forgot it.

But she had to get some kind of job. Eventually she got one, and kept it for several years: sandpapering furniture in George Nakashima's workshop at New Hope. She was the only woman employee. I think Kit must have bullied him into giving her a job in the first place. She told me that several times he had tried to fire her and that she had just laughed at him. She didn't like the job much and didn't think he paid her enough, but she needed the money, so she kept on. Whether Nakashima finally got rid of her, or she just quit, I don't know.

Robert supported a sizable family—actually two families (Nancy and her four children, then Beryl and another four)—not to mention numerous friends and hangers-on, by his pen alone. He had only one salaried job in his life, and that one lasted only a year: the professorship of English at the Egyptian University, Cairo. He must have written as many million words, or thereabouts, as Georges Simenon or Edgar Wallace, but the scope, quality and variety of his writing were far beyond theirs.

Robert Graves must be allowed, as a writer who has tended his trade "with uncessant care" (though his own god will judge how strictly he has meditated the thankless Muse), to be among the most experienced and accomplished of his generation, who long ago left far behind such would-be teachers as Laura Riding. When it comes to writing "clean English," as he calls it, no one can do it better; and in the craft of verse, within his carefully circumscribed limits, few have excelled him. Like Arnold Bennett, he would tackle any question, and he became so seasoned a craftsman that he could turn out a competent job of writing on any subject he chose.

I still remember an epitaph he wrote for his son-in-law's gravestone. Alec Clifford, who married Robert's eldest daughter Jenny, was one of the best British war correspondents in the Second World War, and his foreign correspondence after the war was the brightest feather in the *Daily Mail's* cap. It was Alec who found and rebuilt that marvelous Castelletto at Portofino, where he and Jenny staged our last reunion with Robert in 1949. Julie died later that year, and Alec lived only four years longer: he too died of cancer (Hodgkin's disease) but kept on working till a month or two before his death. This was the epitaph that Robert wrote for him:

OF THOSE CHARGED TO WITNESS VIOLENCE & MISERY FEW HAVE LEFT
SO TRUTHFUL AND COMPASSIONATE A RECORD.*

That revised parable Robert had shown me in Portofino was only a beginning, as I had suspected. The next time I saw him was in Deya in the early 1950s—my first return there since Julie's death. Robert had published *King Jesus,* his fictional account of the life of Christ, and was working on a more serious and ambitious book, *The Nazarene Gospel Restored.* On one of our walks he said to me,

"This book I'm doing now. It frightens me."

"Why, Robert?"

"Because I have a kind of sentimental attachment to the Church I was brought up in, and this book will destroy the Church. It's like having the responsibility for dropping the atom bomb. Christianity will be finished."

"Finished? Now, Robert!"

"Yes, finished, *kaput.* Oh, it may not happen overnight, and everywhere at once. The Catholics will go on telling themselves fairy stories—it may not affect them much. But Protestant Christianity will be wiped out. The only refuge Protestants can find will be to become Jews—and Pharisees at that."

How much of this did he really believe? It's impossible to say; but it was obvious that he had begun to take his "findings" seriously, and was evolving a technique of "historical research" that

---

*The accepted idiom "charged with witnessing" would require five more letters: I suppose Robert was forced into this neologism by limitations of space.

would enable him to discover anything he set out to find. He was like a dowser searching for water, except that he needed no forked stick: he could tell the approach of his quarry, as surely as the witch in Macbeth, by the pricking of his thumbs.

From time to time I have reviewed books by Robert; although then the reviews in *Time* were anonymous, he knew I had written them. I think he must have subscribed to a clipping bureau, for he seemed to read all the reviews of his books, and it became his settled practice to write a letter of protest or correction to the editor whenever he thought the review inaccurate or unfair. Over the years I must have reviewed five or six of his books without rousing his ire, but at last in 1958 I did it.

The book, called *Five Pens in Hand,* was a collection of miscellaneous articles and lectures: not a very good book, but like all Robert's writing, except when he was being a solemn scholar, very readable. This was my review:

Robert Graves is a prose writer of nimble prejudices, coaxing imagination and gap-toothed flashes of disarming charm. He is an old professional who takes care to write cleanly, and his signature is always recognizable. He wishes to be considered, and will probably be remembered, as primarily a poet—a good poet, but not a "great" one (a term which he hates and whose validity he denies).

He will also be remembered, I think, as the author of *Goodbye to All That,* surely one of the best autobiographies ever written and one of the few first-class books about World War I. (A revised version has recently been published in England and America.) And what other writer of our day—with the possible exception of Simenon, who is not in the same class—has shown such unfailing gusto in getting the work out? By his own estimate his "old-fashioned steel nib" has written more than four million words.

His latest book will lose him no friends (he and the Apostle Paul would never have hit it off, in any case) nor, I should think, have much effect on his secure standing as a wit, an accomplished story teller and a grizzled *enfant terrible* among the scholars. . . .

When George Moore wrote *The Brook Kerith* he proved himself an "ignorant old rascal," but nevertheless did base his book on "three bold and accurate guesses: ... that Paul willfully misrepresented Jesus; that Jesus survived the Cross; and that he then considered himself to have offended God by 'forcing the hour.'" Yet, even while Mr. Graves is flying through the air with the greatest of ease, he acknowledges that he does hear an occasional low whistle from skeptical observers: "Scholars speak very cruelly of my work sometimes, accusing me of wild guessing."

He does more. He confesses, in so many words: "My imagination is not that of a natural liar, because my Protestant conscience restrains me from inventing complete fictions; but I am Irishman enough to coax stories into a better shape than I found them." Now, how can you resist that? It's like the Chekhov character who sighs and says: "When I philosophize, I lie terribly." And when Mr. Graves is chuckling out a story, not a complete fiction, but jollied into a better shape than he found it, or writing about himself as if he were the character that indeed he is, there's no denying him. . . .

The book includes twenty of his latest poems (none from my favorite drawer) which speak, as always, for themselves. It also includes a story he says is "ancient," though it was new to me: "An old lady was taking a pet tortoise by train, in a basket, from London to Edinburgh, and wanted to know whether she ought to buy a dog-ticket for it, as one has to do in England if one takes a cat by train—because cats officially count as dogs. 'No,' said the ticket inspector, 'No, mum! Cats is dogs, and rabbits is dogs, and dogs is dogs, and squirrels, in cages, is parrots; but this here turkle is a hinsect. We won't charge you nothing, mum!'"

This here turkle is a hinsect.

My review was intended to pull Robert's leg, but not too hard, about his method of historical dowsing, to which there were several references in this book; I headed the review "This Here Turkle Is a Hinsect." Shortly afterwards Robert wrote me:

Read your review in the N.Y. *Times.* If you feel obliged to prove so convincingly that our friendship does not prevent you from speaking your mind, why go out of the way to review my books? I'm not angry in the least, only curious. I love you dearly. But you do the goddamnedest things sometimes and reduce me to falling back on my superiority-complex. . . .

He said that he himself made it a rule never to review a friend's book unless he could speak only good of it. My suggestion that he cheats is all the more damaging since I'm known to be his friend. None of the points I raised in my review should have been made "to excite ridicule." Why not try to prove him wrong? —that would be more to the point and more helpful.

And he signed himself "Puzzled."

I replied:

Oh, Robert, Robert!

You *were* offended. I'm sorry. But you really shouldn't have been. I've read the review over, anxiously, and got Martha to read it again too. We both think you're being a little prickly.

I've reviewed books of yours before (though never again) and much more critically, and not a word out of you. Whatever faults can be found with this review, it was certainly friendly, and must have been taken so by everyone who read it—though not, obviously, by you.

Tom

I didn't leave it at this, however. A month or so later I was going to Ibiza with friends. Ibiza was only a few hours by boat from Mallorca, so I wrote to Robert and proposed myself for a two-day visit. Before that I had heard from him again:

Thanks for your affectionate letter. Why I wasn't offended by your review of *King Jesus* was that it was offered as fiction; and in fiction one has licence to rearrange events; as also in poetry. But to suggest that a historian takes liberties with his facts is to call him a liar. . . . I don't mind being called crazy, self-opinionated, etc., etc. but if the people to whom you showed your review don't think that it matters whether one tells the truth or not they must be very cynical or even something worse.

Anyhow, everything is straight now I hope. Do *please* come & see us. Much love from us all.

So I went to Canellun for a couple of days, and all was well again. Robert and I went for a walk and talked out our differences —at least to the extent of my promising that I would not review any more of his books. The second day, on another walk, he said, "By the way, have you seen a book of mine called *Five Pens in Hand*"?

I looked at him; he stared, then remembered; and we both laughed.

His connections with Laura were not only severed but all traces of them were now obliterated. In the eight years 1931 to 1938 Robert's entry in *Who's Who* had included a mention of Laura ("partner to* Laura Riding in the Seizin Press since 1927; collaborated with whom in *No Decency Left*, a novel, 1932"). After the 1938 edition no mention of Laura appeared in his *Who's Who* entry, nor did he list any of the books in which he collaborated with her, although he named other collaborators (e.g., Alan Hodge, Joshua Podro).

A question I have many times been asked is: Why did we accept the uncanny domination that Laura exercised over us, and that she could not have exerted without our willing submission? Robert was a special case: he was Laura's lover, as devoted to her as a dog to his master; then and later there was always a stain of masochism in his fidelity to the Muse. But what about John and Lucie and Norman, Julie and me—particularly Julie and me? I knew that Laura, supposedly omniscient, had completely misunderstood my own attitude toward her, so how could I have accepted her as an intellectual—in some sense very nearly a spiritual—guide? And Julie, that resolute paladin of feminine common sense, how could she have let Laura pull the wool over her eyes?

In Norman's case, "laughter supervened," and he escaped; but until the very day of his defection he was as rabidly absolute in Laura's cause as any of Cromwell's image-smashing Saints were in the Protector's. Because Lucie feared Laura, when she was living in Laura's fief she conformed to the necessary rules,

---

*A delicate use of the preposition suggesting "assistant partner to," not "equal partner with."

285

but I think it was only her possessive love for John that out-weighed her mistrust.

Nor did Laura's might and majesty overpower everyone who met her. My sister Peggy, who visited us in Deya for a couple of weeks, was quite immune (perhaps her Gurdjieff vaccination saved her); and my friend Jeffrey Mark, another visitor, was no more impressed by Laura than he was by any bluestocking schoolmarm.

As for Julie and me, and why we acknowledged Laura's sovereignty over us, I cannot give a satisfactory answer, even to myself. I can only say "I don't know." We did feel that there was something occult about her, and this made us uneasy; neverthe-less, as I have said, we told each other that even though Laura might be a bit of a witch, she was a "white witch," definitely on the side of good, not evil.

Was this the same sort of venal mentality that blinded and deafened millions of Germans to the Jewish holocaust in Nazi Germany, and caused "ordinary" Frenchmen to knuckle under to the German occupation, or even collaborate with it? Or could it more accurately be compared to that Jewish meekness that submitted without a struggle to the death camps and the gas chambers, and sometimes even seemed to assist their murderers? The Maccabean Sabras, born and bred in militant Israel, accus-tomed to war and unacquainted with defeat, were puzzled and grieved by this lamblike submissiveness of their fathers and grandfathers. It was said that Ben-Gurion's chief aim in bringing Eichmann to trial in Jerusalem was to teach his young fellow citizens to understand how their forebears could have behaved as they did. This analogy will not hold, for our lives were not at stake.

No, I think it is simpler than that. To the question: Why did we put up with Laura? the answer is: Because people are in general vulnerable to bullying.

And Julie, at least, must be absolved from the charge of complete submission to Laura's will. It was the strength of Julie's innocence, I think, that kept her from being dominated by

Laura. She came along with me into this dangerous territory, but only to keep me company; it was not her line of country. She behaved well wherever she was, and no matter how uncouthly her companions might conduct themselves; she was always happy to get home again, however, to the people she really liked and trusted.

To someone with a good brain (or who thinks he has) and a bad conscience or even the normal amount of self-doubt, people with pretensions, who are *sure* they are superior beings, will always be dangerously attractive. Knowing our own liability to sin and error, admiring and alarmed by their absolute certainty of their own seamless virtue, we tell ourselves that they *might* be right (we are only too well aware of the probability that *we* are not absolutely right about anything that matters). We are weakly and cowardly sane: they are strongly and indomitably crazy. So that when they demand our subjection, complete obedience, and instantly, our tendency is to hear and obey. They are the simulacrum of authority, and for those who crave authority, even if they do not worship and fall down before it, they can seem the surrogate, the deputy, of the Word itself. The world is full of such false prophets, and their bemused (and temporary) followers. Laura was always trying to put me (and everyone else she encountered) in my place; and for a time we both felt she had succeeded. Like most human victories, however, this one too was ephemeral.

We knew—for she let us see—that we provoked Laura constantly by our slowness of understanding, our coarseness of perception, our loose and wavering standards of behavior; yet she was patient with us (all except Robert, a special case, demanding special severity). And we accepted, if we did not openly acknowledge, her sovereignty and her right to judge us. Imperceptibly, before we were aware of where we were, we had become so used to this unquestioning fealty that any qualification of our faith in her would have been like admitting the possibility that God is mad. That possibility *should* be considered, since we take for granted our own sanity as a yardstick for the universe; but at the

287

time it would have seemed a blasphemy even to raise the question of Laura's fallibility. So I suppose you could say that we did believe, in our humanistic (or blasphemous) way, that Laura was God. Or at any rate his Vicar. (Laura would have said "her Vicar.")

How did she reconcile her career as a writer with her role as arch-priestess? I don't think she did reconcile them, or see any reason why she should. In any case, her writing represented only one side of her—she called it her "sun-side," and sometimes spoke of it lightly as her masculine aspect. Her "moon-side," the brooding, all-knowing feminine part of her nature, to which she seldom referred and then only in hushed hints, was the essential Laura, the true core of the sage and prophetess who would change the world.

The instruments of this change could not be the nameless, transient, random little crowd that bought and half-understood or misunderstood her books; they must be individual disciples, chosen and trained by herself. How did she choose them?

Brilliantly clever people think, or appear to think, in a higher mathematics than our simple arithmetic. They play cat's cradle with connections and distinctions invisible to us; they see through the contradictions of paradox to the illuminating enigma at the core; where we stand frozen and perplexed, they are easy and at home.

And how can I know that I am just to Laura? Can anyone ever know? She would say, of my attempts to "tell the truth" about her, that the truth is not in me, that I am incapable of knowing or telling the truth—about her, about anyone or anything. And I should have to agree that this may be. Should I also have to agree that when the shoe is on the other foot, when she tries to draw a just likeness of me (as in her "psychological portrait," which I have unfortunately—she might say "fortunately and deliberately!"—lost), *lust* and *fury*, the words she wrote into the portrait, are my sufficient handcuffs? I think my reply might be that those handcuffs would be enough to make me come quietly to court, but that there—unless it is Laura alone who is to be both judge and jury—I would hope to establish a more adequate likeness.

Laura can always make herself understood, to a certain extent. The rub comes in the *extent.* When she writes: " . . . some of the things that I have already made plain have seemed obscure to people because I have sometimes made too much plain—more than most people are capable of understanding," this will definitely not play in Peoria, where it would rouse guffaws and cries of "Horse-shit!" People who know they are not omniscient tend to dislike those who know they are.

2

Robert has always been a great hand at putting the cat among the pigeons. For example, his various attempts to define or describe poetry ("A poem is the resultant of a conflict in the poet's mind"; "Poetry is the art of avoiding the letter *s*"); or his own literary practice ("I write poems for poets, and satires or grotesques for wits. For people in general I write prose, and am content that they should be unaware that I do anything else.") And in his Clark Lectures at Cambridge in 1954, he intimated that most "great" poets have been overrated phonies and most good poets underrated. (He considered himself a good poet, not a "great" one.)

What tricks our memory plays us! I could have sworn I heard Robert say, in his first lecture as Poetry Professor at Oxford, that every dedicated poet must have a Muse, a live, flesh-and-blood woman whom he worships, and who is not his wife. And that on this occasion both his wife and his Muse were in the audience. But now the nearest thing I can find in the three lectures that have been published is this statement from his third lecture:

"The Muse . . . is 'the perpetual other woman,' never the Poet's wife."

That Muse was Number Two. I don't know how many there were all together; I met only the first two. The first was a tall, coldly handsome, dark-haired Greek-American girl named Margo. I should say she was in her late twenties; Robert was then in his sixties. I remember meeting her only twice, both times in London. I sat next to her at dinner in the flat where Robert and Beryl were staying. She hardly spoke, and we did not exchange a word, but afterwards Robert reported happily that she liked me. Was their love affair a physical one? I think it was. The relation between a poet and his Muse, as defined by Robert, was not the state of romantic chastity pursued by the legendary knights of King Arthur; the poems that mark the progress of his affairs with his Muses are at the same time curiously artificial and sexually explicit.

Since the intimacy of our friendship has long been a thing of the past, it was only from his published poems that I got news of how Robert's love affair with Margo was getting on. I should say: from his poems and from Alastair Reid's. Most of this verse, both Alastair Reid's and Robert's, was published in the *New Yorker,* and it made fascinating but tantalizing reading. Fascinating because I could recognize at least some of the references in these agonized or bitter soliloquies; tantalizing because I could never figure out exactly what was going on, or even who was ahead. Later, from pieced-together bits of news and hearsay, I learned the outline of the story.

Alastair Reid was a handsome, clever, equivocal young Scot, some twenty years younger than Robert, who had played rugby for Scotland (or so it was said), wrote better than competent verse and prose, and had already embarked on a somewhat erratic career by the time Robert took him up. (Alastair Reid was first cousin to Alastair Hetherington, Editor of the *Guardian:* they could not abide one another.) Robert treated Alastair like a favorite son, and gave him a house in Deya to live in. Alastair sat at Robert's feet as a student, not as a disciple; he accepted Robert's bounty with cool appreciation rather than gratitude.

The possible realization of Robert's dream of a successful Hollywood film or a Broadway hit appeared on the horizon during Alastair Reid's incumbency, and he was dispatched to the United States, all expenses paid, to act as Robert's trusted agent. His mission turned out to be a resounding disaster. When I next saw Robert and asked him about the absent Alastair, he answered bitterly and curtly. The fact was that Alastair, instead of bringing home the bacon for Robert, had run off with Margo.

Or had *she* run off with *him?* Whichever way it was, she had left Robert for Alastair, and this was a bitter pill for Robert. Not the bitterest, however—but wait . . . It soon became apparent to a reader of Alastair's verses in the *New Yorker* that all was not well between the runaway pair, and before long it appeared that Margo had bolted again. With whom? Ah, that was the final mouthful that Robert simply could not swallow. For the man whom Margo preferred both to Robert and Alastair was a famous Broadway wit and impresario. She married him and bore him a child (but that marriage didn't last either). This dual betrayal (Muses do *not* get married and they do *not* have children), and with a man whom Robert could not have considered anything but his inferior, retrospectively turned his whole affair with Margo to dust and ashes. He let the milestone poems stand, but the track that joined them he obliterated. Margo, like an excommunicated Communist, was expunged from Robert's history. She no longer was; she had never existed.

It was not long, though, before the second Muse put in her appearance. In fact, she was there already, as one of the band of youths and maidens (poetically speaking) who now danced attendance on Robert in Deya. She too was in her twenties, and of mixed nationality (Mexican-American); though she could not be called beautiful, her face had a knowing, impish stamp that some men, and some women, found alluring. Her name was Aemilia (but he called her "Emile") Laraçuen. We had seen her in Deya when we were there for Robert's sixty-eighth birthday party, and had not found her prepossessing.

In the fall of that year Robert came to England to give his three Oxford lectures (W. H. Auden, his predecessor as Poetry Professor, had hit on the tax-saving device of giving the three annual lectures in one term, and Robert copied him). When he got to London he telephoned me. The conversation went something like this:

"Will you do me a favor, Tom?"

"Of course, Robert. What is it?"

"Well, I'd like you to put up a friend of mine."

"Yes, sure. But you realize there's no one in the house but me. No cook or anything."

"That's all right. We'll be there in ten minutes."

And very shortly arrived at my door Robert and Emile, both wearing Andalusian hats, rarely if ever seen in London, and making them look, I thought, like a family act in a circus; and Robert's daughter Jenny, by now an old friend of mine. Jenny gave me such a look! And I returned it. I knew we would both have given a good deal to be able to voice our thoughts. Robert was brisk and businesslike, Emile all silence and smiles. I showed them her room, explained that she would have to go out for meals, as there was no food in the house, and gave her a latchkey. No mention was made of how long she was to stay.

And that was just about the last I saw of her. Some four days later my conscience smote me: I might at least have given her a glass of sherry. I went home that afternoon determined to do that. When I opened the front door, there was an envelope lying on the floor, addressed to me and sealed with a wad of chewing gum. It was from Emile. She had found some friends of her own age living in Chelsea, she said, and was moving in with them. She would keep my latchkey but I was not to worry: she wouldn't turn my house into a hotel. I immediately telephoned Robert and told him I wanted my key back. And I got it—though not for several days. I saw Emile once again, at Robert's next lecture in Oxford. She was on the other side of the hall, but we spotted each other, and waved.

Robert told this characteristic little ghost story to my wife

Pam: when he gave his last lecture at Oxford in 1966, he and Emile were separated by the Atlantic. She knew that after the lecture there would be a party for him, and she made him fix the precise time when he would be lifting a glass of champagne to drink her health, promising that she would do the same. And at that very instant, said Robert, a glass leapt from the table and shattered itself on the floor. "What power! With 3,000 miles between us. Imagine what the air must be like when we are face to face!"

I don't know how long Emile's Museship lasted, but I think for several years. It was said that Robert once went with her, or followed her, to Mexico. Whether or not he intended to leave home for good, he returned to Beryl eventually. Beryl was durable, and she had to be. For there was always a Muse. For a brief period, when Ava Gardner was living in Spain and occasionally visited Mallorca, it began to look as if *she* might be a candidate, but Robert was not really her type, and nothing came of it.

How or when Emile's Museship ended I never knew, but it did end. Robert must have been well into his seventies when we heard about the next Muse. We were in Venice at the time. A Danish ballet company had been performing at the Fenice, and we heard that Robert had also been in Venice, and that he followed the troupe around, because one of the ballerinas was now his Muse. This girl was in her teens or just out of them.

Robert's love poems still appear, though of late they are not so frequent nor so copious as they were, and they are no longer sexually explicit.

3

In the corner of this Moroccan garden the February morning sun is bright, but not yet hot. Last night the wind dropped; it had been pouring all day up the valley from Agadir, driving the clouds in from the sea and hiding the mountains. Now the peaks of the High Atlas are visible again, covered with fresh snow.

Where you are, 4,000 miles to the westward, it is still night. We are in almost the same latitude, as we are almost the same age. You are a little to the north of me and a few months older. But our tiny planet is so inconceivably tiny a part of the immeasurable universe that whether we like it or not and from any point of view but ours, we are brothers, and our little lives are almost identical. Measured against the lifetime of the sea and the mountains, our careers, which we take so seriously and in which we had hoped to accomplish so much, are finished almost as soon as begun. Does it matter? No, it doesn't matter, except to us. And even to us, very briefly.

We shall not meet again, Schuyler, friend of my youth. I accept the fact—not gladly but because there is no alternative. We are old men now, set hard and wrong in our different ways, and if we did meet we should have to pretend not to notice how different and wrong we had become. You were never very good at pretending. I would find you too sure of yourself, as you always were, and you would see that I am still too unsure. We would have to acknowledge that the good in us had not come to fruition.

I did not approve (though I was expected to applaud) your leaving your wife and children to marry another man's mistress. But what good would it do us now if I granted you my disloyalty and you granted me your madness? No human court could judge between us, and if it could, neither of us would accept the verdict.

Friends for life! How many we remember, with lively and kindly feelings, who years ago have forgotten even our name; and we too are remembered—as it were, watched unawares—by those whom we would no longer recognize if we passed them in the street. If we met again now, it would be like the meeting of two ghosts.

Only yesterday—or was it this morning?—we were young and had a long time to live. Now we are nursed and cossetted by old men's memories, and (on the sly) by regrets, which are at best intoxicating. You might have been one of the mountaineer-poets of our generation; if I had spent my life learning how to write, I might have amounted to something myself.

That bitter taste will always be in my mouth. Would it be less bitter if I knew you were writing poems again? I hope it would; and perhaps you are, though you never publish a word. I would rather go on believing that some day you will become the poet you meant to be than try to believe you were never, for all you said and did, a poet at all. But I no longer know anything about you. For now 4,000 miles of ocean separate us, and the silence of twenty years.

We never said it, in so many words; if we had tried to say what we thought we were up to, I think we might have said that we were looking for the right idea—"the right idea," presumably, of how to live. It couldn't have been called a systematic search: we made our discoveries, such as they were, by happenchance, and we almost always realized later that they hadn't been discoveries after all; that we had been mistaken, we had found the wrong thing—or the wrong person. That was it! It was not so much ideas we discovered as people, the exponents of ideas; and people always turn out to be faulty.

Meantime, while we searched (or told ourselves we were searching) for the right idea, we almost failed to notice that we ourselves were living. Afterwards, looking back, we could see how often and how haphazardly we had changed direction; but at the time we were conscious only of hacking away at the path we were trying to make straight (as we thought) through the thicket and the wilderness. We may not have wandered in circles but we certainly didn't go straight ahead.

4

Life is a tale told by an idiot, true enough; but when he finishes or pauses for breath other voices take up the telling. If life signifies nothing, it also comprehends everything in our tiny universe. If we are included in a greater nothingness than ours, what difference can that make to us who cannot penetrate beyond our own finite nothing? Philosophers cancel each other out. Orage may have been a blind man leading the blind, Gurdjieff half a charlatan, Laura an omniscient who believed she knew all and everything—nevertheless each of them has been part of our lives; and whether or not we are embarrassed or pained to admit it, life does not make sense or ring true or encourage human values: it maims us, kills us, rots us, swallows us and goes on; it is concerned only with its own continuance, in which we are not favored over the spider, the grub or the flora in a rat's intestine.

So perhaps it doesn't matter much, except to our own self-esteem, that our attempts to discover how to live have been so discontinuous, sporadic and zigzag, and apparently came to nothing. We can still hope—I can't help hoping—that we have learned more than we think we have, and may even have found some promissory kind of truth without being aware of it.

Such were the thoughts I had after my farewell to Schuyler. And nine more years went by.

5

Laura is one of those literary curiosities, a poet who renounced poetry—not because it was too much for her but because she was too much for it—a writer whose reputation grew, whose myth took deeper root, during the thirty-six years in which she lived a recluse and wrote, in effect, nothing; word of whom spread (slowly and faintly, to be sure, but as perceptibly as a slight earth tremor is picked up by a seismograph) *after* she stopped writing; whose respectful admirers included much better known poets whom she held in little or no regard (Eliot, Yeats and Auden, to name three).

What, then, was her standing in the world of letters? She herself was in no doubt that it was a high one. Although she had resigned from the poets' Athenaeum, she remained an honorary member of the club and had no hesitation in listing herself as a major poet-emerita. (With equal firmness she relegated Robert Graves to the minor ranks.) And instead of acknowledging any indebtedness to him she strongly hinted that she had attempted (in vain) to teach him truthful ways, and that he owed one of his most famous books, *The White Goddess,* to her suggestions if not to her actual notes. When the two of them had been evacuated from Mallorca in 1936 at twenty-four hours' notice they were allowed to take only a suitcase apiece, and consequently most of their papers had to be left behind in Canellun. Laura wrote to Robert during the war asking him to burn all her papers when he got back to Canellun and he did. (A few that were overlooked were returned to her later.)

Whatever mutual blows beneath the belt were exchanged

by these two who had once been intimate, Laura's old contempt for Robert never changed, while his humble adoration of her ran full circle and turned at last to hate. After reading my autobiography *Name and Address*, in 1960, he wrote to me, congratulating me on not having tried "to put down the Schuyler story in full: one that couldn't be told intelligibly and fairly in cold print. It would have to be told from all angles: but two are incommunicable; and for myself, I prefer to let it go into the bottomless gulf where Laura knowingly cast herself, and into which she nearly dragged me and indeed, all of us." I never told him that in fact I *had* written a chapter about Laura and suppressed it.

If someone of Laura's intelligence and moral force says: *"Yes I am!"* and keeps on saying it with persistence and unremitting intensity all her life long, those within earshot (some of them, not many) are likely to take her seriously, not to say gravely, and her announcement as a piece of weighty intelligence, whether or not they understand *what* she is or why she does not make herself clearer.

The harm that we do to others is never so obvious to us as it is to them; and so buoyant is our self-righting apparatus that it enables us to recover quickly from the slight twinge of uneasiness we may have felt in the midst of our dirty business. The harm we believed Laura did to Kit may have been diminished in Laura's eyes by Kit's extraordinary disregard—as if she ignored or tacitly denied the fact that Laura had harmed her at all; and she continued to evince a devoted affection for Laura—a spooky state of mind that apparently continued until she became a Roman Catholic convert. Then she was able to see that Laura was in fact a forked radish like the rest of us, and Kit was sorry for her.

One of Kit's old school friends, "Izzy" Rockefeller, had married one of Schuyler's, Freddy Lincoln, and it was Izzy who now put an odd sort of job in Kit's way. She had a young niece and nephew, both in their teens, with too much money, no parents (dead or divorced, I can't remember which) and no one to look after them. Kit was to ride herd on this pair and keep them out of mischief. The brother and sister lived, or were supposed to live (they did considerable racketing around), in a large house, staffed with servants, on the outskirts of Greenwich. Here Kit established her headquarters, and when her charges were there—as they were when they felt like it, and only then—I dare say she was to some degree a restraining or at least a mildly beneficent influence on them. But they were thoroughly spoiled and headstrong, and had long ago made up their minds to manage their own lives. I don't remember how or why this "job" of Kit's ended; after a couple of years I suppose both sides agreed that these sophisticated adolescents no longer needed a nanny.

By this time—the 1960s—various things combined to force Kit to move again. The children had grown up and left home— Maria, deserted by her husband, had come back with her two small boys and now lived near Kit; but Raven Rock didn't suit her. It was a back-of-beyond, dead-end sort of place, and Kit felt isolated from her friends and family. And, most compelling of all, Sorby and Jeff now wanted to occupy the rest of their house—so Kit *had* to move. But where on earth should she go? She eventually decided on Boston, perhaps because an elder sister lived there. And in Boston she found a job. All Kit's jobs were odd but this one seemed to suit her (although she never liked it) and apparently she did it well enough. She was house-mother at a girls' vocational college—a fancy name for "training school." The girls were learning to be stenographers or secretaries, but as most of them were boarders the school called itself a college. Kit's job was simply to be there at certain times of day and night, particularly when the girls were going to bed. I think she was expected to be a kind of wardress, disciplining her charges and reporting any rule-breakers, but that was not Kit's way. She was apt to be easygoing on slight infringements of hard-and-fast rules, and I doubt if she ever reported anyone. The girls must have regarded her as a queer old thing, but in time her quality got across to them, and they behaved themselves because they wanted to be in her good graces.

She stayed at that "college" for a year. It was on lower Beacon Street, where the street is no longer a good address. Kit was no snob, but it was an uninteresting part of Boston, and when she got the chance of moving to Cambridge, to a similar but slightly better school, she took it. And there she stayed for four more years. Meantime Maria had settled in Brunswick, Maine—also a college town, though not the equal of Cambridge. Kit used to drive up there for weekends, and took to spending her vacations with Maria. Between them they bought a house on Maine Street, and Kit made the second floor into an apartment for herself, where she intended to live when she retired.

Yes, Robert grew famous, the only one who became a great public figure—which inevitably means, in some respects, a figure of fun. Robert succumbed to greatness. How his uncompromising, hungry youth would have mocked his greedy old age! As an oldster, he talked continually of the triumphs he had won, including two gold medals from Spanish chambers of commerce for *fomento del turismo*. He himself became a tourist attraction in Mallorca. He could still stand on his head when he was seventy-eight, when he wanted to impress a visitor.

Some of the prizes he most wanted never came his way. Several times he thought he was on the short list for the Nobel Prize, but he never got it; and I think he would have liked to be Poet Laureate. (Instead, he had the dubious satisfaction of being ushered by the Laureate, a younger and lesser poet, C. Day Lewis, into Buckingham Palace, where the Queen bestowed on him a gold medal for his poetry. This occasion was included in the official film of the Royal Family, and white-haired old Robert, "easy, smiling, seasoned sound," stole the scene.)

He was delighted to be elected Poetry Professor at Oxford; but long before his five-year term, with its fifteen required lectures, was over, the assignment bored him stiff. He complained to me at the halfway mark that he had said all he knew or wanted to say about poetry, but still had to go on talking about it. He was a poor speaker who never improved much—he looked ill-at-ease and read even his own poems badly—and yet he liked making public appearances, and could often claim a kind of success for them. I remember hearing the first of his Clark Lectures at Cambridge in 1954 and hardly understanding one mumbled word of it, but the alert, appreciative and lynx-eared audience of undergraduates pounced on every slightest twitch of wit with a great roar of delight. Robert was proud of the fact that E. M. Forster came to hear him and that the size of the audience increased with each lecture.

Something of the same sort occurred later at Oxford, during his poetry lectures there. I went to a few of those too, and noticed a recurrence of the same phenomenon in the audience: a tiptoe, patient expectation that Robert would make them laugh, an eagerness to meet his hoped-for sallies more than halfway. In one of the Oxford lectures there was absolutely nothing to laugh at, yet this doglike crowd of hopeful youth crouched there with pricked ears and open mouths, attentively faithful to the boring end, waiting for Robert to say something, anything, that would set them barking. And, though they waited in vain, they did not seem to hold their disappointment against him.

And what became of the Dictionary? When I think of all the work that went into it (three years with five full-time workers, twenty-nine years with two) it makes my head ache. The original project, known as the Dictionary of Exact Meanings, had been backed by an American publisher, Little, Brown & Co.*—who by 1939 had paid Laura several advances against royalties and had developed such cold feet that they wanted to cut their losses and drop the whole thing. A letter from Little, Brown proposing this came to Laura while she and Robert were staying with us in Princeton. Laura's reply (how I wish I had a copy of that outra-

---

*Later bought by Time Inc., the corporation that included *Time*, and not a likely backer of Laura.

geous but masterly letter) ignoring the publisher's proposal and demanding yet *another* advance, was meekly acceded to by Little, Brown! But this, I think, was the last Laura was able to get from that particular source. I don't know the date when Little, Brown canceled the contract, but it must have been no later than the early 1940s.

To Schuyler and Laura's way of thinking, the Dictionary did not so much peter out as delta out: it developed, grew, flowered into a more complex conception. Schuyler made no mention of the Dictionary as such in his entry in *The Class of 1922 after 40 Years.* Neither did he mention Kit. Although he listed his four children, he named only Laura as his wife. He also announced that he had resigned from Ivy, his undergraduate club at Princeton, because of his view "of membership in a social club as being inconsistent with my general life-position."

The final paragraph of his entry indicated that, Dictionary or no, Laura and he were still at it:

She has one general interest which she describes as the self-realization of human beings through the intellectually correct and spiritually full exercise of the instrumentalities of language. Under this head come the study of word-meaning and word-use, and among other things, reevaluation of the linguistics of poetry with incidental reference to her poetic work of past times.

As for himself, he was "expanding and revising a lexicographical complement to Charles M. Doughty's linguistically experimental epic poem, *The Dawn in Britain* . . . and forwarding, in collaboration with my wife, work aimed at increasing the knowledge of words and the principles of linguistic integrity."

What sort of linguistical lingo is this? Its inhuman dreariness is reminiscent of the verbal bogs and quagmires of "Leninist-Marxist" officialese. One good thing about published writing: it is exposed to the testing weather of critical opinion. Schuyler and Laura turned more and more into hothouse or mushroom-cellar writers, and the fungoid growths and leprous distortions of their idiom, even in the small samples that found their way into print,

302

were now painfully or ludicrously apparent to every eye but their own. However else this manner of writing might be characterized, it can certainly lay a strong claim to pomposity. Working and living together as they did in intense isolation, their ways of thinking and writing must have twinned and intertwined like an *algarroba* and an olive tree. Except for the complete absence of irony, this crabbed, sesquipedalian, hyphenated style put me in mind of Orage's flat translations of Gurdjieff.

About this time Robert sent me a poem he had just written:

> How and why do poets die?
> That's a grisly tale.
> Some take a spill on guinea hill,
> Some drown in ale.
>
> Some are lost at sea, or crossed
> In love by cruel witches;
> But some attain long life, and reign
> Like popes among their riches.

Like most of the writers I have known, Robert had a low opinion of almost any other writer you could mention, particularly of his fellow poets. Laura was even more Red-Queenly. In Deya she had disabused me of my admiration for Stephen Crane; she and Robert together tried (unsuccessfully) to wean me from my attachment to Virginia Woolf. Both of them deplored T. S. Eliot, and I think they really hated W. H. Auden. When I was reviewing books for *Time*, Robert suggested that it would be *Time*-ly and just to describe him in print as "Magpie Auden." He told me that when Auden was an undergraduate at Oxford he had a standing order at Blackwell's for all Robert's and Laura's books, and made a practice of stealing phrases or ideas or sometimes whole lines from their poems, to adapt or incorporate in his own.

I didn't fall in with Robert's suggestion; nor, when some time later I met Auden in New York, did I mention Robert's scunner against him. But one evening in London, several years after I first came there, Auden and Nigel Dennis arrived for a drink. Auden knew that I was a friend of Robert's, and said that he was thinking of going to Mallorca and paying a call. I warned him that Robert didn't like him, and told him how Robert had wanted me to call him "Magpie Auden" in *Time*. As they were leaving, Auden said to me, "Tell Robert I'm not a magpie, I'm a woodpecker!"

Robert had a really devoted friend in Ricardo Sicre, a tough young Catalan who had fought against Franco but later, having become a U.S. citizen, returned to Spain with impunity and proceeded to make a fortune as a trader. When Robert asked Ricardo to help him get his property out of Juan Gelat's clutches, Ricardo pitched in and helped. A Catalan knew how to deal with a Mallorquin. When at last Juan Marroig relinquished some of Robert's land (for a price) Robert moved back into Canellun. Before they had left Deya in 1939, Robert and Laura had taken on a secretary, Karl Goldschmidt (who later changed his name to Gay). Karl and his wife Rene now moved into C'an Torrent, next door. Karl meticulously typed all Robert's writing—poems, prose and correspondence—and I should have thought made himself indispensable to Robert.

But there was something chafing in their association. Karl observed, first with a skeptical, then with a disapproving eye, Robert's growing appetite for public acclaim; he muttered and grumbled, and some of his mutterings and grumblings must have been overheard by Robert—or perhaps Karl had the temerity to speak his mind. In any case, some time in the late sixties (or was it even earlier?) Robert announced that he no longer needed a secretary.

Karl and Rene were dismayed, but Robert was adamant. He saw to it, however, that Karl had another job to go to. Robert had sold his poetry manuscripts (for $10,000, according to rumor) to the State University of New York at Buffalo, and he got Karl a job there as custodian of the Poetry Collection in the university library. Sadly Karl and his little family departed for America. He made the best of his unwanted bargain, and settled into the academic life of Buffalo. In the years that followed I had two or three letters from him, and they struck a note of sardonic cheerfulness.

Chronologically, at least, Robert was listed as one of the "Georgian poets"—the young men who had an unconditional date with the year 1914, and most of whom by 1950 were long dead and long forgotten. Robert was one of the very few of his generation who was still read, recognized and liked by those who were young enough to be his grandchildren.

This phenomenon became apparent about the time when Robert was changing from a well-known to a famous figure. Once that high point has been reached and passed, fame is self-propagating. Publicity snowballs. Honors come easily. Everything you do and say is news: and in between times journalists come to write you up and take your picture. A very few famous people, like Charles Lindbergh, hate this kind of treatment and with great effort manage to avoid it; most of them get to like it, to the point of addiction. Robert loved it.

Norman Mailer is not the only writer who writes advertisements for himself; in a sense all writers do it, and Robert was no exception. Though he announced when he turned seventy that he had written enough (by his own count "over 137" books) and would henceforth confine himself to the occasional, unpreventable poem, he found it impossible to stop writing. Articles, lectures, letters-to-the-editor, new heretical theories, kept pouring forth. Some years before, he had told me he had seven books finished and waiting to be published. Presumably this backlog had been used up; but the fire continued to burn.

For years he was in great demand as a public entertainer, a lecturer with bookings in the United States, Mexico, Australia, Greece, "all over the place." And he made a good deal of money. Not from his poetry (and in any case he regarded it as a sin against the Muse to spend money made from poetry for living expenses; it should be spent only on libations, or a party, or something special). On one of my last visits to Deya he told me, with a happy sigh, that he no longer worried about money: he was "affluent." I thought that an excellent thing; for he had a large family to support, and he was incorrigibly and lavishly generous to his friends.

"THE BEST OF FRIENDS MUST PART"

1

I suppose it must have been one of Schuyler's children who gave him the pet name "Bousie" (pronounced *Bow*-zee), and his family—but only his family—almost always called him by this name. With its rather jolly suggestions of bounce and booziness it seemed to me hardly appropriate to Schuyler's iron-clad nature; but his children, and Kit too, continued to use it long after he had left them.

We had come home late, near midnight, from a jolly party in a London suburb. As I walked down the hall towards my study and switched on the light, an ominous feeling came over me that there would be a cablegram lying on top of my typewriter, and that the cable would announce someone's death. There, sure enough, was the yellow envelope.

BOUSIE DIED IN THE EVENING JULY 4 GRISELDA AND I ARE GOING TO WABASSO

BEN

"Ben" too was a nickname. His real name was Schuyler, a name his father forbade him to use, on the grounds that he himself had the exclusive ownership of it, and that Ben had not as yet earned the right even to borrow it.

Schuyler dead! *Schuyler* is dead. I had known that this sentence would some day be spoken, but it had not occurred to me that I would speak it—or that, having spoken it, would know it was a fact but not a fact I could take in. And this numb acceptance was far, far from the same thing as feeling—feeling anything whatever. It was as if a deaf man (as I was deaf) saw a heavy door bang shut but heard no sound.

Later on, this deafness and dumbness of feeling gave way to

a dull sense of disappointment—disappointment that I had been right, after all, in telling myself that I would never see him again; disappointment that his life, and now his death, hadn't meant more to me; disappointment that the rocketing promise of his youth had finally fizzled out. And I was disappointed not to be more disappointed. Yes, his death diminished me, but not by much—not by nearly enough.

I tried to remember what he had been like when we were young men, and friends, closer than brothers. I couldn't remember. He had been intense, wildly gay, affectionate, enlivening, quick, warm—*incandescent!* I could remember that much, if I could no longer feel it. But these memories were cocooned within a dry, deadening, asbestos-like substance composed of absence and time. And as I tried to remember, I found there was more and worse to take into account: when we divorce ourselves, or are divorced, from a loved person, we start instantly, furiously, as though our honor (or self-respect?) depends on it—does it?— to make a case against him (or her); we remember grimly and cite to ourselves with satisfaction small but significant pieces of evidence—of blind and unadmitted bad behavior; of ruthlessness so rhadamanthine it can only be explained as delusions of omnipotent grandeur. Incipient madness, in short, which we now see with cold clarity but brushed aside at the time with embarrassment and anxious pity.

And we? What about us? Since that dignified or ludicrous parting, how has it fared with us? After we managed to rearrange our ruffled egos, did we then climb soberly and sensibly from step to step to reach the moral eminence we stand on now? Only a groan can answer.

Must we all go mad, in order to continue to believe ourselves sane? I had thought Schuyler mad; what had he thought me? And who will now judge between us, or reconcile our quarrel?

I sent a cable to Kit. I thought she might be finding herself in the same wasteland I was in. But perhaps not. She had been his wife; she was the mother of his four children; and now that she had become a Roman Catholic, perhaps she knew how to feel the right things. So I sent a conventional message I hoped she would find comforting, and that I myself hoped, trying to imagine myself a humble, believing Christian, might help my disbelief: MAY LIGHT PERPETUAL SHINE UPON HIM. I wrote to Ben, and to Griselda. Anybody else? Oh, yes, I should let Robert know of the death of my old friend and his old enemy (and that's the way I put it in my letter).

Then I thought: Must I write to Laura? I wanted never to see her again or to have any further dealings with her. But she had been his wife, for twenty-nine years—longer than Kit had been; longer than I had been married to Julie. Was it because he had never sent me a word nor made any sign when Julie died that I thought now of writing to Laura? How do I know? Anyhow, I wrote to her—a short note, trying not to say anything I didn't mean. I wish I'd kept a copy, but I didn't. I think I said that in a small way I shared her sorrow, that he had once been my dearest friend, and I wished that we might have met again. I didn't expect Laura to answer the note. If she did, I asked myself, would it be a great comminatory blast, as was her custom in the old days?

A week or so later, a hasty note from Kit, thanking me for my cable and promising to write at greater length. Then for three weeks no word from anybody. I felt inadequate, uneasy, "surrounded by a conspiracy of silence"—Laura had once used this phrase in a letter to me, accusing me of having thus prevented Schuyler from accomplishing what he might have accomplished.

A few days later I heard from Robert. He'd just been made "adopted son of Deya"— a splendid occasion, with the Civil Guard as godfather and free sherry for all the villagers. Yes, it's too bad about Schuyler, a good honest man . . . . Generous but violent—and not Robert's enemy: they never came to blows.

He'd written six books that year and had been in Australia, Tasmania, the U.S., Russia and Hungary, and is invited by the

Olympic Committee to Mexico in October. In short, he's all right. Family all well too.

Reigning "like popes among their riches"—and he'd rather not remember.

On the heels of Robert's letter came one from Ben:

He was taken to the hospital in the evening of July 4th and died very shortly after arrival; I think it was an easy death if that be possible. . . . Maria and Philip [Ben's six-year-old son] joined Griselda and myself on the journey to Florida. To my surprise Laura not only encouraged our attendance and participation but welcomed it . . . it now appears that the contingency of death was really never admitted by either of them. . . . Laura has no plans and no permanent financial resources; she has no one to turn to beyond her step-children, a few "friends" through correspondence and local Floridians. . . .

His legacy to us is an unavoidable responsibility to her through our duty and love for him which he recognized only in a few brief and fleeting moments. . . .

I will not attempt to describe the service or scene. . . . He was buried in a casket made of some false and pretentious gray material and lowered in the Florida sand by a mechanical device requiring adjustment, shoving and balancing rather than cremated and scattered into the Indian River. However the service was created and conducted entirely by his children and the word Lord was used in spite of Laura's attempt to inject controversy over its appropriateness ("We never recognized the word 'Lord'—'God,' yes, but . . . etc."). I played the flute (*Jesu Joy of Man's Desiring*), the 23d Psalm was read, along with some appropriate words written by Laura, a hymn was sung, and then the final intonation, "Ashes to ashes."

Griselda, the oldest of his four children and the one who most resembled him, wrote of her father: "The best of Bousie was very dear and honorable. Anyway, at his graveside where Ben, Philip, Ria and I made him a service I felt very sad and proud."

Laura did answer my note. The once-familiar handwriting, a little eroded now, had written my name and address on the swollen envelope; I could see that it was a Laura-length epistle.

"THE BEST OF FRIENDS MUST PART"

August 2, 1968
Wabasso, Fla.

I should like to be stronger than I am now, Tom, as I write, for answering your message of July 6th . . . In this matter of strength, I am like Schuyler, in your regard. He felt with unhappiness a deficiency of strength for communicating with you further about your telegram of November 1958*—which lies, browned, on my table as I write, next to your message to me—and the telephone conversation you and he subsequently had. Schuyler was never satisfied with his part in that conversation; he did not alter his view of the character of your telegram-approach, and of your reply to his voiced attitude to it, but he nursed sadness (that had cutting edges of grief) over his (persisting) sense of inadequate strength for saying to you what might possibly dissolve the blockage he felt (had felt from way back) to be in you, and saw you as (from way back) acknowledging and deploring while not of yourself moving to part with it. He never renounced the desire (I believe) to find strength adequate for further effort towards, and about, you. In comparing my problem of answer-approach to you with that of Schuyler's problem in seeking a further way to speak to you (speak to possibly more useful point than he had in the 1958 incident), as a problem tied to the matter of strength, I do not mean that I wish I had strength in relation to that 'blockage': the question of its existence, and possible dissolving, as something of recognized existence, still belongs between him and you—the wish for strength for speaking aright to you on the subject of it is, I am sure, deeply part of his being's lasting bearing towards the course, the fact, of your-and-his friendship. You are owed this knowledge. I deliver it for the further sake of his being, and yours. . . .

You crowd *him* into *your* frame, as you took the liberty of doing publicly in your book. What you tried to do in my regard there, under transparent veiling, I do not comment on except to say that, in whatever you thus succeeded in doing, he was the one more directly hurt.†

---

*It was 1959.
†This must be the passage she refers to:

. . . that was the year I lost my friend Schuyler.

In those days of thirty years ago, I was unsure of myself but sure of him. He was to be a true poet, dedicated to the high craft of verse; poetry was his calling. I had neither his singleness of purpose nor his passion of conviction that only the great heights are worth climbing; my ambitions were timider.

313

She then proceeded to examine, severely and exhaustively, for several pages, my use of the word "small" (in my letter to her I had said that I had a small share in her sorrow over Schuyler's death). She also differentiated in this connection between my feelings and her own: "I cannot, in the sorrow I feel, focus on measurements, divisions—nor in the joy-to-be I feel over the undiminishable, ever-to-grow certainty of his forward living being." This over, she told me that Schuyler had always been grateful to me for the one-volume *Shorter Oxford Dictionary* I had given him (I had quite forgotten about this) and wanted me to have it back; would I please spare her "the expensive consignment of it to England. Perhaps it could be picked up here in time by some car-driving traveler of the number of your friends or family-folk?"

(So, in a way, in his way, he had sent me a message: that he had not forgotten me nor our friendship; that our long estrangement grieved and troubled him too, and that he was grateful to me—if only for a dictionary I didn't even remember giving him! How like him to admit a small indebtedness but not the whole debt! As if it disturbed him that interest on the mortgage was overdue, but he had clean forgotten that the mortgage itself existed.)

This manifesto-message carried the authentic Laura tone—severe, humorless, inquisitorial, authoritarian; but what had happened to her language? Her writing had frequently been obscure, but then it was often thunderous with unshed meaning; it was capable of fierce (and clarifying) lightning flashes. Now it was like a travesty of itself, full of prissinesses, both mincing and awkward, like a bad parody of Henry James. And there was

---

There was nothing timid about him. He was brave, brilliant and assured; I was none of these things, but he made me understand that I too was a kind of poet. Though he was the leader and I the follower, we were friends whom nothing was to part: we thought ourselves devoted to one another for life. We laughed and wept for the same reasons, or understood them. When we married, each was the other's best man, and marriage was not allowed to interfere with our friendship.

What went wrong? Which of us failed the other? Why did he stop writing poetry; and how did our friendship end? The only answer I can give cannot satisfy me: that he and I told ourselves different versions of the same story, not the truth but our truth. In his version, I was disloyal. In my version, he was mad with pride and literally bewitched."
Name and Address (New York: Simon & Schuster, 1960), p. 241.

something else: all those pedantic hyphenated words—what did they call to mind? Gurdjieff!

Had Schuyler reopened her mind "in this regard" (as they would now say)? He himself had left "the Group" thirty years ago and more, when the rest of us did, after Orage's defection or dismissal; but Gurdjieff made a lasting impression on him, and I think Schuyler always kept a soft spot in his mind for that enigmatic quasi-sage. But Laura had once spied the two volumes of "The Book" on my shelves, had taken them away and returned them next day with the flat statement, "Gurdjieff is a very wicked man!" Perhaps, without their being aware of it, some of the tricks of Gurdjieff's style—for he did have a kind of frightful style—had crept into Schuyler's writing, and Laura had caught them from him?

When I read over Laura's letter a second time I noticed some other things about it: touching (at least to me) signs of querulous weakness and age. She wouldn't admit that she felt weak—but she wished she were stronger. She almost confessed her cureless grief by the thin-lipped doggedness with which she announced her "joy-to-be." She could not allow that Schuyler had abandoned her, or even that he was dead—in a letter to the secretary of our Princeton Class she had reported his death thus: "I have the to-me terrible word to tell you that his bodily powers lapsed on July 4th of this month." Now she wrote to me of his "new gathering of presence after the excruciating bodily crisis." Evidently she believed or was clinging to a belief in some sort of personal immortality by which she and Schuyler would continue to be working companions.

In spite of their often disagreeable and complacent self-esteem, is it possible that Schuyler and Laura were at least partly justified in appraising themselves as all-important people—odd and undiscovered but two of the most important persons in the world? It may not be probable, but it's *possible*.

They took themselves with deadly seriousness. They would have phrased it differently: e.g., that they had self-respect. And their accomplishment? They had blown the gaff on poetry (though no one had noticed it). And to have blown the gaff on poetry—or even to suggest that it might be blown—that was indeed something, if only a great big negative something. (Though here again, they were not the only white hunters on poetry's trail: T. S. Eliot had said, more simply if just as darkly, "The poetry does not matter.")

But where now was the magic that had emanated from those two—that others besides me had certainly felt? Had that magic ever really existed? Yes! *That* I would swear to. But could it have existed, would it have had any effect on us, if we had not all been young, if we had not felt that we had a long time to live? Such enormous claims as theirs needed a whole world of time in which to show a result that would justify them. Well, they had had their world, and they had not been justified. Laura was still apparently determined—but perhaps more desperate now than determined—to show that their pride and their labor had not been a vain thing, that Schuyler's life had not been a waste of life.

Can a dedicated life be wasted? Schuyler and Laura were dotty, by common-sense standards, but they were also dedicated. We judge only by results we can see, and in their case we saw no results; that didn't necessarily mean that nothing had happened. It might mean that something happened—or was happening, or was about to happen—that was invisible to our eyesight, accustomed to notice, trained to see, only what we had been brought up to believe was *there*.

Laura's letter to me didn't demand an answer but I thought it asked for one; so, though I knew I ran the risk of bringing another letter down on my head, I wrote to her again (and this time kept a copy):

Dear Laura,

Thank you for your letter of August 2. I was glad to learn from it that Schuyler had not forgotten me, and touched that he and you should want me to have the dictionary I once gave him. I think your suggestion most practical: let it remain where it is until some friend of mine is driving that way and can pick it up. I will let you know in good time when that will be.

Tom

Her answer was prompt and, if not warm, at least with the chill off. She confirmed our agreed arrangement for returning the dictionary to me and concluded:

I write also to thank you for your readiness to act on my suggestion. And, further, to say to you, on behalf of us both, that your wanting the book is welcomed.

Laura

Kit also wrote again:

I too couldn't think of anything to feel and it was only on receiving your cable & your letter that I could grieve—my grief was not for the loss of a beloved person—it was over my dashed hopes and recollection of my grievous faults—I not only hoped but I firmly believed that those two extraordinary people would come to their senses. From what I piece together of Schuyler's final days I would not disbelieve that that was exactly what happened to him and the shock of facing the enormity of his error was more than his heart could stand. The children will miss him, in particular Rya. They have been saddened by his death. I was awfully proud of the way they flew down to Wabasso without delay or deliberation and Ben who had been hurt badly & more or less rejected took the lead as head of the family and was very kind to Laura—they most likely will be writing you. . . . I myself feel totally free and as a member of the church well protected but on my guard—Rya was somewhat apprehensive. . . . Fortunate she recognizes and stays clear herself. Poor Laura—it was very good of you to write to her. I did not nor will I. A few days after his death I had, I guess what you call an inner vision. His face partially illumined by an unusual brilliance and then a cloud dark as pitch drew over the light. He needs our prayers Tom—mine are feeble—I had a Mass said for him at the H.G. Chapel in Boston and there was one said for him at the Benedictine Monastery Mt. Saviour near Elmira—Jimmy [Kit's younger brother] wept when he mentioned Schuyler. He really loved Schuyler and it made me realize that after

317

1924 I never really loved him though I was fiercely loyal and ready to do anything to help him be a happier person. He never knew how to take as I remember. . . .

(Could Kit be right in thinking that at last Schuyler had recognized what had become of his bright promise, and had therefore turned his face to the wall? Can death be an atonement for the harm our lives have caused? It might be some comfort to believe that Schuyler had repented; but I didn't believe it.)

All of us, I think, have made our last move. Kit's was to Brunswick, in Maine. But before she went there she made a longer and more portentous journey: to Rome. I mean it in the religious sense. It was a surprise to everybody. Kit, who had discovered Gurdjieff for us when we were young, as an old lady became a Roman Catholic convert. Her family, on the whole, were delighted. I was told by several of her children that Kit was completely changed—they meant, for the better. When I first saw her after her conversion I thought her exactly the same as she had always been, but more so—vaguer, more absent-minded, more scatter-brained—and just as much of a gentleman. She was continually trying to find the Roman Catholic church in a strange town and continually getting lost; her driving, which had always been somewhat hare-brained, was now dangerous in the extreme, as she paid so little attention to where she was going. Her guardian angel must have worked overtime. But her conversion had made her happy—or so she said; and for that reason I agreed with her children that it was a good thing.

I never would have thought that Kit would remind me of my Aunt Jane, but in this final phase of hers she did. When Aunt Jane was saying goodbye to me she made a habit of saying, *sotto voce*, and with a meaning look, "You know, Tom, I'm still praying!" She meant that she was still praying that I would become a priest— and this when I was a middle-aged man, far gone in journalism and other worldly ways. Kit would say, with an equally sharp look, that she wished I would join "the true Church," and urged me, as a way-station Anglican, to go "all the way."

When last seen, in 1939, Laura was the most prolific as well as the hardest-working writer I had ever encountered. In her thirteen years with Robert she published eight books under her own name, had a guiding hand in many more, and wrote so much of *Epilogue,* the quarterly she founded, that she felt obliged to use several pseudonyms.

In Schuyler this moral force met and acknowledged a greater force than herself. Her almost incessant writing, which had poured from her like an issue of blood, was stanched to a few trickling drops; and this amazing change was not entirely due to the fact that Robert was no longer there to bully unwilling publishers on her behalf; her long silence must have been ordered and enforced by Schuyler. In the twenty-nine years of their marriage Laura published four articles, all of them in a little magazine called *Chelsea,* and a letter to the Editor of the *Minnesota Review.* That was the sum, a tiny total, amounting in effect to zero.

This resounding silence seemed to echo the surmise that without Robert she could no longer find a publisher. Had Robert made it a condition that a book of hers must be accepted with every one of his? It may have been something like that. He was known as "a good publishing property"; Laura, if not quite poison at the box office, roused small enthusiasm in a publisher's breast. But even if she could no longer find her way into print, it seemed incredible that she should have stopped writing altogether. Incredible? Schuyler, whom in pre-Laura days I regarded as a poet of the first water, had forsworn poetry, which he had come to see as only a halfway house, long before he met Laura. And Frank Baisden, who had endured the Schuyler-Laura establishment almost as long as the boy who stood on the burning deck, had told me of a scene he had witnessed in his own house: Schuyler grim-faced and Laura in tears but obediently burning an armful of papers—presumably her poems!

Of course it must have taken a great deal of writing—a very specialized, technical kind of writing—to put together even a fragment of the great, never-published Dictionary* that Laura worked at for more than thirty years, and Schuyler for almost as long. But, to judge by the samples we had seen, their writing had become not so much specialized and technical as unreadable. Laura had never made it easy—she had never made it anything but uneasy—for the reader; all the same, in her heyday her writing, blindingly obscure and abstract as it often was, did now and then flash and reverberate. But now! No lightning, no thunder; her words lay inert, dull, dead on the page. Was this Schuyler's influence on her, or their mutual influence on one another? However it came about, the style in which they both wrote was as heavy as a dead hand.

She had become boringly intelligent, soporifically brilliant, so intent on her own subtleties that she neither knew nor cared what effect they might have on the reader. These barnacled obtundities were not so thick upon her in her younger days; and even now she had her murkily illuminating flashes, her quasi-epiphanies. What was her trouble, her crippling flaw? I think it may have been that she was so in love with herself that she believed every word she said. She was the Moving Finger that never writes anything less than the unalterable truth, and not even she could move herself to cancel half a line.

T. S. Eliot thought (or I think he thought) that the only counterbalance to cleverness, the only means of sanctifying it, is humility—and that was something he was never sure of. This puts him at the opposite pole to Laura. What a fearsome don Laura would have made, what a terrifying head of a college! And what a paradox she is: her extraordinary, brilliant, bladed mind manacled to her ruthless, preposterous, crazy crusade for herself.

This was a kind of Christmas card Laura sent to a select few, five months after Schuyler's death:

*Or "study of word-meaning and word-use," as its authors later called it.

FOR GREETING YOU
"The relation between truth and happiness, in our thinking on the part of language in human life, is a primary one: we see the consciousness that one is speaking at every word with truth, and the companion consciousness of being so spoken to, as the assurance, and the beginning, of human happiness—lasting and general happiness."
From Rational Meaning: A New Foundation
For the Definition of Words
by Laura Jackson and Schuyler B. Jackson
Christmas, 1968   Wabasso

This message, or announcement, although it contains the words *greeting* and *happiness,* has no perceptible concern with either; certainly it does not warm the heart like a Christmas carol. And it gives the inescapable impression that the writer (or writers) no longer commands English idiom.

2

For Laura, Schuyler's death (she avoided the word, particularly in his connection) must have been almost literally an amputation of a vital part of herself. All the same, an ego as formidable and tough as Laura's can survive even so great a severance; and whether or not she would admit it, Schuyler's absence did set her free once more, not only to write but to publish.

Although for some time it had been obvious that the Dictionary (or its linguistic successor) would never be finished, Laura would admit no such thing, and instead threw out hints that the linguistic work, or its equivalent, or something very like it, was in large part completed and might some day soon appear.

In such promissory utterances, particularly in a small book called *The Telling,* Laura, like a sideshow barker, held out the promise of great things, marvelous things, to be seen and experienced inside the tent; and like all such performances, hers ended before a single customer had entered. Her spiel carried a tone that was peremptory, overblown and meaningless, at the same time awesome and nonsensical. It was like hearing the veritable voice of God (or its plausible facsimile) in a dream caused by indigestion.

Meantime articles and letters, some very lengthy, signed "Laura (Riding) Jackson" began to pop up in various little magazines—*Antaeus,* the Denver *Review*—and in *The New York Times Book Review,* the *Times Literary Supplement,* the *New York Review of Books.* At least once an article by her was announced and then failed to show up. What frightful scenes behind the scenes did this non-appearance indicate? I knew from bruising experience what Laura was like as an editor. It was inconceivable that Laura herself should be revised, cut, or edited in any way. Can God be corrected or improved—except by God herself? (In the dual godhead that existed while Schuyler was alive, the feminine aspect might, God willing, be occasionally admonished by the masculine partner, or vice versa.) Laura was certainly not going to have her writing tampered with by an ordinary mortal.

A case in point was the memorial of Schuyler that was published in the Princeton *Alumni Weekly.* Our class secretary asked me to write it, and I did; but it had to be shown to Laura for her approval, and I was sure she would never pass it if she knew I was the writer. The class secretary, a friend of mine, kept my name out of it; but he had a terrible time with Laura all the same. The *Alumni Weekly* limited these memorials to 350 words, and Laura's mere outline was nearly 10 times that length. She and the secretary never actually met, but she so buffeted him with letters that at last he abandoned his deadline, and their correspondence, dragging on and on, held up the publication of the memorial for more than a year.

Then, two years after Schuyler died, Laura published (in England) a selection of her poems,* none of them new, with a

---

Selected Poems in Five Sets (London: Faber & Faber, 1970).

preface justifying this apparently inconsistent act: " . . . No poet before me has gone to the very breaking-point. . . . I know of no one besides myself and my husband Schuyler . . . who has put feet across the margin on the further ground—the margin being the knowledge that truth begins where poetry ends."*

I was made aware of this event by my old friend Maisie Somerville, now retired from her long labors at the BBC and living in Selsey, who wrote me an agitated letter saying that she had just heard Laura on the radio, that her voice was "chillingly" the same, and that she must have, lo and behold, returned to England.

Could it be true? I investigated. The BBC let me listen to a playback of the program, and I too heard Laura's voice. It was recognizable, and chilling indeed, but not the same: although the old tone of implacable, absolute authority still smoldered there, like a bad-tempered empress's on the edge of cold rage, the anglicized accent had completely worn off.

Yet where had all that manic energy gone? Why had she ceased to write? Schuyler might have converted her—apparently he *had* converted her—to his view that poetry is an impure art. But there are other forms of writing: scripture, for example.

In any case, this voice that I was hearing now was no meek little *hausfrau*'s. She spoke for several minutes longer on the theme that poetry could not be the highest form of human expression, because poets are incapable of speaking the truth and nothing but the truth—let alone the whole truth. The necessary gospel, she implied, had not yet been written (although she gave a strong hint that she had the matter in hand). The poems we were to hear (her own) had not attained the perfection of absolute truth; she was allowing them to be read, however, because insofar as poems *could* embody truth, these did.

Then several of her poems, all of which I remembered, were read—and read very well—by an English voice, I think an ac-

*Why couldn't she let this pithy phrase stand? No, she had to translate it into her Ozymandias-English: "wanting, in its peculiar linguistic character, the authority attributed to it as a final linguistic norm." *Ugh!*

tress's. *World's End, The Wind Suffers,* and *Be Grave, Woman:* I recall those three. As I say, there were no new ones.

But she had a few good things to say for these poems she was presenting again, and for their author as well:

I have initiated enough poets into the idea of linguistic discipline for truth's sake, in the past, to know how verbally insensitive to considerations of truth poets can be, though behaving as persons born privy to it. . . . A word, now, as to Rimbaud's quitting poetry, and mine. In the poetic adventure, I had a structure of hope for shelter, whatever happened; and my inspiration came from everywhere. He was inspired by desperation; he flung it out, it narrowed fast back upon him, and would have destroyed him eventually had he not run away from it. . . . And just what is the sequel to my poems? I have written that which I believe breaks the spell of poetry; but I must be in no hurry as to that . . . my poems are good illustrations of poetry . . . I judge my poems to be things of the first water as poetry. . . .

This small reprinted book of Laura's did not knock the wind out of an astonished world, but in the little literary kingdom of Cockaigne it did rattle a few window frames. This book and *The Telling* were reviewed, not widely but too well—and that gave Laura ammunition for a further assault. No review could satisfy her, because no reviewer could sufficiently recognize or sufficiently acknowledge her godhead.

The points her letters-to-the-editor aimed at making were often obscure; they had a schoolmarmish asperity and their knotted phraseology gave off a somewhat antique air, as if the schoolmistress had been absent so long that her pen had grown rusty and her tongue unaccustomed to addressing a class. But their severe intention was clear; Laura wished to set an ignoramus straight or to tighten the attention of a careless reviewer.

When Laura laid out one of her reviewers by dropping a Cyclopean letter on him, it was almost always a technical knockout: if he knew what was good for him he went down for the count and lay still, saving his breath to cool his porridge. But in one case her usually crushing avalanche of codswallop did—as

the inelegant phrase has it—hit the fan. When Paul Amster reviewed her in the *New York Review of Books* (August 7, 1975),
she blasted him in a long letter: "The underlying tone . . . is
whining. . . . It is an attempt to extinguish me graciously. . . . His
reading of my poems is linguistically and poetically illiterate.
. . . The whine swells at the close."

This was Paul Amster's reply:

Mrs. Jackson seems to feel that anything less than total acceptance of
her position is to be interpreted as an outright rejection of everything
she stands for, that praise tempered by criticism amounts to nothing
more than a devious form of ridicule.

She refuses to understand that one can be of two minds about
something. Her work is both admirable and difficult, and it cannot fail
to elicit strong reactions. I do not see why she should object to this. For
to challenge her ideas is certainly not to dismiss them. If I had wanted
to do that, I would not have taken the trouble to write the article in the
first place.

The tone of Mrs. Jackson's letter exhibits the same self-righteous-
ness that I find so disagreeable in much of her writing, and just as my
article was in no way condescending to her accomplishments, I will not
now condescend to answer her personal attacks.

At least one member of the silent audience breathed a
"Bravo!"

3

I suppose everyone feels in himself, in relation to "reality," an
inadequacy, an uncertain comprehension, partial and insuffi-
cient, a broken unity. Laura says, in effect: "Yes, I know this
feeling (or have known it); but I have left it behind. I have become adequate, I comprehend wholly and sufficiently, my broken unity is reunited." There was a time when we believed her

—or almost believed her. We should all like to know for certain
—we would give anything to know—that this state is humanly
attainable. In any case we cannot disprove Laura's claim that she
has attained it, so we say, "Well, perhaps. Anyhow, she's got
something."

Nevertheless, we cannot fail to see also her conceit and ego-
mania. She suspects, accuses and judges everyone but herself.
Yet, she is also a human being, no matter how she chooses to deny
or qualify that status; and as a human being she, inevitably, shares
our common nature and its weaknesses. What is her life like, now,
in Wabasso, where truth begins? I think she must be lost—alone
and old, and unaccustomed to being either. All those years of
incessant activity, plying her self-taught art of bossing other people and their projects; and then the many years with Schuyler,
when both she and their interdependent project were bossed by
him. And now, all his support gone, and nothing to replace it but
the disused freedom to be alone.

One word that must be applied to Schuyler and Laura is
uncompromising. And this word, as we all know, has in it ele-
ments of nobility, a quality which in turn carries connotations of
bravery, independence, backbone, unyielding moral principle—
all admirable qualities, and rare enough among human beings to
be remarkable. People who are really uncompromising, as uncompromising as Schuyler and Laura were, would stop there,
and say that this is the whole meaning of the word. But for the
rest of us, this is not so: the word has further associations which
we have to consider.

For an unyielding position is sometimes unsuccessful: like
the Spartans' at Thermopylae or the Texans' at the Alamo, it can
be overborne. And an unyielding position can also be by-passed
or ignored: this is one of the myriad tricks the world uses in its
dirty fighting.* A blank, uncomprehending stare can be a suffi-

---

*And which General Sherman used again and again in his famous march from Atlanta

cient weapon, or a guffaw, or a whisper behind the hand ("He's *crazy!*"). Although a man may be absolutely sure he is right, and a genius, the consensus of his fellow men may be that he is mad. If Schuyler and Laura had been sufficiently well known to be the subject of a popular poll, they would almost certainly have been voted mad as hatters. I go along with that hypothetical consensus. For I think that, although they were in a sense noble to remain so uncompromising, they were also blinded by pride in their own uniqueness. They accepted the universe, but only on their own terms, and if he had dared to put in a word (he was silent, as usual) they would have told God where to head in. If this is not madness, what would you call it?

While Schuyler was alive, he and Laura had a fixed income from his father's trust; but at his death the income from the trust reverted to his children. How did Laura manage then? She applied for a Guggenheim Fellowship ($2,400 a year at the time and in some cases renewable) and got it. She was a name not widely known but deeply admired by those who knew her work, and I supposed her still able to strike terror into timid hearts. When I heard this news, I wondered whether the Guggenheim Foundation had longterm plans in her regard. Laura would certainly apply for a renewal of her Fellowship when the time was up, and unless I missed my guess she would get it. Remembering the number of advances she had had from Little, Brown for the Dictionary, I foresaw the likelihood that the Guggenheim Foundation would be involved with her for a long time.

Like most heavy smokers, Schuyler and Laura smoked cigarettes continually, every waking hour. But by 1957 they had given up the habit. I followed suit (though I didn't know about them) a year later. As converts from smoking they were fiercely

---

to the sea in 1864, avoiding battles when he could, as a showy waste of time and manpower. The defeated South still hates him as a dirty fighter who scrapped the accepted conventions of head-on battle in favor of winning the campaign.

intolerant of the unconverted; as was I. I looked on all cigarette smokers with contempt (kindly in the case of old friends) and did my best to keep out of range of their noxious exhalations; Schuyler and Laura would not grant smokers even the hope of salvation.*

4

Once in a great while Robert and I write to each other. I get occasional reports of his doings and sayings—usually, alas, from the newspapers. As a famous and eccentric poet he has become fair game to the press. My son Tommy, who first saw Deya when he was five, has often returned there on his annual holiday, and always pays his respects to Robert. After a recent visit he reported that Robert has aged perceptibly and that his memory is playing him tricks. He had stared at Tommy and then said, "I know you! Your father was a bishop. Very nice man." (The fact was that my father couldn't abide Robert, and Robert had never thought him "a very nice man.")

This report of Robert's failing memory was borne out by others. John Aldridge, whose friendship with Robert dated back forty years, told me that when he and Gretl had last visited Deya and were staying as Robert's guests in a house he owned in the village, he had come to see them and asked if this was their first visit to Mallorca. And my son John—who met Robert and Beryl in Budapest in 1974 ("They came down from Warsaw just to see me and were going back to Krakow a few days later") and had a high old time with Robert, drinking and singing Irish songs—thought his mind "as sharp as ever and he still talks a streak," but said that Beryl would interrupt him:

*Thus equating them with Gurdjieff's damned souls, the "hasnamuss individuals."

328

"Now, darling, you just told him that."
"Oh, did I?"

One hot summer day in London in 1975, Len and I met for, I suppose, the last time. He had come over with his wife to a meeting of documentary film makers at Annecy, and stopped off on the way home to visit old haunts in London. I went up from the country to have lunch with him. He must have found me much aged, but I could see no change in him.

What an innocent old con man he is! His besetting notion is still with him (he'll never let go of it) but the key word now is "body" (genes?). Even his clothes—what *was* he wearing?—reminded me of those Irish tweeds in which he had appeared when he first arrived in New York. We looked at each other sideways, and talked of old times. His rolling, watchful, evasive eye! The *Guardian* had a piece the next day in which he was mentioned as "the legendary Len Lye"—and that's what he is. I'm glad we met again. I think it was our last time.

Len showed his sense of the occasion by saying in his casual drawl but with a solemn look that he was grateful for what I had done for him in the past. I wonder what he meant. And what *did* I do for him?

Nothing Robert and I can say to each other now has the ring of truth. We are two old men who like to be humored, and expect to be. I think Robert's expectations are more demanding and continual than mine, because he is a famous man, long accustomed to being the center of attention, hopelessly addicted to coddling and flattery. My only claims to special regard are that I am usually the oldest person present, and the richest. Both Robert and I have long ceased to be attractive to women, or even likable. But we cannot bear to believe this. Robert has even convinced himself that he is still capable of arousing passionate love in young girls—a classically comic situation. Have I changed as much in fifty years as it seems to me Robert has changed? It is more than probable, whether I can see it or not. And have I changed as much for the worse as I think he has? That probability also I must allow.

The last time he was in my house in London was at an evening party to which for some reason he came alone, and where he was not recognized nor made much of. This turned the old lion surly: he complimented my wife ironically on the *paella*, which, he said, though it might have been concocted by our Spanish cook, would never have passed muster in Spain. Ironic compliment has become such a habit with him that now, I am told, his only comment on anything that displeases him (and many things these days displease him) is to cry "Hurray!"

Next week Robert celebrates his eightieth birthday. It is to be a great occasion. Printed invitations have been sent out:

Robert Graves
requests the pleasure of your company
on the occasion of his 80th birthday
on Thursday, the 24th of July 1975
at Canellun, Deya, Mallorca
from 8–12 p.m.
R.S.V.P.

The *Times Literary Supplement* advertises a memorial volume. (I have not been asked to contribute, and all but one or two of the contributors are unknown to me.) We hear that BBC Television will send a team to witness the event, and that such notables ("Beautiful People," in the current argot) as Spike Milligan and Peter Sellers will be there, with bells on. We got an invitation (I suppose Beryl saw to that) but nothing could induce us to join that rout of sycophants and publicity-seekers. It will very likely be Robert at his worst, and having known him at his best I don't want to see it.

What are we like, in these last years—perhaps months—of our lives? Well, none of us is up to much, and at our advanced age nothing further is expected of us. Robert still sprouts poems the way a dead man sprouts hair and fingernails. He no longer resists the rib-cracking hug of fame, and at last admits that he is a great man. He is sure to be remembered after the rest of us are forgotten, but not so much, I think, for his poems as for what he and Laura considered potboilers: *Goodbye to All That* and the two *Claudius* novels. Schuyler died with all his promise still unperformed; Laura continues to protest her unique sanity. Even now she occasionally emits a kind of galvanic sparkle, but the manifestoes she continues to publish, at rarer and rarer intervals, are so reticulated and decussated, with such interstices between the intersections, that they induce, they almost demand, the immediate inattention of the reader. In short, she has become a cranky old fusspot. I quit my job in New York twenty-one years ago and went to live in England, "to learn to write"—but it was too late or I was too lazy. Since I regard my fellow survivors as mad or next door to it, very likely I am to be found at the same address.

I still believe that Laura and Schuyler had the two most brilliant minds I ever encountered. And what did those minds accomplish? Very little.

Great wits are sure to madness near allied . . .

Ah, John Dryden, how right you were!

What has become of us? We, who once took ourselves quite seriously as the hope of the world—not the only hope, to be sure, but nothing was genuine without our signature—we are all, without exception, dead, dying or mad. In short, defeated and out of it. We are no longer expected to take an active part or even a responsible interest in any going concern; we sit on our benches at the edge of our world and watch. We are "senior citizens," walking euphemisms, old people, pensioners, zombies, struldbrugs. Though our apparently empty days are full enough with the fading but still delectable pleasures of sleep, food and drink, and some of us (Laura, I feel sure) may give the impression of grimly fevered activity, in fact we are all just waiting—waiting to die. Our story is told, our lives are over, the curtain is coming down. We do not agonize over our collapsing civilization, be-

331

cause we know we shall be collapsing before it does.

In a blink of time, brief even by our minuscule measurements, all that will be left of us will be contained in the distorted and dwindling flashes of memory, less and less frequent, in the minds of fewer and fewer people.

The six main characters in this story—if you can call it a story, for it has a beginning, an undistributed middle and no end—were together only briefly, a matter of a few months. The short duration of that friendship still seems amazing to me, when I consider how intense our relationship was and how lasting its repercussions. Yet during that period we would have said, with complete confidence, that we were "one another's best," and that we expected our friendship to endure as long as we lived.

If we had all remained at close quarters—for, let us say, forty years—would we have continued to "love," or even like, one another? Alas, I cannot think so. Under the recurrent, cumulative battering of daily life, and its abrasive attrition, the best which human beings can manage is forbearance, tolerance and charity, whose faint and evanescent scent is the only hope of drowning out that stinking dislike of their fellows that masks their own self-hatred and despair. This disciplined temper may seem weaker and more colorless than "love" but in fact is stronger, more continuous, more durable.

When we were young and were all so intensely friends, we were—we were quite sure of it—good enough to open any poker hand (we all had Jacks or better), good enough to win most pots. What happened in that poker game, and what happened to us?

None of us won the jackpot, though we all had promising openers. It might be said that Robert won it. Schuyler and Laura, if they had condescended to accept the metaphor, might claim to have won it (though no other living person would have allowed the claim). I should say that Julie ended up far ahead of the rest of us.

But *was* there a jackpot?

In due course we all died and the poker game went on

without us; but some of us lived a long time. I was one: when I wrote these words I was seventy-four. All of us live far apart, and most of us have not met for many years. Robert, a bit of a bore now, is interested only in the fantasy-figure of himself. Laura, the absolute despot of a nonexistent empire, is also a bore. Kit is an impoverished eccentric duchess whose vagueness verges on wandering wits. She is still, God bless her, a gentleman. And I— what am I? I sometimes wish I knew, or wish I wished it; but on the whole, perhaps it's better not to know. I do know that I've developed characteristics (some no doubt boring and some undoubtedly mad) that arouse quite violent hostility, even in strangers who know me only from my writing.

CLOSING REMARKS

A good judge in a court of law, summing up facts and probabilities—inferences that may properly be drawn from the evidence, assumptions that can reasonably be made about the characters of the defendant and the witnesses, conclusions that must not be jumped at—may make it seem a simple matter to let the truth be shown, a matter of bringing in common sense to enlighten the rules of law. But the judge himself knows, if he is an honest and intelligent man, that justice and truth are not identical; that they may sometimes overlap but very rarely coincide. Justice, as man understands it and administers it, is seldom more than a rough approximation of a limited and partial truth. Truth may be more damning, more merciful, more inconclusive than justice.

Telling your own story can only be an attempt to do oneself justice: not to tell the truth.

I have lived in a mold that does not fit me; I have done many things I did not want to do; I have said No when I meant Yes and Yes when I meant No, I have felt guilty when I might have felt pleased and pleased when I might have felt ashamed. I have been at war with myself all my life. I know much more about hate than I do about love.

The divisions in my life seem endless. I could tell the story of anyone else's life with infinitely less trouble, for the divisions in other people's lives are much less perceptible and less painful to me, and I feel that I could reconcile them with less difficulty. I am told that I should consider my life as a story: but a story has a plot, a hero, major and minor characters (who merely contribute their bit to the hero's story), and events that move from a beginning to a climax. I am also told that the story of my life (if I can discover what it is) can only be interesting and worth telling if I present myself as a type—a representative product of my social class and educational background—a horrible example of misdirected upbringing. The result would presumably make salutary reading, like a crow nailed to a tree.

Early in my life I learned—or was taught, or submitted to the idea—that higher authorities exist, and that they are to be respected and obeyed. I have questioned the nature and extent of those authorities, at least in my own mind, up to the highest level my imagination can reach, and I have evaded or transgressed their rules, or what I understand to be their rules, whenever I dared or whenever it suited me; but I have never doubted that those authorities exist and reign, whoever they (he, she, it) may be, nor that I am their (his, her, its) most disloyal, unloving but submissive subject. Though it may be like the stupid shrilling of an insect to say so, I acknowledge that higher authority (god, goddess or gobbet) and my complete and helpless subjection to it.

A poem of Robert Graves's begins with the wonderful line, *There is one story and one story only:* it has always meant to me more than I think he meant by it, or at any rate something different. I take it as an absolute statement, whereas he qualifies its absoluteness in the next line *(that will be worth your telling).* The unqualified statement, to me, has the ring of unexpected but suddenly obvious truth. I believe that there is one story and one story only; but I cannot say I understand what it is I believe, and I do not know what the story is.

C. G. Jung, who I think made discoveries about truth, seems to say that there are two stories, or perhaps two aspects to the "one story": one that can be seen and is apparently understandable (at least when it is forced into a pattern); the other—"the shadow," as he calls it—that can be seen only in glimpses, in dreams, in impulses pushed down below awareness, a story that is not understood, that is in fact so horrifying that we deny its

335

existence. The *idea* of this duality does not horrify me: I know and can admit, at least in theory, that I am at odds with myself; but the *nature* of this "shadow," unknown to me although within me, alarms and disturbs me, like a dog hearing the far-off howling of a timber wolf. Though this shadow may be my real kinship with the real world, all my conscious life, all my training, has unfitted me for perceiving or dealing with this world. If I could reconcile my domesticated dog-self with my brother the wolf— would I know my own story then? Perhaps I would.

Whenever I have seen a pattern in nature, or a piece of it, it has almost equally fascinated and repelled me. The fascination has come from the pattern itself, and the fact that I could recognize it as a pattern; the repulsion, from the pattern's irregularity —it was never absolutely symmetrical, absolutely orderly, and seemed to carry within it a threat, a warning, that the design I thought I saw might be merely an illusion—that it might be only a piece, in effect a formless piece, of a bigger or different pattern that I couldn't see at all. I think this possibility very likely. The reality of nature must have more in common with my shadow-self than it has with what I call "me"—my conscious perception, my eyesight, my reason.

The willow pattern on a Chinese plate is more symmetrical than the garden it represents, which in turn is more symmetrical than the garden itself, which in turn is more symmetrical than the trees, shrubs and rocks that make up the garden, which in turn are more symmetrical than . . . ? Asymmetrical, imperceptible, un-understandable as it may be, we won't give up the idea of an underlying pattern, a pattern that finally underlies all patterns. No, we won't give up the idea, but we have to admit that we don't know it and can't see it.

So then what? If we want to make something with any kind of shape to it—a plate or a story or a picture—we'll just have to make do with the best sample we can find, admitting that the one we hit on will be artificial and may have nothing in common with the shadowy, invisible pattern of "reality." If I want to make a story out of my life, there must be a better pattern for it than a crow nailed to a tree. That ugly picture suggests a more terrible one: a man, who is somehow more than a man, nailed to a tree. But that is not anything like the picture I see of myself. I see more likeness in the picture of the dog chained in the farmyard who hears the far-off howling of his feared and hated blood-brother.

Human kind cannot bear very much reality. Bear it? They can't get anywhere near it! This famous "reality" we talk about is the momentary, glancing realization that we shall die—that's all. *O dark dark dark. They all go into the dark.* And somewhere deep in that darkness, millions of light-years (or dark-years) distant from our little life, it may be that reality (the real reality), faintly, imperceptibly, sparsely begins.

The warts, the moles, the liver spots, the horny excrescences and harsh spurs of hair that emerge and proliferate on our sagging, wrinkled bodies, have their counterparts in the blemishes that mottle our aging spirits. I try to think of exceptions to this inexorable and debasing process, and I am sure, or almost sure, of one or two. I wish to be an exception myself. But how can you take the great leap forward from cleverness to goodness? And why does this question only present itself seriously when you can no longer leap? Perhaps it can't be done so suddenly, but only by stumping along on your knees for as long as you can keep going. Is that my answer from the saints?

My thoughts turn back to the past and my attention wanders: soon I hear myself (or fail to hear myself) groaning and muttering the same old imprecations and complaints, a Mr. Punch who glares and jerks as the strings are pulled. I am broad in the beam and short of breath. My legs ache, my knee hurts, I cannot turn my stiff neck even as far as I used to. I am deaf in one ear and could hardly hear without an electronic aid; I cannot read without spectacles. Half-blind, half-deaf, half-crippled, nearing my end. And yet I wake with gladness every precious morning, and would like to praise God that I am alive, if I knew how to address him.

Fools are born every minute, and so are the rest of us. The human race, they say, is producing too many babies, at least in other countries. We are told on the highest authority that if the bombs don't get us we shall infallibly be crushed to death by our own numbers. One way or another the present generation is doomed: it is certain that not one of us will survive.

There really isn't much to choose between human beings, although human beings think there is. From only a slight distance, the plot of their individual stories is identical: they are born, they live, they die. With few exceptions, so few that they are statistically negligible, they are all born one at a time in the same manner, head first from between their mother's legs. They live, if they survive that experience, all in the same way: by swallowing food every day, excreting most of it, breathing all the time, sleeping a third of their lives. When they stop breathing they die.

Infants of the human species not only look alike but act alike. In this early chapter of their lives they are helpless and must be considered innocent. They did not ask to be born, they were literally forced into life by other beings, they cannot be held responsible for their appearance, their outcries, the messes they make. Later they begin to learn some sorts of control: to command the muscles of the sphincter and the bladder until they feel against their buttocks the cold permissive circle of the pot. Gradually they learn to accomplish further feats of strength and will.

At what point can they be considered responsible creatures, doers of good and evil? No one can say for sure, least of all themselves. But the more they learn, the more is required of them. They come, much more quickly than they are prepared for, under the system of rewards and punishments from a higher authority whose superior strength they have to acknowledge but whose justice they sometimes fail to understand and often question. If they live, some will be servants and some masters, or will "find their own level" in between. A few will become saints or will sit in the seats of the mighty; some will blow out their brains or end on the gallows. They will all die: every man jack, every girl-jill.

But just now, they are all babies, squalling, red-faced, helpless, ugly and innocent.

For the past ten years, at least, I don't suppose I have said anything that I haven't said before. Occasionally, when something in the conversation reminds me or tempts me to tell one of the few funny stories I can remember, I am uneasily aware that my wife has heard it many times, and I look at her apologetically as I start to repeat it, or even, with some embarrassment, ask her if she minds hearing it all over again. If she minds! Nothing could stop me from telling it. Every time this happens, however, I feel a slight twinge of remorse, shame—even fear, perhaps? for it is a kind of *déjà vu* that I have summoned up myself, deliberately: a form of mental suicide.

Repeating stories and anecdotes is bad enough, but even worse is my almost automatic repetition of thoughts, words and phrases. I can seldom catch myself in the act, or before the act, and in the heat of talk I never catch myself at all; it's only afterwards and only sometimes that I recall, with faint horror and dull dread (the words are not too strong), that once again I have been parroting the same old squawks and cackles that have served me, and served me badly, all my life. Mention a topic and if it "rings a bell" the pinball machine goes into helpless automatic action: lights flash, buzzers rasp, the ball is flung from pillar to post; nothing can stop it until it thumps down a hole and disappears.

Fear is never groundless: it is grounded in the deepest feeling we know—fear itself. Franklin Roosevelt's famous phrase was a piece of rhetoric: it sounded like a trumpet-call, as rhetoric should, and meant the opposite of what it said, as rhetoric often does. President Roosevelt meant, and was understood to mean:

"Be brave!" But what he said was, "All we have to fear is fear itself." Exactly. It's all we have to fear, and it's more than enough.

If a man could be truthful about his life, he would have to say that he had forgotten most of it. What we remember of our past is partly a blurred, partly an edited version. We sometimes remember things our friends have done or said which they have quite forgotten and which embarrass or anger them to have recalled. No, we cannot be truthful about our lives. And yet what else have we to tell the truth about?

What can we do with the past, even with the tiny fingernail paring of it that we call our own? We cannot "recall" it, let alone remember it as it was. We cannot altogether invent it, because we keep bumping into things we think we remember. Though we cannot see it clearly, the past is not only directly behind us but all around us and in us: it is not only what we wish to forget and think we have succeeded in forgetting but also (and much more poignantly) what we wish we could remember.

The scraps and broken shards that form the record of human history go back only a few thousand years, and masses of them must be forever unrecoverable, their sites not only unknown but buried under the sea, under glacial moraines, absorbed again into the dust and rock and marshes of the earth. Of those still hidden human traces that remain to be found, entombed, embalmed, preserved and waiting for the lucky digger, it is very unlikely that most will ever be discovered. And without every scrap of this scanty evidence our knowledge of man's early history, let alone prehistoric times, must be full of guesswork and gaps.

But history purports to be the story of man, and what sort of story is it that consists of bits and pieces, guesswork and gaps? There will always be men who want the *whole* story. Edmund Wilson once said that every small town in America had its eccentric who had written or was writing a universal history. And there's the rub: no one seems to be able to write a coherent and continuous account of man's life on earth without some sort of plot to justify the story; and every such thesis is either subjective to the point of eccentricity or seems so to other people. Humanists, drawing themselves up to their full 72 inches and cockadoodling to make the sun rise, assert that history (i.e., what happens to human beings) is *not* the result of blind forces (i.e., something they don't understand).

Though Gibbon did not attempt what H. G. Wells or Arnold Toynbee did, and aimed to write a classical (i.e., objective) account of the Roman Empire's decline, he was so much the child of his "enlightened" age that he couldn't refrain from showing an anti-Christian thesis. Wells, a curable optimist, preached the march of scientific progress until he had progressed to the end of his tether. And Toynbee, the only historian so far who has admitted that historians cannot help being affected by the cant of their own day, and that the only thing they *can* do is to try to lift themselves up by their own bootstraps (i.e., use their imaginations), has been widely attacked by most of his fellow historians for letting his imagination run wild. His *Study of History* enrages historians because they think it overweeningly ambitious.

We know enough of how current history is recorded—in the warped gossip, fictitious adulation and lying affidavits of newspapers, official announcements and the controlled propaganda of governments and corporations—to agree with Henry Ford that history is mostly bunk. For the records of our times, with all their suppressions, misunderstandings, mistaken interpretations and plain lies, will become the basis of history. We do well to disbelieve in it, to take it with so many grains of salt that we become thirsty for something truer.

The present—that is, the time when these words are being written—is regarded by many of the people who live in it with something very like horror: they cannot help comparing it with a more hopeful past and they see in it the preview of an even more dreadful future. And it may well be true that life was easier and more pleasant, for a good many people, in bygone ages, even or perhaps particularly in those we call "dark."

I suppose we are lucky, those of us who are alive now rather than later. Though our century has been nominated the cruelest and most savage in recorded history, the victims of our famines and mass murders are numbered only in the millions, not yet in billions. If any record of us should survive, future historians may smile at our complaints and laments, and decide that we lived in the last sinking light of a Golden Age. If any distinction is made between us and the Victorians, whose grandchildren we are, it may be said of them that they enjoyed the solider happiness of being well deceived, for they thought their civilization as firm as Gibraltar, but we know that ours is as incurable as New York. Nevertheless, like nomads camping among ruins, some of us can still use and take pleasure in the scattered relics of an earlier order.

The passage of time, which I am now old enough to have experienced, is a wonderful cooler of ambition. I am too old now to use the word *love* in the active mood, the present tense. Nevertheless I still have the noun in my pocket, where I keep my change: a little, dried-up black nugget as small and shapeless as a withered and petrified heart. When my fingers, fumbling for a coin, encounter this stony lump, it is an unexpected comfort to feel it there, that small hard noun. But it is more a keepsake than a talisman.

I have made an old lady laugh; I have told her anecdotes and reminded her of some. We have had a high old evening. I have not given myself away, I have successfully pretended that everything is just about as it should be, that nothing surprising or untoward has happened or could possibly happen, that there may be squalls of rain or frost on the hills but that most of us can expect the usual bright intervals. I have given no indication that . . . Now I am by myself, whatever that means. I think it means, among other things, that I am surrounded.

The truth comes at night. In the dead hours of early morning when pain or restlessness wakes you, the thoughts that visit you

342

then are thoughts with no color; incontrovertible, hard and immovable as rock. Thoughts like these: that there is no escape from what you are; that you have just squandered another twenty-four hours of your irreplaceable and dwindling capital; that you are going to die and that it doesn't matter.

For the moment I have had everything I want: a cigarette, two vodka martinis, a good slice of roast beef, a seidel of Michelob beer. The pain in my belly has moved back, nearly out of sight, with only a paw on the threshold.

After our elders reach a certain age, the age of retirement, they go into a kind of hush, almost a state (it seems to us) of suspended animation. While our busy world hums on around them, they simply wait—for what? They don't seem to know, but we do. When the news comes at last that they have died, we are not at all surprised and only momentarily concerned. It was about time. At last they have encountered what they were waiting for, done what they were expected to do.

Try as I may, I cannot altogether shake off my habitual awe of the Church nor completely dissociate it from the far more fearful God to whom the Church makes its ritual obeisances. I still think of God—no, not *think* but apprehend, as I was trained as a child to envision the idea—as a watchful, vengeful, enormous, omniscient policeman, instantly aware of the slightest tinge of irreverence in my innermost thought, always ready to pounce (though with ominous patience he might hold his hand for a time) if I curse, if I mention him in anger, fun or mere habit, if I (O hell-fire and horror!) blaspheme his holy name.

And how can that kind of fear of that kind of God be the beginning of wisdom?

Who cares? (The old man coughing his life out in a freezing garret, the stoat biting the terrified rabbit's neck, the drowning kitten sucking in the oily waters of the canal, the young widow

343

sobbing for the beloved lost body of her husband.) Who cares? Nobody.

Before death tackles a man head-on and brings him down, he trips and stumbles over small obstacles he often doesn't even notice, any more than he notices that the terrain he walks on is made up, more and more, yard by yard, of nothing else but these small obstacles. In short, his landscape (or himself?) is changing, although he is unaware of the fact. He doesn't see, he fails to notice, that the slight bulges in his body's profile, its ugly late growths of moles and warts, the eccentric or peculiar habits that cover his invisible submerged underside like barnacles, have changed him out of all knowledge from the ways of his youth: his own mother wouldn't know him. As far as *he* can see he is just the same as he always was—or at any rate he has turned out, he thinks, more or less as he had hoped. He will not admit even the possibility that the innocent or charming child he was has turned into the hollow scarecrow, the nasty and frightening person, that he is now.

Where did we go wrong? What happened? There must have been some point where each of us took a fatal turn for the worse. We all started off as blameless babies; and look at us now! When did it begin, that creeping corruption that has changed the good children, the promising material we were, into the self-satisfied or self-hating or otherwise mad human beings we have become? There must have been a moment—was it the same one for all of us?—when we stood on the very peak of our promise, our lives before us and our world to conquer. What happened to those promises and those worlds?

Must we believe that all human beings deteriorate as they grow, not only bodily but in every other way? Yet, if we do not quietly, obviously or imperceptibly go mad, how else can we explain our continuing belief in ourselves, or even our ineradicable delusion that we still have a chance—to live always a little longer, to be crowned with laurel, to find the bluebird? How can we pretend to think of ourselves, or accept the pretense that others think of us, as "mature people," let alone "true poets," "great men" or "pure souls"? If we are not mad, how can we believe or cling to the hope that we, though others haven't, have found The Way to salvation, or even the way to live?

And yet it may be that we cannot tell the difference between growth and decay. Whoever or whatever planted us presumably knows, though, and might say (of one nearing the end of his season): "Ah, that's coming on quite nicely."

INDEX

Note: The following abbreviations have been used: RG for Robert Graves; SJ for Schuyler Jackson; TM for T. S. Matthews

T. S. MATTHEWS was born in Cincinnati and educated at St. Paul's School, Princeton, and New College, Oxford. He worked for the *New Republic* during Edmund Wilson's tenure, and in 1929 joined *Time* magazine, eventually becoming its editor. His previous books include poetry, literary criticism, and autobiography. He lives in Suffolk, England.